THE BEST SOFTWARE WRITING I

Selected and Introduced by

Joel Spolsky

Apress®

The Best Software Writing I: Selected and Introduced by Joel Spolsky

Copyright © 2005 Edited by Joel Spolsky

ISBN (pbk): 1-59059-500-9

Printed and bound in the United States of America 9 8 7 6 5 4 3 2 1

Trademarked names may appear in this book. Rather than use a trademark symbol with every occurrence of a trademarked name, we use the names only in an editorial fashion and to the benefit of the trademark owner, with no intention of infringement of the trademark.

Lead Editor: Gary Cornell
Editorial Board: Steve Anglin, Dan Appleman, Ewan Buckingham, Gary Cornell, Tony Davis,
    Jason Gilmore, Jonathan Hassell, Chris Mills, Dominic Shakeshaft, Jim Sumser
Assistant Publisher: Grace Wong
Project Manager: Beth Christmas
Copy Edit Manager: Nicole LeClerc
Copy Editor: Liz Welch
Production Manager: Kari Brooks-Copony
Production Editor: Kelly Winquist
Compositor: Dina Quan
Proofreader: Nancy Sixsmith
Indexer: Broccoli Information Management
Cover Designer: Kurt Krames
Manufacturing Manager: Tom Debolski
Licensing: Tina Nielsen

Distributed to the book trade in the United States by Springer-Verlag New York, Inc., 233 Spring Street, 6th Floor, New York, NY 10013, and outside the United States by Springer-Verlag GmbH & Co. KG, Tiergartenstr. 17, 69112 Heidelberg, Germany.

In the United States: phone 1-800-SPRINGER, fax 201-348-4505, e-mail orders@springer-ny.com, or visit http://www.springer-ny.com. Outside the United States: fax +49 6221 345229, e-mail orders@springer.de, or visit http://www.springer.de.

For information on translations, please contact Apress directly at 2560 Ninth Street, Suite 219, Berkeley, CA 94710. Phone 510-549-5930, fax 510-549-5939, e-mail info@apress.com, or visit http://www.apress.com.

To my sister Ruth, כִּי אֵשֶׁת חַיִל אָתְּ, כִּי יוֹדֵעַ כָּל-שַׁעַר עַמִּי

CONTENTS

ABOUT THE EDITOR

Joel Spolsky is a globally recognized expert on the software development process. His website, *Joel on Software* (www.joelonsoftware.com), is popular with software developers around the world and has been translated into over 30 languages. As the founder of Fog Creek Software in New York City, he created FogBugz, a popular project management system for software teams. Joel has worked at Microsoft, where he designed VBA as a member of the Excel team, and at Juno Online Services, developing an Internet client used by millions. He has written two previous books: *User Interface Design for Programmers* (Apress, 2001) and *Joel on Software* (Apress, 2004). Joel holds a BS from Yale in computer science. Before college he served in the Israeli Defense Forces as a paratrooper, and he was one of the founders of Kibbutz Hanaton.

ABOUT THE AUTHORS

Ken Arnold has loitered around the computing field for decades, including attending Berkeley where he worked on the BSD project, creating the curses library and helping on rogue; writing the "The C Advisor" column for *Unix Review* (later "The C++ Advisor" as progress led us down the garden path); coauthoring *The Java Programming Language* and other books; designing JavaSpaces and helping design Jini; and occasionally (as shown here) pretending to be hip by blogging. His current dalliances include the human factors of programming languages and APIs, electronic voting systems your mother could trust, and the Napkin pluggable look and feel for Java that makes provisional GUIs look, well, provisional.

Leon Bambrick is a prolific programmer, satirist, and pugilist, working out of the southern hemisphere. He first met Joel Spolsky when they were stranded together on a desert island, with nothing but an 8086 and a copy of Kernigan and Ritchie. His website, secretGeek.net, has a small cameo in *Star Wars Episode III – Revenge of the Sith*—as an Imperial Guard's codpiece.

Michael Bean is a software developer and entrepreneur. He is currently president and one of the founders of Forio Business Simulations. Before Forio, Michael held senior management posts at consulting and software firms in the United States and Europe. Michael was also a research associate for the System Dynamics Group at MIT, where he developed simulations that analyzed the strategic implications of manager decisions. Michael has consulted with corporations and government agencies nationally and internationally on transfer pricing, competitive strategy, emerging technologies, and customer migration. He has conducted scenario planning, systems thinking, and computer simulation seminars to corporations and government agencies worldwide. In addition, Michael has presented at national conferences on strategy, software, and computer simulation.

Rory Blyth works for Microsoft as a corporate stooge. In his spare time, he keeps a blog at www.neopoleon.com, ponders the universe, and considers himself to be one of the three missing Sankara stones, although he probably isn't, but it makes him feel better about being so bloody insignificant.

Adam Bosworth joined Google recently as vice president of engineering. He came to Google from BEA, where he was chief architect and senior VP of advanced development and responsible for driving the engineering efforts for BEA's Framework Division. Prior to joining BEA, he cofounded Crossgain, a software development firm acquired by BEA. Known as one of the pioneers of XML, he held various senior management positions at Microsoft, including general manager of the WebData group, a team focused on defining and driving XML strategy. While at Microsoft, he was responsible for designing and delivering the Microsoft Access PC Database product and assembling and driving the team that developed Internet Explorer 4.0's HTML engine.

danah boyd is a PhD student in the School of Information Management and Systems at the University of California, Berkeley, where she studies how people negotiate a presentation of self in mediated social contexts to unknown audiences using ethnographic methods. She is particularly interested in how youth develop a culturally situated understanding of self and the role of technology in this process. Prior to Berkeley, danah received a master's in sociable media from the MIT Media Lab and a bachelor's in computer science from Brown University. Her work has ranged from psychological studies of how depth cue prioritization is dependent on levels of sex hormones to design installations of interactive social visualizations. danah blogs extensively at Apophenia (www.zephoria.org/thoughts) and Many-to-Many (www.corante.com/many).

Raymond Chen has worked in Microsoft's Windows division since 1992 and has seen a lot of things come and go. His blog deals with the history of Windows and the dying art of Win32 programming.

Kevin Cheng is an independent user experience specialist and global nomad. He holds a master's in human-computer interaction and ergonomics from the University College London Interaction Centre (UCLIC) and has spoken at UXNet, UPA, and ACM-SIGCHI. He is the cofounder and cocreator of OK/Cancel (www.ok-cancel.com), an online site believed to be in the top five of usability and HCI-themed comics.

Tom Chi has a Masters Degree in Electrical Engineering, which probably means he's qualified neither to talk about HCI nor to write any sort of funny thing. Yet, week after week he dreams the impossible dream at ok-cancel.com. As for credentials, there is the small matter of having designed UI features for two releases of Microsoft Outlook, as well as his dark history of consulting for F500 clients—but these are topics that civilized people shouldn't speak of. Shhh.

Cory Doctorow (craphound.com) is European Affairs Coordinator for the Electronic Frontier Foundation (www.eff.org), a member-supported non-profit group that works to uphold civil liberties values in technology law, policy, and standards. He represents EFF's interests at various standards bodies and consortia, and at the United Nations' World Intellectual Property Organization. Doctorow is also a prolific writer who appears on the mastheads at *Wired*, *Make*, and *Popular Science* magazines, and whose science fiction novels have won the Campbell, Sunburst, and Locus Awards. His novel *Down and Out in the Magic Kingdom* is a finalist for this year's Nebula Award. He is the coeditor of the popular weblog Boing Boing (boingboing.net). Born in Canada, he now lives in London, England.

Bruce Eckel (www.BruceEckel.com) is the author of *Thinking in Java* (Prentice Hall, 1998, 2nd edition, 2000, 3rd edition, 2003, 4th edition, 2005), the *Hands-On Java Seminar CD-ROM* (available on the website), *Thinking in C++* (PH 1995; 2nd edition 2000, Volume 2, with Chuck Allison, 2003), and *C++ Inside & Out* (Osborne/McGraw-Hill, 1993), among others. He's given hundreds of presentations throughout the world, published over 150 articles in numerous magazines, was a founding member of the ANSI/ISO C++ committee, and speaks regularly at conferences. He provides public and private seminars and design consulting in C++ and Java.

Paul Ford is an editor at *Harper's* magazine, a frequent commentator on NPR's *All Things Considered,* and the sole proprietor of Ftrain.com. He has fooled with computers for the last two decades, and feels no inclination to stop. He lives in Brooklyn, New York.

Paul Graham is an essayist, programmer, and programming language designer. In 1995 he developed with Robert Morris the first web-based application, Viaweb, which was acquired by Yahoo in 1998. In 2002 he described a simple Bayesian spam filter that inspired most current filters. He's currently working on a new programming language called Arc, a new book (probably) for O'Reilly, and is one of the partners in Y Combinator. Paul is the author of *On Lisp* (Prentice Hall, 1993), *ANSI Common Lisp* (Prentice Hall, 1995), and *Hackers & Painters* (O'Reilly, 2004). He has an AB from Cornell and a PhD in computer science from Harvard, and studied painting at RISD and the Accademia di Belle Arti in Florence.

John Gruber is a freelance writer, web developer, designer, and Mac nerd. He combines those interests on his website, Daring Fireball (http://daringfireball.net/). John lives in Philadelphia with his wife and son.

Gregor Hohpe leads the Enterprise Integration practice at ThoughtWorks, Inc., a specialized provider of application development and integration services. Gregor is a widely recognized thought leader on asynchronous messaging architectures and coauthor of the seminal book *Enterprise Integration Patterns* (Addison-Wesley, 2004). Gregor speaks regularly at technical conferences around the world and maintains the website www.eaipatterns.com.

Ron Jeffries has been developing software longer than most people have been alive. He holds advanced degrees in mathematics and computer science, both earned before negative integers had been invented. His teams have built operating systems, compilers, relational database systems, and a large range of applications. Ron's software products have produced revenue of over half a billion dollars, and he wonders why he didn't get any of it.

Eric Johnson graduated from the University of Illinois with a BS in computer science in 1993 and has worked at FactSet Research Systems ever since. Currently he is the director of market data engineering and lives with his wife and two kids in southwestern Connecticut. He can be reached at johnson.eric@gmail.com.

Eric Lippert has been a software developer at Microsoft since 1996. He spent his first five years working on VBScript, JScript, Windows Script Host, and other scripting technologies and more recently has been working on Visual Studio Tools For Office. He also writes a blog, where he dispenses advice about scripting, security, and (occasionally) romance. When not writing software or writing about software, Eric can be found playing old songs on old pianos, trying to keep the mast of his tiny sailboat upright, building kites, or talking his friends into helping him fix his 97-year-old house.

Michael "Rands" Lopp is a Silicon Valley–based software engineering manager. He's ridden a variety of high-tech roller-coasters, including Borland International, Netscape Communications, Apple Computer, and a start-up you've unfortunately never heard of. In his spare time, he writes a weblog at www.randsinrepose.com, where he optimistically contemplates the fact that the world continues to get uncomfortably smaller.

Larry Osterman has been working at Microsoft since 1984. In that time, he's worked as a software engineer deep in the plumbing of various Microsoft® products, including MS-DOS, MS-NET, LAN Manager, Windows NT, Exchange, and eHome, and is currently working in the Windows Multimedia Technologies group. Larry lives just north of Seattle with his wife Valorie and their two kids, four cats, and two horses.

Mary Poppendieck is a seasoned leader in both operations and new product development with more than 25 years of IT experience. She has led teams implementing lean solutions ranging from enterprise supply chain management to digital media, and built one of 3M's first just-in-time lean production systems. Mary is currently the president of Poppendieck LLC in Minnesota. Her book *Lean Software Development: An Agil   ~lbit*, which brings lean principles to software development, won th Development Productivity Award in 2004.

Rick Schaut grew up in Green Bay and Milwaukee, Wisconsin, where he spent his childhood watching Paul Hornung score touchdowns and Hank Aaron hit home runs. At one point, he believed that our national anthem ended with, "the land of the free and the home of the Braves," and he had a hard time figuring out why every American League umpire was named "Al." After graduating from high school, Rick studied economics at the University of Wisconsin, Milwaukee, and computer science at the University of Wisconsin. Rick joined Microsoft in 1990, and has been working on versions of Microsoft Word ever since.

Clay Shirky teaches at NYU's graduate Interactive Telecommunications Program, and works with clients, including the Library of Congress, Connecting for Health, and Nokia, on network design issues. He writes about the cultural and economic issues of the Internet (archived at shirky.com).

Eric Sink is the founder of SourceGear, a developer tools ISV. More of Eric's writings and rants can be found on his weblog at software.ericsink.com. Eric and his wife live in central Illinois with their two young daughters and one old cat.

Aaron Swartz is a teenage writer, hacker, and activist. Formerly the Metadata Advisor to Creative Commons and member of the W3C's RDF Core Working Group, he is currently a student at Stanford University, where he authors his popular weblog and is beginning work on a technology startup.

why the lucky stiff is a computer progg'er and aspiring author with no true achievements under his belt. Except there was that time when he tore a building in half with his bare feet.

INTRODUCTION

New York City is a blast.

Just the other day, as I was walking the four blocks from my office to the subway entrance, interesting things kept happening.

Not *really* interesting things, just modestly interesting things.

So, for example, some guy was running down the sidewalk frantically, looking very much like a character in an R. Crumb comic, flapping his arms broadly and making chicken sounds. Running isn't the right word. He was kind of pratfalling repeatedly and then catching himself right before he hit the ground.

Then a taxi turning the corner nearly knocked over an old man who was crossing the street a little bit too slowly for the taxi driver's taste.

A couple of chubby, red-faced out-of-towners asked me if there was a bar anywhere nearby. (There was. We were in front of it.)

Someone was handing out little advertising cards at the entrance to the subway. Of course, the inside of the subway station was completely *littered* with the cards because everybody who took one immediately hurled it on the ground as violently as you can hurl a four-by-six postcard. I almost slipped on one on the steps down.

Modestly interesting stuff, but quite forgettable in New York.

The next day I was talking to one of the summer interns we just hired. For some reason, this year's summer intern class consists of 75% people who are either from Indiana or who went to school in Indiana. Indiana, for those of you not familiar with our American landscape, is somewhere in the middle—a state of farms, wholesome colleges with corn-fed basketball-playing kids, Norman Rockwell towns, and the occasional rust-belt hellmouth industrial city gasping its last breath. (As I write these words I brace for the slew of angry letters from the Indiana Department of Tourism and Infrastructure promoting the exciting cultural scene, the many picturesque lakes, the world-class telephone system, and the variety of ethnic restaurants. You might find a Mexican restaurant and an Italian restaurant on the same block!)

Anyway, the intern said he had never lived in New York City, and asked me what it was like. I didn't really have a good answer, but I said, "New York is the kind of place where 10 things happen to you every day *on the way to the subway* that would have qualified as interesting dinner conversation in Bloomington, Indiana, and you don't pay them any notice."

Feeling smug with myself, I pulled down an atlas from the bookshelf to find another state to insult.

*Any*how, I can't remember why I told you that story.

Oh, wait, yes I can, but first I have to tell you *another* story.

A few months ago, I got a review copy of a book from another publisher, other than the publisher of this book, who will remain anonymous, and the book will remain anonymous, and the author will remain anonymous, because I'm afraid I just have *nothing* good to say about said book.

The publisher wanted to get a quote from me to put on the back cover talking about how wonderful his book was. Normally I'd be happy to do that; I'm a complete publicity slut and will do just about anything to get my name in front of the reading public. My hope is that if I do this enough, telemarketers who call me at home will be able to pronounce my name.

The book started out looking promising. It filled a real need. I remember several times standing in bookstores desperately trying to find a book on the very topic, but there was nothing to be found. So I started reading the manuscript full of high hopes.

Bleah.

I could hardly bear to keep reading.

The author kept saying smart and interesting things.

He even wrote clearly.

But the book was thoroughly, completely, *boring*. And worse, it was completely unconvincing.

The author had violated the number one rule of good writing, the "Show, don't tell" rule. There was not a single story in the book. It was chock-full of sentences like "A good team leader provides inspiration by setting a positive example." What the eff?

Pay attention. Here's the way to say "A good team leader provides inspiration by setting a positive example" without putting your audience to sleep:

> For a few months in the army I worked in the mess hall, clearing tables and washing dishes nonstop for 16 hours a day, with only a half-hour break in the afternoon, if you washed the dishes really fast. My hands were permanently red, the front of my shirt was permanently wet and smelly, and I couldn't take it any more.
>
> Somehow, I managed to get out of the mess hall into a job working for a high-ranking Sergeant Major. This guy had years of experience. He was probably 20 years older than the kids in the unit. Even in the field, he was always immaculate, wearing a spotless, starched, pressed full dress uniform with impeccably polished shoes no matter how dusty and muddy the rest of the world was around him. You got the feeling that he slept in 300-threadcount Egyptian cotton sheets while we slept in dusty sleeping bags on the ground.
>
> His job consisted of two things: discipline and the physical infrastructure of the base. He was a bit of a terror to everyone in the battalion due to his role as the chief disciplinary officer. Most people only knew him from strutting around the base conducting inspections, screaming at the top of his lungs and demanding impossibly high standards of order and cleanliness in what was essentially a bunch of tents in the middle of the desert, alternately dust-choked or mud-choked, depending on the rain situation.
>
> Anyway, on the first day working for the Sergeant Major, I didn't know what to expect. I was sure it was going to be terrifying, but it *had* to be better than washing dishes and clearing tables all day long (and it's not like the guy in charge of the mess hall was such a sweetheart, either!).
>
> On the first day he took me to the officers' bathroom and told me I would be responsible for keeping it clean. "Here's how you clean a toilet," he said.
>
> And he got down on his knees in front of the porcelain bowl, in his pressed starched spotless dress uniform, and scrubbed the toilet with his bare hands.
>
> To a 19-year-old who has to clean toilets, something which is almost *by definition* the worst possible job in the world, the sight of this high-ranking, 38-year-old, immaculate, manicured, pampered discipline officer cleaning a toilet completely reset my attitude. If he can clean a toilet, I can clean a toilet. There's nothing wrong with cleaning toilets. My loyalty and inspiration from that moment on were unflagging. *That's* leadership.

See what I did here? I told a story. I'll bet you'd rather sit through 10 of those 400-word stories than have to listen to someone drone on about how "a good team leader provides inspiration by setting a positive example."

Anyway, I called up the editor of the book that they wanted me to praise, and said I couldn't, in good faith, recommend a boring book without any stories in it, even if it was 100% correct and otherwise well-written. I think they hate me now.

So be it.

The software development world desperately needs better writing. If I have to read another 2000-page book about some class library written by 16 *separate* people in broken ESL, I'm going to flip out. If I see another hardback book about object-oriented models written with dense faux-academic pretentiousness, I'm not going to shelve it any more in the Fog Creek library: it's going right in the recycle bin. If I have to read another spirited attack on Microsoft's buggy code by an enthusiastic nine-year-old Trekkie on Slashdot, I might just poke my eyes out with a sharpened pencil. Stop it, stop it, stop it!

And that's why when Gary Cornell suggested this book, I leapt at the idea. It would be a chance to showcase some of the best writing about software from the past year "or so." The original idea was to make it an annual, so the volume you're holding would be "The Best Software Writing of 2004," but there were a bunch of great articles from 2003 that we wanted to include, and we were afraid bookstores would return it at the end of the year if there was a date in the title. I solicited nominations from the faithful readers of my website, *Joel on Software,* and selected the final stories myself, so the blame for what's included and what isn't included is entirely my own, but full credit for really incredible writing in a field that doesn't normally get any goes to the contributors.

Ken Arnold

STYLE IS SUBSTANCE[1]

Python did something really interesting: it made whitespace matter for the first time in a major programming language since FORTRAN on punched cards. In Python, the way you create a block is not by surrounding it with begin and end or { and }, but by indenting it. That's all.

A lot of geeks instinctively cringed. "Whitespace should never matter!" they claimed, without remembering why. The main reason was that you couldn't always see whitespace, because it's, um, white. So, for instance, in the standard Unix Make, where certain lines must begin with a tab character, if you or your editor replaced such a tab character with eight spaces (how helpful!), you would suddenly find your makefile didn't work, and without any explanation. So we all learned: whitespace mustn't matter!

Well, yeah.

Maybe we went too far.

Here's the beauty of Python.

In C-like languages (C, C++, Java) the human eye sees indentation as defining a block, but the compiler sees the { and the }. So in cases where the indentation and the braces disagree, the one that is less visible to humans—the braces—wins out. But why do we need two ways to indicate a block, one for humans and one for compilers? Why not stick with one way, so code always looks like what it does?

---

1. Ken Arnold, "Style Is Substance," Artima Weblogs, Notes from Underfoot (http://www.artima.com/weblogs/index.jsp?blogger=arnold), October 6, 2004. See http://www.artima.com/weblogs/viewpost.jsp?thread=74230.

Ken Arnold took this small idea from Python all the way. He proposes something even more radical—which, like many great ideas, is so crazy it just might work. – Ed.

~

. . . wherein I decide to wade into the programming language equivalent of TV wrestling: coding style . . .

I'm sure this will cause me no end of grief, but I'm about to confess publicly here that I am a heretic. (In this particular case I'm only confessing to heresy in computer language design. Other heresy confessions will have to await another time.)

I'll state it right out: For almost any mature language (C, Java, C++, Python, Lisp, Ada, FORTRAN, Smalltalk, sh, JavaScript, etc.) coding style is an essentially solved problem, and we ought to stop worrying about it. And to stop worrying about it will require worrying about it a lot at first, because the only way to get from where we are to a place where we stop worrying about style is to enforce it *as part of the language.*

Yup. I'm really saying that. I'm saying that, for example, the next ANSI C update should define the standard K&R C programming style[2] into the language grammar. Programs that use any new features should be required to be in K&R style or be rejected by the compiler as syntactically illegal.

I'm gonna pause here. When I was talking about this on a mailing list I had to go through this several times. People didn't quite get me because they couldn't believe someone was saying this. I mean this literally. For example, I want the next C grammar to define that a space comes between any keyword and an opening parenthesis: if (foo) would be legal, but if(foo) would not. Not a warning, not optionally checked, but actually forbidden by the language parser. Flat-out illegal. Can't compile.

---

2. From Brian Kernighan and Dennis Ritchie's *The C Programming Language* (Prentice Hall, 1988), the standard and founding tome for the language.

Here is the logic in its simplest form:

- **Premise 1: For any given language, there are one or a few common coding styles.**

  Typically one is set by the founder(s) or earliest documenter, but others will evolve over time. But even for C there are only a handful of commonly used styles, ignoring trivial variations.

- **Premise 2: There is not now, nor will there ever be, a programming style whose benefit is significantly greater than any of the common styles.**

  Get real. Discovering a style that improves your productivity or code quality by more than a few percent over the common styles is about as likely as discovering a new position for sex. (Astronauts need not apply, unless they want to invite me along.)

- **Premise 3: Approximately a gaboozillion cycles are spent on dealing with coding style variations.**

  Think about it: How many reformatter/pretty-printers projects are there on SourceForge[3] alone? How many options does any given IDE (including emacs) have for formatting code? How many cycles are spent deciding on a style, documenting it, enforcing it, and updating it? How many history logs for CVS, ClearCase, etc., have a lot of noise from varying format changes? How many brain cycles are spent on arguing about this topic?

- **Premise 4: For any nontrivial project, a common coding style is a good thing.**

  I really think this is pretty well agreed on. How constraining the style is varies, but having several folks hacking on the same code with conflicting coding styles introduces more pain than any single style imposes on any single person. Every project I know of has a style, if not spelled out at least by custom.

- **Conclusion: Thinking of all the code in the entire world as a single "project" with a single style, we would get more value than we do by allowing for variations in style.**

---

3. See http://sf.net.

Think of it. All the programming examples in one style. Web pages, journals, papers, emails use one style. Reformatting issues gone. Arguments over whose style is better gone. Reformatters become a quaint historical artifact.

And most of all: *No More Style Wars!* Really! Think of all those cycles that we could then plow into something more productive, like vi/emacs wars! Or world peace! Or a *really* good chocolate cookie recipe! You choose!

Of course, you will never enforce any style globally unless people have literally no choice. How many C programmers use "during" as a stylistic preference to the keyword "while"? (Preprocessor abusers need not apply. On second thought, please do: We need to identify you for our eugenics program.) Or skip the parentheses around an if clause? They don't because they *can't*. You know some would if they could. The thing that stops these "personal styles" is that the C compiler will not accept them. If you can't compile your code you fix it. It's so simple it's stupid. And therefore it works.

So I want the owners of language standards to take this up. I want the next version of these languages to require any code that uses new features to conform to some style. Let the standards committees gnash and snarl and wring their hands over which of the common styles is the winner. Sell tickets. We all get to comment and the language standards geeks decide. We know where they'll go—C will go to K&R; C++ will go with Bjarne's style (excuse me while I cringe); Java will go with the Sun style as shown in the language spec and most of the Java books from Sun (including mine); Lisp style is almost already set mostly in stone. Perl is a vast swamp of lexical and syntactic swill and nobody knows how to format even their own code well, but it's the only major language I can think of (with the possible exception of the recent, yet very Java-like C#) that doesn't have at least one style that's good enough.

Some things are either uncheckable (Hungarian notation, using "get" and "set" method prefixes) or not widely agreed upon (such as import/#include ordering). These can be left for future standards. Or not. The owners of the standard decide. But whatever they do, they should set the style and build it into the actual freakin' grammar.

This heresy encompasses one major sub-heresy: That whitespace should matter.

Most style rules have to do with the placement of whitespace: new-lines before or after curly braces, whitespace around operators or not, etc. So I'm saying that languages should indeed care about whitespace. A lot.

Yet one of the things we supposedly learned from languages like FORTRAN was that whitespace should only matter to mark boundaries between tokens. This was accepted wisdom because FORTRAN had columns—the first five columns were reserved for a statement number or a comment indicator, the sixth column with any character in it meant a continuation of the previous line, seven through 72 had the code, and the last eight were reserved for sequence numbers useful for reordering the card deck if it was dropped. Yes, I mean cards, the physical type, with rectangular holes. So if you put something in the wrong column, a statement could become a comment or whatever, which was really annoying. Also, `DO10I=1,100` was the same as `DO 10 I = 1, 100` because `DO` was a keyword followed by a number and so the space wasn't required, although it made `DO10I=1` interesting, as that assigned `1` to a variable named `DO10I`.

I lived this ugliness, so I felt the pain. But this didn't prove that whitespace shouldn't matter. All it really proved was that FORTRAN's whitespace rules sucked. Freedom to put whitespace anywhere has proven to be expensive and cycle-wasting in practice. We're not editing on punched cards anymore, and reformatters are as common as spam. We can use this power: type code however you want to but before you compile it, reformat it (or reformat on the fly, whatever).

In the end, this requires only that editors and IDEs will let you type stuff and make it look right. This is basically just reformatting on the fly, which many editors already do. We don't need you to type zero, one, or 17 spaces between an `if` and its open parenthesis, we just need the editor (assuming K&R C style) to put exactly one space there. And getting even this right will be easier if there is only one style to worry about. It's one of the things that those reformatting or style-adapting cycles can go to.

Basically, freedom for formatting style has proven extremely expensive, and does not deliver much value for cost. Think of it this way: could you honestly fill in the following:

I, *[insert name here]*, know of a programming style whose impact on programmer productivity and/or program quality is large enough that my freedom to choose it over any major common style validates the programmer productivity and investment used industry wide in arguing about style, imposing style, and reformatting to match styles. That style is *[insert style description here]* and its benefits are *[insert benefits here]*.

Or even the less demanding:

> I, *[insert name here]*, know of a programming style whose impact on pro-
> grammer productivity and/or program quality is ≥ 5% when compared to
> any major common style. That style is *[insert style description here]* and its
> benefits are *[insert benefits here]*.

I think you will mostly get snickers even suggesting that this can be
filled out. And on a single project alone you can spend 5% on coding
style issues—mostly up front, but it's a continuous bleeding: style wars
cropping up over things as yet undefined; new tools being suggested,
written, or integrated; people forgetting to put it in the right style getting
corrected, polluting the change history; training new people in the style;
disciplining engineers who are uncooperative; and general bitching,
whining, and moaning.

So 5% doesn't even touch the opportunity costs and other pain associated with not having a mandated style across all the code in the world.

Or if you prefer the question the other way 'round: What benefits do
we get from freedom of style that outweighs the cost we pay for it?

To me the answer seems obvious: nowhere *near* enough.

Leon Bambrick

AWARD FOR THE SILLIEST USER INTERFACE: WINDOWS SEARCH[1]

Why is a dog asking me questions?

Who's been putting the mescaline in the Microsoft Koolaid?

What if Google used this approach?

Would Google still be number one?

1. Leon Bambrick, "Award for the Silliest User Interface: Windows Search," secretGeek (http://www.secretgeek.net). See http://www.secretgeek.net/ms_search.asp#.

Google™

So You'd Like to Search for Something!

- Do you know where you last saw it? <u>Yes</u> or <u>No</u>
- Is it bigger than a <u>breadbox</u>? Or <u>smaller</u>?
- Is it <u>animal</u>, <u>mineral</u>, or <u>vegetable</u>?
- Maybe you should <u>buy a personal organizer</u>! Then you won't keep losing things.
- Did you check <u>under the bed</u>?

©2004 Google - Searching 8,058,044,651 web pages

Unless Microsoft can correct this wrongheaded approach to search, WinFS promises to be so overengineered as to be completely unusable.

Michael Bean

THE PITFALLS OF OUTSOURCING PROGRAMMERS

Why Some Software Companies Confuse the Box with the Chocolates[1]

Offshoring and outsourcing have become hot topics over the last year, as the least creative U.S. companies rush to dump their software development tasks on bright, educated programmers in India, China, and Eastern Europe, and newly unemployed American programmers surprise themselves by making heartfelt arguments in favor of protectionism.

I've read entire books about outsourcing, and fundamentally nobody seems to understand that software development is design, not manufacturing. Every single line of code that gets written involves making a decision about the design of the software. And for software companies, and any other company that derives competitive advantage from proprietary software, outsourcing design is, eventually, fatal.

In 2001 I wrote:

[D]uring the recent dotcom mania a bunch of quack business writers suggested that the company of the future would be totally virtual—just a trendy couple sipping Chardonnay in their living room outsourcing everything. What these hyperventilating "visionaries" overlooked is that the market pays for value added. Two yuppies in a living room buying an e-commerce engine from

1. Michael Bean, "The Pitfalls of Outsourcing Programmers," Forio Business Simulations (http://www.forio.com). See http://www.forio.com/outsourcing.htm.

company A and selling merchandise made by company B and warehoused and shipped by company C, with customer service from company D, isn't honestly adding much value. In fact, if you've ever had to outsource a critical business function, you realize that outsourcing is hell. Without direct control over customer service, you're going to get nightmarishly bad customer service—the kind people write about in their weblogs when they tried to get someone, *anyone*, from some phone company to do even the most basic thing. If you outsource fulfillment, and your fulfillment partner has a different idea about what constitutes prompt delivery, your customers are not going to be happy, and there's nothing you can do about it, because it took 3 months to find a fulfillment partner in the first place, and in fact, you won't even know that your customers are unhappy, because they can't talk to you, because you've set up an outsourced customer service center with the explicit aim of *not* listening to your own customers. That e-commerce engine you bought? There's no way it's going to be as flexible as what Amazon does with obidos, which they wrote themselves. (And if it is, then Amazon has no advantage over their competitors who bought the same thing). And no off-the-shelf web server is going to be as blazingly fast as what Google does with their hand-coded, hand-optimized server.[2]

Bean's essay is the clearest and least politically charged writing I've seen. It's a pleasure to see such a lucid explanation that really cuts to the heart of the issue, especially in a year of so much morbidly bad writing on the topic. – Ed.

~

Clothing and toys are manufactured overseas. So why not make software there too, where labor is cheaper?

In the last few years, many U.S. technology companies have moved their software development to India. In 2004, Hewlett-Packard became India's largest multinational IT employer,[3] with more than 10,000 employees.

The enthusiasm for overseas outsourcing mirrors the enthusiasm for Internet companies in the 1990s. Ravi Chiruvolu, a partner at Charter Venture Capital, wrote that "Venture Capitalists decided that because of

---

2. Joel Spolsky, *In Defense of Not-Invented-Here Syndrome*. First published on the Web October 14, 2001. http://www.joelonsoftware.com/articles/fog0000000007.html.

3. See http://news.zdnet.co.uk/business/employment/0,39020648,39118282,00.htm.

cheap engineering talent in countries like India it would be more cost effective to outsource software development. If Nike could outsource sneaker manufacturing, we could do the same with code."[4] Following similar logic, Oracle decided to double the number of software engineers it employs in India to 6,000.[5]

Much of the writing on outsourcing asserts that companies that outsource have an ethical obligation to retain jobs locally. Although the outsourcing trend has resulted in a net transfer of jobs outside of the United States, this isn't about job losses in the U.S. We live in a global economy. People in India deserve jobs as much as people in the United States or anywhere else, and it's worrisome when companies are criticized for outsourcing solely because they have hired people overseas.

Although outsourcing isn't unethical, software companies that outsource are making a strategic blunder when they decide to move development away from the rest of the organization. Outsourcing fails when software companies confuse *operational effectiveness* and *strategy*. Operational effectiveness is about working cheaper or faster. Strategy is about the creation of a long-term competitive advantage, which, for software companies, is the ability to create innovative applications.

Outsourcing programmers works when the software developed isn't a key part of the pipeline of innovation for products a company actually sells. For example, when website design or back-office software such as payroll or inventory control is outsourced, that can be good because it improves operational effectiveness.

But writing innovative software cannot be done on an assembly line. It requires hard-to-find development and design skills. Farming out development to legions of programmers overseas will not create a differentiation advantage. When a software company outsources development, that company loses its capacity to innovate and its competitive advantage.

This isn't because Indian programmers are less skilled or less creative than programmers elsewhere. Outsourcing hurts innovation when people aren't able to communicate frequently and casuall Frequent and

4. See http://www.charterventures.com/news/vcj_techtalk_2003r

5. See http://www.zdnet.com.au/jobs/news_trends/story/0,20000

casual conversations are impossible across nine time zones.[6] Innovation is also sacrificed when the programmers who are making discoveries and thinking of new ideas for your software aren't around for the long term because they don't work for you. It doesn't matter where your company is based or where you outsource your programmers: if your software company outsources its programmers developing your core software, then it can't support innovation.

If you're building an innovative software company, you need to retain your best and brightest programmers internally. Software companies entirely based in India can successfully innovate over the long term, as can U.S. companies or companies based anywhere else. It's the trend of U.S. software companies outsourcing all their development that's bad strategy.

~

Why Some Software Companies Confuse the Box with the Chocolates

I live near North Beach in San Francisco. North Beach is known for its Italian restaurants, its nightlife, and for its little specialty shops. Recently, I bought some chocolates from XOX Truffles, one of these specialty shops in North Beach. These chocolates are fantastic. Owner Jean-Marc Gorce makes them by hand, and his small shop has been rated as one of the top 10 in the United States.

Jean-Marc recently started selling his chocolates in gold and blue boxes. I like the new design. When I asked him about the boxes, he told me that his wife designed them and he found a company in the Philippines that could produce the boxes in the small volume they needed for a good price.

---

6.   The difference in time zone between the United States and India usually means there is no overlap between the working days of each country. Teams that need to coordinate their work via email usually find that a simple back-and-forth conversation that would take a handful of emails and 20 minutes in the same time zone takes several weeks when communicating with someone who won't read your message until the next morning, while asleep. – Ed.

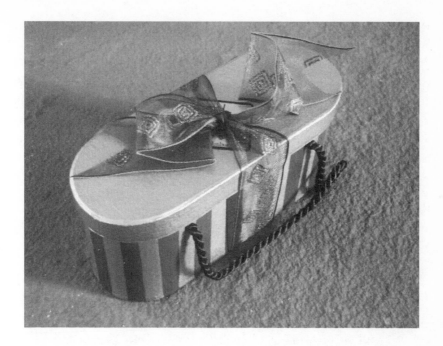

Jean-Marc's gold and blue boxes are an example of successful out-sourcing. Jean-Marc sells chocolates, not boxes. The design and production of chocolates is his core competency. Jean-Marc can outsource box production, improving his operational efficiency without sacrificing his reputation as a maker of superlative chocolates.

While outsourcing boxes improves Jean-Marc's operational effectiveness, he would never consider outsourcing his chocolate truffle production because he would lose his core differentiation advantage. Yet, in their enthusiasm for cost savings, many U.S. software companies have done precisely that—outsourcing their core technology and key strategic differentiator.

~

Design and Assembly Are Different

This isn't the first time companies have tried to commoditize software development. In the '80s, Japanese companies unsuccessfully attempted to set up software factories to manufacture programs. They discovered that just throwing a lot of programmers together doesn't create innovative software.

But, as I've stated, not all outsourcing is bad. And in some industries, outsourcing may be essential to stay competitive. For example, it makes sense to outsource the manufacture of clothing and toys. Most of the cost of clothing and toy manufacturing is in the assembly, not the design. Those products can still be designed close to corporate headquarters but assembled elsewhere to keep costs low.

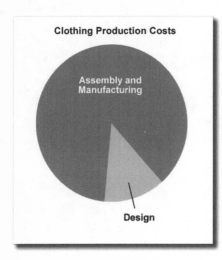
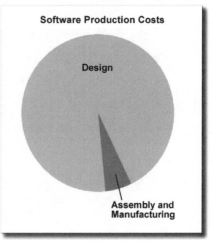

But writing a software program is primarily a design challenge. Nearly all of the costs of creating software come from writing the program, not the assembly. The assembly stage for software is really just copying the final program onto a disk and enclosing it with a manual in a box.

Harvard Business School's Michael Porter,[7] an expert on strategy and competitive advantage, nicely summarized the problem with competing solely on operational effectiveness:[8]

"If all you're trying to do is essentially the same thing as your rivals, then it's unlikely that you'll be very successful. It's incredibly arrogant for a company to believe that it can deliver the same sort of product that

---

7. See http://dor.hbs.edu/fi_redirect.jhtml?facInfo=bio&facEmId=mporter.

8. See http://www.fastcompany.com/online/44/porter.html.

its rivals do and actually do better for very long. That's especially true today, when the flow of information and capital is incredibly fast. It's extremely dangerous to bet on the incompetence of your competitors— and that's what you're doing when you're competing on operational effectiveness."

The software outsourcing fad is bad for companies not because of the short-term programmer layoffs but because technology companies will lose their capacity to innovate. Software companies that outsource their programming talent will fail to innovate as rapidly as their competitors. Ultimately, competitors that have in-house developers and can innovate more rapidly will replace these companies.

Rory Blyth

EXCEL AS A DATABASE[1]

Just wait until you find out that your corporate firewall strips the pictures from incoming email. – Ed.

∿

As a developer, you've probably, at some unfortunate point in your life (possibly several points, actually), been handed an Excel file that has been crammed full of "data" by someone in marketing and been told to "do something with it."

Columns probably didn't line up, and a thousand different fonts were used. Every feature of Excel was probably abused and abused again to avoid having to use an actual database application for storage of the data.

Of course, it's up to you to make sense of the layout, and marketing could just give a bleepity-bleep about what a pain it is to suck weird data out of Excel and "do something with it" when little or (more often) no thought has been given to possibly making the data consistent or, dare I say, orderly.

To this end, I've put together an art project to illustrate the process. What you will see unfold before your peepers is a process of discovery— my thoughts on how these files are created.

---

1. Rory Blyth, "Excel as a Database," Neopoleon.com (http://www.neopoleon.com), September 29, 2003. See http://neopoleon.com/blog/posts/434.aspx.

Note I wound up drawing one of the characters with fangs and, eventually, "crazy eyes"—I don't know why I did this. It just felt right.[2]

---

2. It's because you're a complete lunatic, Rory. – *Ed.*

Hey—I know what you're thinking: "That was a little weird, Rory."
Yup.

Adam Bosworth

ICSOC04 TALK[1]

Adam Bosworth is probably the most important software designer you've never heard of, and one of the leading thinkers about software architecture of our time. His point is simple: smart computer scientists create marvelous edifices of rigid complexity that are simply too complicated for humans to really understand, so they never go anywhere. But the really smart computer scientists use their intelligence to simplify their designs, making them workable for the masses, and those are the architectures that matter.
Back in 2002 I wrote:[2]

Whenever somebody gives you a spec for some new technology, if you can't understand the spec, don't worry too much. Nobody else is going to understand it, either, and it's probably not going to be important. This is the lesson of SGML, which hardly anyone used, until Tim Berners-Lee dumbed it down dramatically and suddenly people understood it. For the same reason he simplified the file transfer protocol, creating HTTP to replace FTP.

You can see this phenomenon all over the place; even within a given technology some things are easy enough to figure out and people use them (like COM's IUnknown), while others are so morbidly complicated (IMonikers) when they should be simple (what's wrong with URLs?) that they languish.

---

1. Adam Bosworth, "ICSOC04 Talk," Adam Bosworth's Weblog: Thoughts on computing (http://www.adambosworth.net), November 18, 2004. See http://www.adambosworth.net/archives/000031.html. Originally presented at the 2nd International Conference on Service-Oriented Computing in New York City.

2. *Joel on Software* entry for April 2, 2002. On the Web at http://www.joelonsoftware.com/news/20020402.html.

The thing about the too-complicated specs is that nobody wants to look stupid, so they never call the designers on designing something too complicated. For years and years as C++ became increasingly Byzantine and incomprehensible, nobody was willing to say, "Stop it, this is too hard for any human being to understand," because they didn't want to look dumb, but they did quietly vote with their feets by switching to Visual Basic and PHP and Perl, which were understandable by mere mortals. You don't have to feel bad if you don't understand CORBA and don't quite get what all those WS-* things are all about, because nobody else will, either, and they're unlikely to be important outside of a small niche. VoIP languishes for years and years because H.323 is beyond the ability of mere mortals, until the Skype designers toss the whole thing and make a doohickey that lets you place phone calls over the Internet. There, was that so hard? – Ed.

~

I gave a talk yesterday at the ICSOC04.[3] It was essentially a reminder to a group of very smart people that their intelligence should be used to accommodate really simple user and programmer models, not to build really complex ones. Since I was preceded by Don Ferguson of IBM and followed the next day by Tim Berners-Lee, it seemed especially wise to stick to simple and basic ideas. Here is the talk.

I'm sandwiched by smarter and more august speakers. Don Ferguson of IBM builds edifices of such sophistication and elaboration as to daunt the designers of the extraordinary archways of the Alhambra. Tim Berners-Lee created the Web as we know it today and preaches a sort of religion about the semantic Web from his aerie at MIT that is totally over my head. These are very smart gentlemen. One would be foolish to try to appear smart when speaking between them. Accordingly, I'm going to take the opposite tack. I'm going to talk about the virtues of KISS (which I'll conveniently describe as keeping it simple and sloppy) and its effect on computing on the Internet.

There has been, of course, an eternal tension between that part of humanity that celebrates our diversity, imperfectability, and faults as

---

3. See http://icsoc.dit.unitn.it.

part of the rich tapestry of the human condition and that part which seeks to perfect itself, to control, to build complex codes and rules for conduct which, if zealously adhered to, guarantee an orderly process.

This talk is about this conflict as it relates to computing on the Internet. This talk is also a polemic in support of KISS. As such it is unfair, opinionated, and perhaps even unconscionable. Indeed, at times it will verge on a jeremiad.

It is an ironic truth that those who seek to create systems that most assume the perfectibility of humans end up building the systems that are the most soul destroying and most rigid—systems that rot from within, until like great, creaking, rotten oak trees, they collapse on top of themselves, leaving a sour smell and decay. We saw it happen in 1991 with the astonishing fall of the USSR. Conversely, those systems that best take into account the complex, frail, brilliance of human nature and build in flexibility, checks and balances, and tolerance tend to survive beyond all hopes.

So it goes with software. That software which is flexible, simple, sloppy, tolerant, and altogether forgiving of human foibles and weaknesses turns out to be actually the most steel-cored, able to survive and grow, while that software which is demanding, abstract, rich but systematized turns out to collapse in on itself in a slow and grim implosion.

Consider the spreadsheet. It is a protean, sloppy, plastic, flexible medium that is, ironically, the despair of all accountants and auditors because it is virtually impossible to reliably understand a truly complex and rich spreadsheet. Lotus Corporation (now IBM), filled with Harvard MBAs and PhDs in CS from MIT, built Improv. Improv set out "to fix all this." It was an auditor's dream. It provided rarified heights of abstraction, formalisms for rows and columns, and in short was truly comprehensible. It failed utterly, not because it failed in its ambitions but because it succeeded.[4]

---

4. I remember Improv because it came out while I was working on Excel, and claimed to be "the future of spreadsheets." Rather than giving you a free-form grid of cells, Improv required you to define strict n-dimensional hypercubes for your data. Rather than allowing you to enter any formula in any cell, Improv only allowed you to define new rows and columns whose values were computed from existing rows and columns. There was none of the flexibility of traditional spreadsheets. Improv assumed that spreadsheets were used for the kind of models made by MBA students. In fact, when we did a little market research we found that most spreadsheet users are just making lists, and the real world never fits into n-dimensional hypercubes as well as it did at Wharton. – Ed.

Consider search. I remember the first clunky demos that Microsoft presented when Bill Gates first started to talk about Information At Your Fingertips[5] with their complex screens for entering search criteria and their ability to handle Boolean logic. One of my own products, Access, had the seemingly easier Query by Example.[6] Yet, today half a billion people search every day and what do they use? Not Query by Example. Not Boolean logic. They use a solution of staggering simplicity and ambiguity, namely free-text search. The engineering is hard, but the user model is simple and sloppy.

Consider user interface. When HTML first came out it was unbelievably sloppy and forgiving, permissive and ambiguous. I remember listening many years ago to the head, then and now, of Microsoft Office, saying contemptuously in 1995 that HTML would never succeed because it was so primitive and that Word would win because Word documents were so rich and controlled in their layout. Of course, HTML is today the basic building block for huge swathes of human information. What's more, in one of the unintended ironies of software history, HTML was intended to be used as a way to provide a truly malleable plastic layout language that would never be bound by 2-dimensional limitations—ironic because hordes of CSS fanatics have been trying to bind it with straightjackets ever since and bad-mouthing tables, and generations of tools have been layering pixel-precise 2-dimensional layout on top of it. And yet, ask any gifted web author, like Jon Udell, and they will tell you that they often use it in the lazy, sloppy, intuitive human way that it was designed to work. They just pour in content. In 1996 I was at some of the initial XML meetings. The participants' anger at HTML for "corrupting" content with layout was intense. Some of the initial backers of XML were frustrated SGML folks who wanted a better, cleaner world in which data was pristinely separated from presentation. In short, they disliked one of the great success stories of software history, one that succeeded because of its limitations, not

---

5. Information At Your Fingertips, or IAYF, was the "vision" Bill Gates laid out for Microsoft to work on in the early 1990s, before the Internet happened. – *Ed.*

6. Query by Example is a user interface that lets you search a database for rows by entering a new row with some of the values filled in and the rest of the values left blank. Then you press a button and the database engine returns a list of all the rows that match those particular values. So for example if you entered a row with "<18" in the age field and "NY" in the State field, you'd get a complete list of people under the age of 18 in New York. – *Ed.*

despite them. I very much doubt that an HTML that had initially shipped as a clean layered set of content (XML, layout rules—XSLT, and formatting—CSS) would have had anything like the explosive uptake.

Now I backed XML in 1996, but as it turns out, I backed it for exactly the opposite reason. I wanted a flexible, relaxed, sloppy human way to share data between programs, and compared to the RPCs and DCOMs and IIOPs of that day, XML was an incredibly flexible, plastic, easy-going medium. It still is. And because it is, not despite it, it has rapidly become the most widely used way to exchange data between programs in the world. And slowly, but surely, we have seen the other older systems collapse, crumple, and descend toward irrelevance.

Consider programming itself. An unacknowledged war goes on every day in the world of programming. It is a war between the humans and the computer scientists. It is a war between those who want simple, sloppy, flexible, human ways to write code and those who want clean, crisp, clear, correct ways to write code. It is the war between PHP and C++/Java. It used to be the war between C and dBASE. Programmers at the level of those who attend Columbia University, programmers at the level of those who have made it through the gauntlet that is Google recruiting, programmers at the level of this audience are all people who love precise tools, abstraction, serried ranks of orderly propositions, and deduction. But most people writing code are more like my son. Code is just a hammer they use to do the job. PHP is an ideal language for them. It is easy. It is productive. It is flexible. Associative arrays are the backbone of this language, which, like XML, is therefore flexible and self-describing. They can easily write code that dynamically adapts to the information passed in and easily produces XML or HTML. For them, the important issue is the content and the community, not the technology. How do they find the right RSS feeds? How do they enable a community to collaborate, appoint moderators, and dynamically decide whose posts can go through and whose should be reviewed? How do they filter information by reputation? These are the issues that they worry about, not the language.

In the same way, I see two diametrically opposed tendencies in the model for exchanging information between programs today:

On the one hand we have RSS 2.0 or Atom. The documents that are based on these formats are growing like a bay weed. Nobody really cares which one is used because they are largely interoperable. Both are essentially lists of links to content with interesting associated metadata. Both enable a model for capturing reputation, filtering, standoff annotation, and so on. There was an abortive attempt to impose a rich abstract analytic formality on this community under the aegis of RDF and RSS 1.0. It failed. It failed because it was really too abstract, too formal, and altogether too hard to be useful to the shock troops just trying to get the job done. Instead, RSS 2.0 and Atom have prevailed and are used these days to put together talk shows and play lists (podcasting), photo albums (Flickr), schedules for events, lists of interesting content, news, shopping specials, and so on. There is a killer app for it, blog-readers/RSS viewers. Anyone can play. It is becoming the easy, sloppy lingua franca by which information flows over the Web. As it flows, it is filtered, aggregated, extended, and even converted, like water flowing from streams to rivers down to great estuaries. It is something one can get directly using a URL over HTTP. It takes one line of code in most languages to fetch it. It is a world that Google and Yahoo are happily adjusting to, as media centric, as malleable, as flexible and chaotic, and as simple and consumer focused as they are.

On the other hand, we have the world of SOAP and WSDL and XML SCHEMA and WS_ROUTING and WS_POLICY and WS_SECURITY and WS_EVENTING and WS_ADDRESSING and WS_RELIABLEMESSAGING and attempts to formalize rich conversation models. Each spec is thicker and far more complex than the initial XML one. It is a world with which the IT departments of the corporations are profoundly comfortable. It appears to represent ironclad control. It appears to be auditable. It appears to be controllable. If the world of RSS is streams and rivers and estuaries, laden with silt picked up along the way, this is a world of Locks, Concrete Channels, Dams, and Pure Water Filters. It is a world for experts, arcane, complex, and esoteric. The code written to process these messages is so early-bound that it is precompiled from the WSDLs, and as many have found, when it doesn't work, no human can figure out why. The difference between HTTP, with its small number of simple verbs, and this world, with its innumerable layers that must be composed together in Byzantine complexity, cannot be overstated. It is, in short, a world only IBM and Microsoft could love. And they do.

On the one hand we have Blogs and Photo Albums and Event Schedules and Favorites and Ratings and News Feeds. On the other we have CRM and ERP and BPO and all sorts of enterprise-oriented, three-letter acronyms.

As I said earlier, I remember listening many years ago to someone saying contemptuously that HTML would never succeed because it was so primitive. It succeeded, of course, precisely because it was so primitive. Today, I listen to the same people at the same companies say that XML over HTTP can never succeed because it is so primitive. Only with SOAP and SCHEMA and so on can it succeed. But the real magic in XML is that it is self-describing. The RDF guys never got this because they were looking for something that has never been delivered, namely universal truth. Saying that XML couldn't succeed because the semantics weren't known is like saying that relational databases couldn't succeed because the semantics weren't known or text search cannot succeed for the same reason. But there is a germ of truth in this assertion. It was and is hard to tell anything about the XML in a universal way. It is why InfoPath[7] has had to jump through so many contorted hoops to enable easy editing. By contrast, the RSS model is easy with an almost arbitrary set of *known* properties for an item in a list, such as the name, the description, the link, and MIME type and size if it is an enclosure. As with HTML, there is just enough information to be useful. Like HTML, it can be extended when necessary, but most people do it judiciously. Thus, blogreaders and aggregators can effortlessly show the content and understanding that the value is in the information. Oh yes, there is one other difference between blogreaders and InfoPath. Blogreaders are free. They understand that the value is in the content, not the device.[8]

RSS embodies a very simple proposition that Tim Berners-Lee has always held to be one of the most important and central tenets of his revolution, namely that every piece of content can be addressed by a URL. In the language of RSS we call these "permalinks."[9] This idea has profound value. Dave Sifry of Technorati pointed out to me recently that one of the most remarkable things about RSS and weblogs (blogs) is the

---

7. A Microsoft product for filling out forms that is, essentially, a glorified XML editor. – *Ed.*

8. Well, some of them are. InfoPath is really so expensive that it is never touched outside of corporations who are already paying a large annual license fee to Microsoft for the complete version of Office. – *Ed.*

9. When a blogger wants to link to something another blogger wrote today, rather than linking to their home page, which will change tomorrow, they link to the "permalink," a permanent link that will always display the same content. – *Ed.*

manner in which they have started to solve one of the most tragic things about the Web, namely the incivility of the discourse. The Web, in many ways, today represents a textbook example of the tragedy of the commons. Because sending email is virtually free, we have spam. Because posting messages is virtually free and anonymous, we have groups where a small number of people can overwhelm the discussion with loud and senseless chatter. But one of the values of being able to reference every element is that now comments about elements can be distributed over the Web. The Web becomes something like a giant room in which people comment on other people's thought via posts in their own weblogs. In so doing they put their reputation on the line. These are hardly cheap and anonymous posts. They take up real estate in a place that is associated with your own point of view and reputation. And thus the comments tend to be measured, thoughtful, and judicious. Furthermore if they are not, either you can decide that it is OK or you can opt out. It is like dueling editorials in a pair of newspapers.

By contrast, the rigid abstract layers of web service plumbing are all anonymous, endless messages flowing through under the rubric of the same URL. Unless they are logged, there is no accountability. Because they are all different and since the spec that defines their grammar, XML Schema, is the marriage of a camel to an elephant to a giraffe, only an African naturalist could love these messages. They are far better, mind you, than the MOM messages[10] that preceded them. Since they are self-describing, it *is* possible to put dynamic filters in to reroute or reshape them using XPATH and XSLT and XML Query and even other languages, all of which can easily detect whether the messages are relevant and if so, where the interesting parts are. This is goodness. It is twenty-first century. But the origination and termination points, wrapped in the Byzantine complexity of JAX RPC or .NET, are still frozen in the early-bound[11] rigidity of the twentieth.

I would like to say that we are at a crossroads, but the truth is never so simple. The truth is that people use the tools that work for them. Just as for some programmers the right tool is PHP, and for others the right

---

10. Messaging-Oriented Middleware. I don't know what it is, but it sounds horrible. – *Ed.*

11. I think what Adam means here by *early-bound* is that you write code assuming you know exactly what all messages will look like, and the code is compiled to deal only with messages of exactly that format, and if anything ever changes, you get a nice exception and nothing runs. – *Ed.*

tool is Java, so it is true that for some programmers the right tool is RSS and for others it is WS-*. There is no clear "winner" here. What I am sure about is the volumes and the values. The value is in the information and its ability to be effortlessly aggregated, evaluated, filtered, and enhanced.

What does this mean to you? Think of the radio. When it was a novelty, the real value was in the radio itself. There was relatively little content, but lots of people wanted the radio. At a certain point, however, radios got good enough and transmission got good enough and the value ineluctably swung to the content. This is why the DRM[12] fights are so bitter, why podcasting is so revolutionary, why Howard Stern was paid so much to play on a private radio model. That's where the value is. We have arrived at the same point for computing. The value is neither in the computers nor in the software that runs on them. It is in the content and the software's ability to find and filter content and in the software's ability to enable people to collaborate and communicate about content (and each other). Who here really cares if Excel adds a new menu item unless it is one that lets you more easily discover information on the Web, and possibly update and interact with it or with others about it?

What about mobile phones? What do they mean? Is it really interesting to have a spreadsheet or a PowerPoint on your mobile phone? Or is it more interesting to know where the nearest ATM is, where the nearest Indian restaurant that your friends like is, which are the CS books in the store for a given course, which course has the best section person and what its schedule is, or what the reviews of the books say? Is it really interesting to have an address book that is synced to your PC, or is it more interesting to see the presence of the people who are involved in your class, your project, your party plans, and be able to coordinate and plan an event with them? And if it is the latter, then isn't the value really coming from the knowledge of with whom you are working, socializing, and studying; what they think about things you care about, such as movies, classes, restaurants, and news articles, rather than the software on the device itself? Isn't the device really just a sort of n-way radio/classified? Soon as you deliver context and content and community and collaboration over the Web, 2 billion people will be able to see and interact with your solutions.

---

12. Digital rights management – *Ed.*

There is a lot of talk about Web 2.0. Many seem to assume that the "second" Web will be about rich intelligent clients who share information across the Web and deal with richer media (photos, sound, video). There is no doubt that this is happening. Whether it is Skype[13] or our product Hello,[14] or iTunes,[15] people are increasingly plugging into the Web as a way to collaborate and share media. But I posit that this isn't the important change. It is glitzy, fun, entertaining, useful, but at the end of the day, not profoundly new.

What *has* been new is information overload. Email long ago became a curse. Blogreaders only exacerbate the problem. I can't even imagine the video or audio equivalent because it will be so much harder to filter through. What *will* be new is people coming together to rate, to review, to discuss, to analyze, and to provide 100,000 Zagat's,[16] models of trust for information, for goods, and for services. Who gives the best buzz cut in Flushing? We see it already in eBay. We see it in the importance of the number of deals and the ratings for people selling used books on Amazon. As I said in my blog

> My mother never complains that she needs a better client for Amazon. Instead, her interest is in better community tools, better book lists, easier ways to see the book lists, more trust in the reviewers, librarian discussions since she is a librarian, and so on.

This is what will be new. In fact, it already is. You want to see the future. Don't look at Longhorn. Look at Slashdot: 500,000 nerds coming together every day just to manage information overload. Look at Bloglines.[17] What will be the big enabler? Will it be Attention.XML[18] as Steve Gillmor and Dave Sifry hope? Or something else less formal and more organic? It doesn't matter. The currency of reputation and judgment is the answer to the tragedy of the commons, and it will find a way.

---

13. A service providing free over-the-Internet phone calls – *Ed.*

14. Google's picture-sharing application – *Ed.*

15. Apple's online music store – *Ed.*

16. A restaurant guide with reviews contributed by readers. – *Ed.*

17. An online blog aggregator now owned by InterActiveCorp. – *Ed.*

18. An XML standard for keeping tracking of what you're supposed to be paying attention to. – *Ed.*

This is where the action will be. Learning Avalon[19] or Swing[20] isn't going to matter. Machine learning and inference and data mining will. For the first time since computers came along, AI is the mainstream.

I find this deeply satisfying. It says that in the end the value is in our humanity, our diversity, our complexity, and our ability to learn to collaborate. It says that it is the human side, the flexible side, the organic side of the Web that is going to be important and not the dry and analytic and taxonomical side, not the systematized and rigid and stratified side that will matter.

In the end, I am profoundly encouraged and hopeful that the growth on the Web is one that is slowly improving the civility and tenor of discourse. Just as porn seems to be an unpleasant leading user of technology, so does crude and vituperative communication seem to be a pattern for early adopters, and it is a relief to see that forms of governance, trust, and deliberation are now emerging.

There are those who will say that all this is utopian. If utopian means not being afraid to dream, then indeed it is. So was Tim's initial vision of universal access to information. So is Google's mission. T. E. Lawrence wrote in the *Seven Pillars of Wisdom*, "All men dream: but not equally. Those who dream by night in the dusty recesses of their minds wake in the day to find that it was vanity: but the dreamers of the day are dangerous men, for they may act their dream with open eyes, to make it possible."

I encourage all of you to act on your dreams with open eyes. I encourage all of you to dream of an Internet that enables people to work together, to communicate, to collaborate, and to discover. I encourage all of you to remember that, in the long run, we are all human and, as you add value, add it in ways that are simple, flexible, sloppy, and, in the end, everything that the Platonists in you abhor.

---

19. The graphical programming library for Microsoft's planned "Longhorn" operating system. – *Ed.*

20. A graphical programming library for Java. – *Ed.*

danah boyd

AUTISTIC SOCIAL SOFTWARE[1]

I think 2004 will be remembered as the year that socially dysfunctional Silicon Valley nerds started getting venture capital to codify their own Asperger's Syndrome in the social interfaces that they created with services like Orkut and LinkedIn, and demonstrated thoroughly just how completely they don't understand human–human interaction, let alone computer-mediated human–human interaction. I noticed on danah's blog recently that AOL only lets you have 200 friends. First of all, 200? Not even a base two number! What's going on there! I can just hear Dustin Hoffman in Rainman: "Can't have more than 200 friends. Must discard a friend. Kmart sucks." – Ed.

~

A s technologists, we often frame technological use rather than build technology based on users' practices and needs. In this talk, I step back and offer a different framing for what we technologists and entrepreneurs have done and what kinds of values we have instilled in users. My goal is to challenge us to reconsider our approach so that we can truly meet the needs of people.

---

1. danah boyd, "Autistic Social Software," talk given at Supernova Conference, June 24, 2004. See http://www.danah.org/papers/Supernova2004.html.

~

Sociable Media, Sci-Fi, and Mental Illness

While "social software" has recently emerged as a phenomenon in the tech community, "sociable media" has been around since the beginning of the Internet. Email, BBSes, Usenet, chat rooms, MUDs, and MOOs all captured the imagination of technologists throughout the 1980s and '90s. Alongside the development of these technologies, academics and pundits spouted off about the utopian dreams that could be fulfilled by these innovations. Their prescriptions mirrored the particular concepts set forth by science fiction, often without the richness that the writers were trying to convey. Idealists envisioned a world where embodied identity would not matter because online, no one would know that you're a dog.

While many science fiction writers try to convey the nuances of human behavior, their emphasis is on the storyline, and they often convey the social issues around a technology as it affects that story. Building universal assumptions based on the limited scenarios set forth by sci-fi is problematic; doing so fails to capture the rich diversity of human behavior. Science fiction is not trying to understand human psychology in general; the authors are trying to tap into some aspect of human behavior in order to convey a story.

Extending those conceptual models to the world at large fails to handle the reality that our lives do not play out in a cleanly packaged narrative. From a human psychology perspective, sci-fi models are often naive and simplistic, tools for the story. Outside of sci-fi, human psychology has been a topic of contemporary cultural discourse for the last two decades, and topics of human dysfunction and mental illness have captured the mainstream imagination through science news articles and films. Remember, George Bush Sr. declared the 1990s "The Decade of the Brain."

Although all types of mental disorders hit the mainstream press, multiple personality disorder in particular captured the imagination of the public during the 1980s and '90s. Multiple personality was perceived to be the canonical psychiatric disorder, and films tried to capture what the disorder was about. Even *Newsweek* titled one of its articles on MPD "Unmasking Sybil: A re-examination of the most famous psychiatric patient in history."

Discussions of human psychology, mental disorders, and multiple personality also appeared in studies of the Internet. Both Sandy Stone and Sherry Turkle, two famous sociable media researchers, considered the potentials brought on by digital interactions in terms of multiple personality. They saw the opportunity for "parallel lives" and "multiple selves" as empowering, freeing the subject from the restraints of the physical body in everyday life.

Sociable technologies not only supported but encouraged pseudonymous participation; even today, we talk about it as a protective tool against privacy invasion. People were encouraged to fragment their identity into different pseudonyms so that they could properly contextualize their online participation. They were encouraged to develop multiple selves.

Guess what? People aren't that fragmented. While they may lead faceted lives, their control over what information to present when is very nuanced and cannot simply be partitioned into multiple identities.

Unfortunately, though, our earliest ideas about multiple personality have pervaded not only the discourse around but also the actual technologies of sociable media. Whenever I raise concerns about privacy or vulnerability, I'm often told that people should just create separate identities.

Think about how asinine that is. Why on earth should we encourage people to perform a mental disorder in the digital world? We do so because we've built technology that does not take into consideration the subtle nuances of the identity faceting with which people are already accustomed. As geeks, we were trained to separate policy and mechanism through systems courses. We rely on people to figure out the policies, not realizing that we've framed what is possible through our technology.

As we know, the Internet did not live up to the fantasy of a world where social identity no longer mattered. In a project called "The Turing Game,"[2] Amy Bruckman showed that people performed their everyday

---

2. See http://www.cc.gatech.edu/elc/turing/.

identity through their personas even when they were trying to perform otherwise. Today, there is a technological tension between having a federated identity[3] (such as Passport) and continuing to build systems that make users build new identities with each new system. The debate around this has turned pseudo-religious, but every effort that I've seen still focuses on the technology, not the people and practices. Because of this inverted focus, things like access control lists (ACLs) and open Friend of a Friend (FOAF) protocols are bound to fail. They aren't situated in people's lives.

$\sim$

Autism and Attention Deficit Disorder

While earlier sociable media was couched in representations of science fiction and metaphors of popular psychology, contemporary sociable media is not devoid of these references. Social disorders, albeit different ones, still frame many of our conceptions about human psychology. Consider the plethora of articles about autism and Asperger's during 2003–2004. For those who aren't familiar with Asperger's, it is a mild form of autism marked by normal intelligence and poor social and communication skills. Asperger's patients often systematize social activity in order to give it the structure necessary to be procedurally performed in everyday life. Recently, researchers have argued that Asperger's and autism run rampant in the Bay Area. It is important to note that Asperger's is often conflated with another one of mainstream media's pet "mental illnesses": Attention Deficit Disorder. ADD is often marked by an inability to focus on a given task, or, in the case of ADHD, a tendency to hyperfocus and then lose complete focus. Just as with multiple personality, mainstream media has made autism and ADD appear to be commonplace and everywhere.

Technologists have also adopted and promoted these concepts, marking them as valuable to the way of geek life. Many of you are

---

3. A hypothetical system, never successfully built, in which a single database holds all your
    account information so that you can use the same logon information to access every web-
    site and account. – *Ed.*

staring at your laptops, multitasking.[4] Although you will only remember a fragment of this talk, you will probably tell me that you remembered the important part or that you were practicing your continuous partial attention. Some of you may already be ninja masters at this, but the majority of you are probably paying poor attention to both the computer task and to me. But you *want* to be a continuous partial attention ninja master because you've been told that all of the cool kids are.

While autism is not nearly as chic as ADD, there are aspects of it that are promoted in our culture. Geek culture has always eschewed ideas of acceptable social interaction, and its members pride themselves on having the right to act any way that they want. Don't get me wrong—I've been a rebel all of my life. But there is a value in understanding social life and figuring out how to interact with people on shared terms.

~

Socially Inept Computers

Just like their creators, computers are notorious for being pretty socially inept. Yet, with sociable media, computers take on a social role or become mediators between people engaged in social interaction. Their position in social life does not inherently make technology any more sociable; their functions are intimately entwined with what people enable them to do. Thus, the onus is on the programmers to empower technology to operate in social life.

What does this mean for sociable media? We do not understand how social life really works. Thus, we make crude approximations for it, and we make crude approximations for human psychology, too. In the tech world, we often make these assumptions based on material like science fiction and pop psychology because we pride ourselves on being removed from an understanding of social life. A simplistic or mechanical understanding of social life is the mode of functioning for autistic individuals.

---

4. At computer conferences these days, like the one where this talk was given, it's not unusual for 80% or 90% of the audience to be using laptops for *something* during the presentations. – *Ed.*

From an autistic perspective, social life can and must be program-matically and algorithmically processed and understood on simplistic categorical levels. The nuanced relationships that people regularly man-age in everyday life are boiled down to segmented possibilities. When we teach autistic children to engage in social life, we teach them things like facial expressions. We tell them that a smile means goodness, that a frown should be concerning. Step by step, we dissect social affect and try to formalize it so that these kids can understand the world. This is also what we do with computers. How different is this from asking, "Are you my friend, yes or no?"

Consider, for a moment, the recent surge of interest in articulated social networks such as Friendster, Tribe.net, LinkedIn, Orkut, and the like. These technologies attempt to formalize how people should con-struct and manage their relationships. They assume that you can rate your friends. In some cases, they procedurally direct how people can engage with new people by giving you an absolute process through which you can contact others.

While this approach certainly has its merits because it is computa-tionally possible, I'm terrified when people think that this models social life. It's so simplistic that people are forced to engage as though they have autism, as though they must interact procedurally. This approach certainly aids people who need that kind of systematization, but it is not a model that makes sense universally to all people. Furthermore, what are the implications of having technology prescribe mechanistic engage-ment? Do we really want a social life that encourages autistic interactions?

We technologists are notorious for building software based on our own practices and values instead of constructing them based on people's values and needs. Yet, such an approach can often leave the mainstream at a loss, forced to subscribe to the views set forth by developers or fail trying. If we are really trying to build sociable media that supports social interaction, shouldn't we do it based on what social life looks like? Shouldn't we allow for the vast array of nuances that enable people to interact differently depending on their needs?

None of the articulated social networks model everyday life. Feel free to read my other work[5] if you want to understand how these networks

---

5. See http://www.danah.org/papers

diverge from social life and the theoretical knowledge that they're purportedly built on. But realize that creating an open source federated identity across these networks doesn't solve the underlying problems embedded in the technology. You can't cure multiple personality disorder in order to address autism. This is exactly what we're trying to do when we talk about FOAF.

This does not mean that simplistic models of daily life are not fun and cannot be toyed with. People love to see such slices of themselves. Why do you think quizzes like "Which Star Wars character are you?" are so popular? They're not insightful, but they provide for interesting reflection, an opportunity for sharing and social play. They afford us the same opportunity for internal and shared conversation as tarot cards. That's not the same as having a meaningful model of someone's social psychology.

Simplistic models of human interaction pervade our industry. When technologies based on them are rapidly adopted, we tout the merits of those technologies, without stopping to consider what people are actually doing with them.

～

Friendster's Success

Consider Friendster. It was developed as a dating site. The expected usage scenario was simple: get people to map out their social network so that single people could be introduced to other single people in a trusted environment. Guess what? For the majority of users, this scenario did not resonate. Even those who used the "introduce" feature often did so to introduce mutual friends so that they could connect on the site.

What was successful about Friendster had nothing to do with its original purpose or design. Instead, users saw it as a flexible artifact that they could repurpose to reflect their social practices. As I learned how people embedded Friendster into their daily lives, I was fascinated by how it manifested itself as so many different tools to so many different people. Some saw it as an information-gathering tool, allowing them to learn about friends and strangers. Others saw it as a performance tool and a venting site. It was also used as a gaming device, a distribution channel for the drug dealer, an antidepressant for the voyeur, a popularity contest for the wannabe prom queen. Many also saw it as a cultural artifact necessary for all watercooler discussions.

For a while, Friendster decided to limit acceptable behavior on its site. Their reason was valid: server load problems. Due to ever-increasing downtimes and poor performance, access was limited. Yet, efforts were made to control what users did and how. This stopped the load problem by putting off early adopters. Many of the earliest adopters grew bored and disenchanted with the site; it no longer provided them with the range of interactive opportunities that drew them there. Yet, it continued to spread to new user groups whose practices differed, and they found new mechanisms for interaction on Friendster.

Consider the hundreds of students from Singapore and Indonesia who create Friendsters for their teachers so that they can write testimonials about them. While the myriad of Fakesters haunted Friendster a year ago, today's Friendster is filled with underage users and fraudulently constructed people who represent the arch nemeses of these teens' lives.

The simplicity of Friendster allowed it to be repurposed over and over again. Its popularity did not validate its underlying model, articulated social networks, or the values embedded in the technology. Its success validated that people love flexible artifacts that allow them to reflect on their identity and their social situation. Friendster's popularity was viral because of its flexibility, not because people bought into the values set forth by the company.

In the last year, hundreds of companies have decided that social networks are the hot thing and must be incorporated into everything. I'm often told that social networks are the future of the sociable Internet. Guess what? They were the cornerstone of the Internet, *always*. What is different is that we've tried to mechanically organize them, to formalize them. Doing so did not make social networks suddenly appear; formalization meant that they became less serious, more game-like. All other Internet social networks are embedded into another set of practices, not seeking an application to validate their existence.

In their current version, social networks are a performance device. We construct our identity in terms of other people. We collect friends and communities to signal who we are, what we believe in. We pad our blogrolls[6] with people that we admire. These signals say a lot of things, but they do not say anything about our actual social network—our trust relationships or information flow.

People often ask me where those early adopters of Friendster went. Sure, some went to Tribe.net or MySpace or other social networking tools, but the vast majority of them just went back to their pre-Friendster lives, no longer using any such tool. They weren't into Friendster for its social networking capabilities; they were into it because it fit into their lives.

~

Situating Technology in Practice

I was asked to talk about the future, and I have to say that I'm a little frustrated. There's a tendency to follow the hype, perfect it, fix technological problems. But, in doing so, I fear that we lose track of the bigger picture. What makes sense in this domain is not to perfect the technology and deal with the social consequences later or to build a bazillion replications, as though mimesis will bring cash flow. Instead, we must step back and think about what social practices we're aiming to address and what values we're inserting while trying to address them. We've learned a lot during this iteration, but yet we have learned nothing.

The most successful sociable technologies are those that fit into people's lives and practices; they fill the gaps that people have rather than creating artificial needs. Email and Usenet emerged to provide geeks with a mechanism for communicating one-to-one and one-to-many; they filled a need. Youth in Europe and Asia figured out how SMS could be manipulated to meet their needs, and the technologists followed their lead as new versions were developed. Even LiveJournal was based on a standard practice: journaling. It too evolved based on what it was that LiveJournal users were doing both online and off, and the practices that exist there no longer resemble journaling.

---

6. A blogroll is a list of *other* blogs that you put in the margin of your blog, usually blogs you read frequently, or blogs of friends, or blogs that you hope will link back to you. – *Ed.*

In other words, it is not to say that we can predict what technology will fit into people's lives, but we can learn from the technologies out there in order to evolve our own.

There are three ways to make technology work in the context of people:

1. Make a technology, market the hell out of it, and demand that it fit into people's lives. When this fails, logroll. In other words, bundle it with something that they need so that they're forced to use it. Personally, I think that this is pretty disgusting, although I recognize that it is the way that the majority of our industry works.

2. Make a technology, throw it out to the public, and see what catches on. Follow the people who use it. Understand them. Understand what they are doing and why and how the technology fits into their lives. Evolve to better meet the needs and desires of the people who love the technology.

3. Understand a group of people and their needs and then develop a technology that comfortably embeds itself within the practices of those people. Make technology ubiquitous.

Personally, I believe that the latter two approaches are the conscientious way of designing sociable technology. The third approach is the common mechanism used by researchers in industry, while the second can be the contribution that social software makes when it stops and pays attention to what it has produced rather than just throwing out more technology to fix technology problems.

We are talking about technology meant for people to engage with other people. Users may do the darndest things, but they're only peculiar when you try to understand it in your framework. Reframe what they are doing in their framework. Instead of demanding that they behave like we want them to behave, try to understand why they chose a path that is different from ours. When we can understand their perspective, we're halfway there.

The trick then is to design from that perspective, to truly get it, not just be tolerant of it, to iterate our technology based on their perspective since they're the ones who are evolving the practices. When we ::groan:: about those darn users, we're missing the point. They're not interacting with technology to prove a point to us. They're interacting with technology because it fits into their framework of the world. Understanding that, really getting that . . . that is the key.

I'd like to conclude with a quote by Douglas Adams in his article "How to Stop Worrying and Learn to Love the Internet":

> Working out the social politics of who you can trust and why is, quite literally, what a very large part of our brain has evolved to do.

Social software has the potential to truly reform the technology development process. Startups all around us are throwing technology out to the masses and they're using it, challenging us with their unexpected uses. We can either turn our backs on them as we beg for venture capital money using our frame of reference, or we can be true to them and convince the world that this is a more conscientious and valuable long-term approach for everyone involved. I vote that we focus on the people and stop asking them to engage in autistic practices. Let's empower them to use their nuanced approaches to social life in a meaningful way.

[Thanks to Cory Doctorow, Scott Lederer, Kevin Marks, and many others for good pointers and conversation.]

Raymond Chen

WHY NOT JUST BLOCK THE APPS THAT RELY ON UNDOCUMENTED BEHAVIOR?[1]

Windows includes quite a few sneaky and beautiful hacks to make sure that when you upgrade to a new version of the operating system, all your old applications will continue to run.

I first learned about this from one of the developers of the hit game SimCity, who told me that there was a critical bug in his application: it used memory right after freeing it, a major no-no that happened to work OK on DOS but would not work under Windows where memory that is freed is likely to be snatched up by another running application right away. The testers on the Windows team were going through various popular applications, testing them to make sure they worked OK, but SimCity kept crashing. They reported this to the Windows developers, who disassembled SimCity, stepped through it in a debugger, found the bug, and added special code that checked if SimCity was running, and if it was, ran the memory allocator in a special mode in which you could still use memory after freeing it.

Young and inexperienced engineers are driven crazy by hacks like this. But it's precisely this kind of hack that made Windows successful. Raymond Chen, an old-timer on the Windows team at Microsoft, explains it best. – Ed.

---

1. Raymond Chen, "Why Not Just Block the Apps That Rely on Undocumented Behavior?" *The Old New Thing* (http://blogs.msdn.com/oldnewthing), December 24, 2003. See http://blogs.msdn.com/oldnewthing/archive/2003/12/24/45779.aspx. Used with permission from Microsoft Corporation.

~

Why not just block the apps that rely on undocumented behavior? Because every app that gets blocked is another reason for people not to upgrade to the next version of the Microsoft® Windows® operating system. Look[2] at all these programs that would have stopped working when you upgraded from Windows 3.0 to Windows 3.1.

```
HKEY_LOCAL_MACHINE\SOFTWARE\Microsoft\
          Windows NT\CurrentVersion\Compatibility
```

Actually, this list is only partial. Many times, the compatibility fix is made inside the core component for all programs rather than targeting a specific program, as the entries in this list do.

(The Windows 2000-to-Windows XP list is stored in your C:\ WINDOWS\AppPatch directory, in a binary format to permit rapid scanning. To browse it, you can use the Compatibility Administrator that comes with the Application Compatibility Toolkit.[3])

Would you have bought Windows XP if you knew that all these programs were incompatible?

It takes only one incompatible program to sour an upgrade.

Suppose you're the IT manager of some company. Your company uses Program X for its word processor and you find that Program X is incompatible with Windows XP for whatever reason. Would you upgrade?

Of course not! Your business would grind to a halt.

"Why not call Company X and ask them for an upgrade?"

Sure, you could do that, and the answer might be, "Oh, you're using Version 1.0 of Program X. You need to upgrade to Version 2.0 for $150 per copy." Congratulations, the cost of upgrading to Windows XP just tripled.

And that's if you're lucky and Company X is still in business.

I recall a survey taken a few years ago by our Setup/Upgrade team of corporations using Windows. Pretty much every single one has at least

---

2. In the system registry; run regedit. – *Ed.*

3. See http://www.microsoft.com/windows/appcompatibility/.

one "deal-breaker" program, a program that Windows absolutely must support or they won't upgrade. In a high percentage of the cases, the program in question was developed by their in-house programming staff, and it's written in Microsoft Visual Basic® (sometimes even 16-bit Visual Basic), and the person who wrote it doesn't work there any more. In some cases, they don't even have the source code any more.

And it's not just corporate customers. This affects consumers too.

For Windows 95, my application compatibility work focused on games. Games are the most important factor behind consumer technology. The video card that comes with a typical computer has gotten better over time because games demand it. (Microsoft Office Outlook® certainly doesn't care that your card can do 20 bajillion triangles a second.) And if your game doesn't run on the newest version of Windows, you aren't going to upgrade.

Anyway, game vendors are very much like those major corporations. I made phone call after phone call to the game vendors trying to help them get their game to run under Windows 95. They didn't care. A game has a shelf life of a few months, and then it's gone. Why would they bother to issue a patch for their program to run under Windows 95? They already got their money. They're not going to make any more off that game; its three months are over. The vendors would slipstream patches and lose track of how many versions of their program were out there and how many of them had a particular problem. Sometimes they wouldn't even have the source code any more.

They simply didn't care that their program didn't run on Windows 95. (My favorite was the one that tried to walk me through creating a boot floppy.)

Oh, and that Application Compatibility Toolkit I mentioned earlier. It's a great tool for developers, too. One of the components is the Windows Application Verifier: if you run your program under the verifier, it will monitor hundreds of API calls[4] and break into the debugger when you do something wrong (like close a handle twice or allocate memory with the GlobalAlloc function but free it with the LocalAlloc function).

---

4. An API call is a request, made by a program, for Windows to do something. – *Ed.*

The new application compatibility architecture in Windows XP carries with it one major benefit (from an OS development perspective): See all those DLLs in your C:\WINDOWS\AppPatch directory? That's where many of the compatibility changes live now. The compatibility workarounds no longer sully the core OS files. (Not all classes of compatibility workarounds can be offloaded to a compatibility DLL, but it's a big help.)[5]

---

5. A DLL is a file, ending with the extension .DLL, containing code that can be used by a program that's already running. For example, if you wanted to write a spell-checker that could be used by all your programs but that did not take up any memory while it was not in use, you could write it as a DLL and then call it from your word processor and your spreadsheet as needed. Most of the functionality of Windows is provided by DLLs, and you'll find hundreds of them in the Windows directory. – Ed.

Kevin Cheng and Tom Chi

KICKING THE LLAMA[1]

1. Kevin Cheng and Tom Chi, "Kicking the Llama," OK/Cancel (http://
    www.ok-cancel.com). See http://www.ok-cancel.com/comic/4.html.

Cory Doctorow

SAVE CANADA'S INTERNET FROM WIPO[1]

Here's a neat trick. Try it at home.

Pick someone you hate. Doesn't matter why.

Find their website.

Find some random paragraph on their website.

Send a letter to their Internet provider complaining that that paragraph is a copyright violation, and invoke the DMCA. You don't even have to know what DMCA stands for. And of course the paragraph doesn't have to be a copyright violation. Just say that you're the copyright holder and the paragraph in question was copied out of your senior thesis in high school without your permission.

Nine out of 10 times, that's all it takes. Your enemy gets kicked off his Internet provider and his account is closed down. Ta-da! Instant vigilante justice.

Many, many years ago when the phone system was a government-regulated monopoly, copyright owners tried to sue Ma Bell when telephone users tried to use the phone system to transmit copyright material. Why did they sue the phone company and not the person sending the copyright material in the first place? For the same reason Willie Sutton robbed banks: that's where the money was.

---

1. Cory Doctorow, "Save Canada's Internet from WIPO," boingboing.net, A Directory of Wonderful Things (http://boingboing.net), November 6, 2004. See http://www.boingboing.net/2004/11/06/save_canadas_interne.html.

The phone companies, of course, weren't responsible and couldn't possibly serve as copyright police for every phone conversation, and the law grew to recognize this. In the case where someone is merely acting as a common carrier, carrying all data regardless of content without prejudice, they can't be held responsible for the legal ramifications of that data.

In the early days of the Internet the same legal principle was brought over from telephony. If you hire me to deliver bits from point A to point B, no matter what those bits are—completely random bits, copyright violations, ransom notes, love letters, or music videos—I'm not responsible for the content; you are. I'm just deliverin' bits. It's really the only legal principle that makes sense.

Unfortunately, making sense wasn't good enough for the music industry, already apoplectic in rage at the amount of money they weren't able to divert from artists into their own pockets because of MP3 trading. They wanted more power to prevent piracy, and they wanted to be able to go after the responsible businesses that contract to move bits from point A to point B, because, as Willie Sutton said, that's where the money was. So they lobbied hard and long and won the passage of the DMCA, a nasty bit of legislation that adds one innocuous-seeming provision: if you move bits from point A to point B, you won't be held responsible for the content you deliver, but only if you agree to take down anything anyone complains about.

Never mind if that makes sense, never mind if that gives every schmuck with a grudge the practical ability to censor anything they want on any website they want merely by sending a letter. It doesn't matter if the gripe is legit or not; the carrier needs to be able to use their "get out of jail free card" so usually they'll comply with your censorship request without investigating.

It's crappy law, but that's what we get when we let the entertainment industry lobbyists write our laws. – Ed.

~

Canada is strongly considering ratifying the 1996 WIPO "Internet Treaties." These are the treaties that caused the United States to implement the loathsome Digital Millennium Copyright Act (DMCA), and they've wrought untold damage around the world. What will this mean for Canada? Well, for starters, the *Globe and Mail* notes that a notice-and-takedown regime is inevitable:

> In what is bound to be a controversial element, the committee recommended that Internet service providers (ISPs) must be held liable for copyrighted material that goes through their systems. To be exempt from that liability, the ISPs must show they are acting as true "intermediaries," without actual or constructive knowledge of the content.
>
> ISPs should be required to comply with a "notice and takedown" system against subscribers who violate copyright laws.

Boing Boing's incomparable sysadmin, Ken Snider, a Canadian geek, wrote

> It is extremely important to me that our government not bow to CIRA. I have high hopes that the current minority gov't means they won't deal with this anytime soon, but I *want* to get the message out to every damned MP I can get my hands on. The problem is, I don't have any *specific* information on these provisions. I was hoping you would, or at least, could point me in the right direction (or even champion the cause with me! Woo!).
>
> It's *critically* important to me that Canada doesn't follow the US in this process. I'm prepared to do whatever it takes to make the reasons *why* this is a shitty idea known, I just need some help making my points clear and concise, as well as containing the appropriate amount of "politik" that they'll make a difference.

So, Ken, here are some answers for you.

Copyright is a system for regulating technology—it regulates technologies used to make and distribute copies. We have lots of technology regulation in the world: there are rules that govern the operation of automobiles and rules that govern the marketing of electrical appliances. This isn't wrong per se.

But when the 20-horsepower locomotive was invented, the black-smiths weren't able to successfully lobby to have 80 horseshoes welded to each engine, despite the rule that said that every "horse" used for transport needed four shoes. When you invent a railroad, you need rail-road rules for it, not horse-and-buggy rules. The fact that the railroad doesn't need shoes, or oats, or currycombs doesn't reflect bugs in rail-roading: those are the features of railroading.

The Internet has one overarching feature that makes it superior to the technologies that preceded it: it can copy arbitrary blobs of data from one place to another at virtually no cost, in virtually no time, with virtually no control. This is not a bug. This is what the Internet is sup-posed to do.

It was really foresighted in 1996 for WIPO to sit down to update copyright law to suit the Internet. They recognized that the Internet was a fundamentally different thing from the technologies that came before it, and of course, a new technology needs new rules and regulation.

But WIPO got it horribly wrong. The approach that WIPO took to regulating the Net was to create a set of rules that tried to make the Internet act more like radio, or TV, or photocopiers—like all the things that it had already made rules for. The WIPO approach treated the ease of copying on the Net as a bug, and set out to fix it.

Notice-and-takedown is an area where WIPO got it drastically, terri-bly wrong.

If you own a restaurant, you're not responsible for policing your cus-tomers to ensure that none of them are carrying stolen bank loot. If someone burst in and pointed at the guy at the back table and said, "He's wearing my hat!" no one would blame you if you didn't wrestle the hat away from him and give it back to the accuser.

But under notice-and-takedown, this is what we ask of our ISPs. If you allow users to host stuff, you're responsible for what they host. If they put an infringing file on your server, you're required to know what they've put online, and you'll share in their punishment if you fail to block them from posting infringing material.

Now what is and isn't a copyright infringement isn't anything like a clear-cut issue. ISPs aren't equipped to evaluate what's infringing and what isn't—hell, even Supreme Court judges have a hard time figuring it out. Operating a server doesn't qualify you to understand and evaluate copyright law.

So there's a get-out-of-jail in notice-and-takedown. If you respond to accusations of infringement by taking your customers' materials offline quickly, you won't share in their liability. Now, given the kinds of penalties available to rights-holders for online infringement (in the U.S., it's $150,000 per infringement!), it's not surprising that most ISPs avail themselves of this "safe harbor," removing stuff whenever a complaint comes in.

But a complaint isn't proof—someone who rings up your ISP and says, "That file infringes on my rights" is like the guy who busts into a restaurant and shouts, "That guy is wearing my hat!" There's no way for an ISP to evaluate whether he's genuinely aggrieved, whether he's nursing a grudge, whether he's just a nut. In the U.S., nuts, grudge-nursers, and flakes all use notice-and-takedown to censor the Internet and get material removed.

Usually rights-holders will counter that this can be addressed through something called "counter-notification," where an ISP that's removed something is given the right to contact its customer and say, "This guy says you infringed his copyright. If you disagree, let us know and we'll put your file back online and you two can sort it out in court."

But in practice, counter-notification is a rare beast. Most ISPs just do the math and decide that sending a single counter-notification letter will cost them more in lawyer-hours than the customer in question will ever make for them. They just invoke the termination clause in nearly every ISP contract and shut down the account.

This is why notice-and-takedown is a near-perfect tool for censorship. Don't like what your critics have to say? Just sent a takedown notice and poof, it's gone! The Scientologists *love* this tactic—they even get Google to remove links to sites that are critical of their "church" by asserting copyright infringement. Have a look at the truly chilling annals of ChillingEffects,[2] which gathers up takedown notices and other nasty-grams. The takedown notice is the favorite tool of the crank, the censor, and the bully.

Even when applied to genuine copyrighted works, takedown is dangerous to the point of unusability: the Business Software Alliance, MPAA, and RIAA send out automatically generated takedowns by the thousands, using software that does half-assed pattern matching on files

2. See http://chillingeffects.org.

available on the Net and then sending off letters to universities, ISPs, and other entities demanding the takedown of book reports about Harry Potter, Linux distributions with the same names as movies, and academic work by professors with the same name as musicians.

What's more, notice-and-takedown is almost always accompanied by systems for piercing Internet users' anonymity: if you want to find out your stalking victim's new address and number, you need only find the message board where she's posting about her troubles and write to the ISP as an infringed-upon rights holder, demanding her info.

If Canada wants to "solve" the problems of the Internet, it should be looking to find "Internet-native" solutions. Canada's Internet laws should treat copying as a feature, not a bug. It should empirically evaluate which sectors are negatively impacted by file sharing (mounting evidence suggests that almost none of the entertainment industry's woes can be blamed on the Net) and then solve those industries' problems with blanket licenses and other tools that don't seek to regulate copying, something that's impossible to do without breaking the Internet.

Solutions that approach the Internet as a problem are no solutions at all.

ea_spouse

EA: THE HUMAN STORY[1]

There is a major school of thought in software development, of which I am a member, that says that programmers who work more than 40 hours a week for extended periods of time actually get less work done than programmers who are not in crunch mode all the time. This is well studied and documented in books like Peopleware[2] *by Timothy Lister and Tom DeMarco. When people work more than about eight hours a day at programming tasks, the quality of their work suffers so much that they need to do two hours of bug-fixing for every hour of coding that they do. The work they do after eight hours is actually negative work.*

Another core belief of mine is that an experienced employee is worth much more than a new employee, and that it can take a new employee a year to get fully up to speed and be as productive as the senior members of the team. If ea_spouse is correct that EA's employee turnover is running 50% a year thanks to the long hours, this company has a serious problem.

ea_spouse's perspective is the human one, the perspective of the employees and their families, which is important.

But I'd like to point out that even if all you cared about was the employer's perspective, if all you cared about was what Electronic Arts should do to maximize their profits, the permanent crunch time policy is still *completely counterproductive.*

1. ea_spouse, "EA: The Human Story," Live Journal (http://www.livejournal.com/users/ea_spouse), November 10, 2004. See http://www.livejournal.com/users/ea_spouse/274.html.

2. DeMarco, Tom and Timothy Lister. *Peopleware: Productive Projects and Teams, 2nd Ed.* Dorset House, 1999.

Let's do a little math.

When you force programmers to work 90-hour weeks, they can't do all the little errands that are a part of everyday life. If they're at work from 9 a.m. to 10 p.m., 7 days a week, when are they supposed to get the emissions test for their car? When are they supposed to pay their credit card bills? Or call their mom?

I'll tell you when: when they're at work. All this stuff happens during work, so immediately subtract 10 productive hours from the real workweek. OK, we're down to 80.

Now, those 40 hours of overtime? Probably worthless. Most programmers, when forced to stay at work until late, will use the extra time surfing the Web, chatting on IM, or doing anything but writing code, not because they are lazy sloths, but because their brain has shut down for the day. But I'll give EA management the benefit of the doubt: let's assume that somehow, all evidence to the contrary, you get 10 hours worth of coding done in those extra 40 hours. So now we're down to 50 useful hours.

Now let's add back the cost of recruiting to replace employees who burn out. Recruiting and training a new employee is usually estimated to cost about 12 months' salary, total. This includes the actual recruiting expenses, but it also includes the decreased productivity of the new employee while they get up to speed, the time they soak up from other employees who have to interview them and show them the ropes after they're hired, moving expenses and startup bonuses, etc., etc.

If EA is losing 50% of their employees every year, rather than the industry standard of about 5%, that extra turnover costs as much as having 45% more employees. Or to put it in terms of our 50-hour workweek, we're down to a little bit more than 25 productive hours a week out of the average employee, because almost half of the employee population is still in their first year and therefore they haven't yet earned back their startup costs.

So not only would 40-hour workweeks be more humane, they would actually be significantly more profitable for Electronic Arts. I'm not just saying this due to some misconstrued ideology: I have a software company of my own and we are pretty strict about 40-hour workweeks, so I'm willing to put my money where my mouth is.

In March 2005, Electronic Arts announced that "it will depart from tradition by beginning to pay overtime to some workers. Those workers would no longer be eligible for options or bonuses." Mmhmm. Well, it's a start, but it sounds like they're doing the minimum necessary to comply with the law, and they don't fully understand just how unproductive a software sweatshop really is. – Ed.

~

My significant other works for Electronic Arts, and I'm what you might call a disgruntled spouse.

EA's bright and shiny new corporate trademark is "Challenge Everything." Where this applies is not exactly clear. Churning out one licensed football game after another doesn't sound like challenging much of anything to me; it sounds like a money farm. To any EA executive who happens to read this, I have a good challenge for you: how about safe and sane labor practices for the people on whose backs you walk for your millions?

I am retaining some anonymity here because I have no illusions about what the consequences would be for my family if I was explicit. However, I also feel no impetus to shy away from sharing our story, because I know that it is too common to stick out among those of the thousands of engineers, artists, and designers that EA employs.

Our adventures with Electronic Arts began less than a year ago. The small game studio that my partner worked for collapsed as a result of foul play on the part of a big publisher—another common story. Electronic Arts offered a job, the salary was right and the benefits were good, so my SO took it. I remember that they asked him in one of the interviews, "How do you feel about working long hours?" It's just a part of the game industry—few studios can avoid a crunch as deadlines loom, so we thought nothing of it. When asked for specifics about what "working long hours" meant, the interviewers coughed and glossed on to the next question; now we know why.

Within weeks production had accelerated into a "mild" crunch: eight hours, six days a week. Not bad. Months remained until any real crunch would start, and the team was told that this "pre-crunch" was to prevent a big crunch toward the end; at this point any other need for a crunch seemed unlikely, as the project was dead on schedule. I don't know how many of the developers bought EA's explanation for the extended hours; we were new and naive, so we did. The producers even set a deadline; they gave a specific date for the end of the crunch, which was still months away from the title's shipping date, so it seemed safe. That date came and went. And went, and went. When the next news came it was not about a reprieve; it was another acceleration: 12 hours, six days a week, 9 a.m. to 10 p.m.

Weeks passed. Again the producers had given a termination date on this crunch that again they failed. Throughout this period the project remained on schedule. The long hours started to take their toll on the team; people grew irritable and some started to get ill. People dropped out in droves for a couple of days at a time, but then the team seemed to reach equilibrium again and they plowed ahead. The managers stopped even talking about a day when the hours would go back to normal.

Now, it seems, is the "real" crunch, the one that the producers of this title so wisely prepared their team for by running them into the ground ahead of time. The current mandatory hours are 9 a.m. to 10 p.m.— seven days a week—with the occasional Saturday evening off for good behavior (at 6:30 p.m.). This averages out to an 85-hour workweek. Complaints that these once more extended hours combined with the team's existing fatigue would result in a greater number of mistakes made—and an even greater amount of wasted energy—were ignored.

The stress is taking its toll. After a certain number of hours spent working the eyes start to lose focus; after a certain number of weeks with only one day off fatigue starts to accrue and accumulate exponentially. There is a reason why there are two days in a weekend—bad things happen to one's physical, emotional, and mental health if these days are cut short. The team is rapidly beginning to introduce as many flaws as they are removing.

And the kicker: for the honor of this treatment EA salaried employees receive a) no overtime; b) no compensation time! ("comp" time is the equalization of time off for overtime—any hours spent during a crunch accrue into days off after the product has shipped); c) no additional sick or vacation leave. The time just goes away. Additionally, EA recently announced that, although in the past they have offered essentially a type of comp time in the form of a few weeks off at the end of a project, they no longer wish to do this, and employees shouldn't expect it. Further, since the production of various games is scattered, there was a concern on the part of the employees that developers would leave one crunch only to join another. EA's response was that they would attempt to minimize this, but would make no guarantees. This is unthinkable; they are pushing the team to individual physical health limits, and literally giving them nothing for it. Comp time is a staple in this industry, but EA as a corporation wishes to "minimize" this reprieve. One would think that the proper way to minimize comp time is to avoid crunch, but this brutal crunch has been on for months, and nary a whisper about any compensation leave, nor indeed of any end of this treatment.

This crunch also differs from crunch time in a smaller studio in that it was not an emergency effort to save a project from failure. Every step of the way, the project remained on schedule. Crunching neither accelerated this nor slowed it down; its effect on the actual product was not measurable. The extended hours were deliberate and planned; the management knew what they were doing as they did it. The love of my life comes home late at night complaining of a headache that will not go away and a chronically upset stomach, and my happy supportive smile is running out.

No one works in the game industry unless they love what they do. No one on that team is interested in producing an inferior product. My heart bleeds for this team precisely *because* they are brilliant, talented individuals out to create something great. They are and were more than willing to work hard for the success of the title. But that goodwill has only been met with abuse. Amazingly, Electronic Arts was listed #91 on Fortune magazine's "100 Best Companies to Work For" in 2003.

EA's attitude toward this—which is actually a part of company policy, it now appears—has been (in an anonymous quotation that I've heard repeated by multiple managers) "If they don't like it, they can work someplace else." Put up or shut up and leave: this is the core of EA's Human Resources policy. The concept of ethics or compassion or even intelligence with regard to getting the most out of one's workforce never enters the equation: if they don't want to sacrifice their lives and their health and their talent so that a multibillion-dollar corporation can continue its Godzilla-stomp through the game industry, they can work someplace else.

But can they?

The EA Mambo, paired with other giants such as Vivendi, Sony, and Microsoft, is rapidly either crushing or absorbing the vast majority of the business in game development. A few standalone studios that made their fortunes in previous eras—Blizzard, Bioware, and Id come to mind—manage to still survive, but 2004 saw the collapse of dozens of small game studios, no longer able to acquire contracts in the face of rapid and massive consolidation of game publishing companies. This is an epidemic hardly unfamiliar to anyone working in the industry—though, of course, it is always the option of talent to go outside the industry, perhaps venturing into the booming commercial software development arena. (Read my tired attempt at sarcasm.)

To put some of this in perspective, I myself consider some figures. If EA truly believes that it needs to push its employees this hard—I actually believe that they don't, and that it is a skewed operations perspective alone that results in the severity of their crunching, coupled with a certain expected amount of the inefficiency involved in running an enterprise as large as theirs—the solution therefore should be to hire more engineers, or artists, or designers, as the case may be. Never should it be an option to punish one's workforce with 90-hour workweeks; in any other industry the company in question would find itself sued out of business so fast its stock wouldn't even have time to tank. In its first weekend, Madden 2005 grossed $65 million. EA's annual revenue is approximately $2.5 billion. This company is not strapped for cash; their labor practices are inexcusable.

The interesting thing about this is an assumption that most of the employees seem to be operating under. Whenever the subject of hours comes up, inevitably, it seems, someone mentions "exemption." They refer to a California law that supposedly exempts businesses from having to pay overtime to certain "specialty" employees, including software programmers. This is Senate Bill 88. However, Senate Bill 88 specifically does not apply to the entertainment industry—television, motion picture, and theater industries are mentioned in particular. Further, even in software, there is a pay minimum on the exemption: those exempt must be paid at least $90,000 annually. I can assure you that the majority of EA employees are in fact not in this pay bracket; ergo, these practices are not only unethical, they are illegal.

I look at our situation and I ask "us": why do you stay? And the answer is that in all likelihood we won't; and in all likelihood if we had known that this would be the result of working for EA, we would have stayed far away in the first place. But all along the way there were deceptions, there were promises, there were assurances—there was a big fancy office building with an expensive fish tank—all of which in the end look like an elaborate scheme to keep a crop of employees on the project just long enough to get it shipped. And then if they need to, they hire in a new batch, fresh and ready to hear more promises that will not be kept; EA's turnover rate in engineering is approximately 50%. This is how EA works. So now we know, now we can move on, right? That seems to be what happens to everyone else. But it's not enough. Because in the end, regardless of what happens with our particular situation, this kind of "business" isn't right, and people need to know about it, which is why I write this today.

If I could get EA CEO Larry Probst on the phone, there are a few things I would ask him. "What's your salary?" would be merely a point of curiosity. The main thing I want to know is, Larry: you do realize what you're doing to your people, right? And you do realize that they *are* people, with physical limits, emotional lives, and families, right? Voices and talents and senses of humor and all that? That when you keep our husbands and wives and children in the office for 90 hours a week, sending them home exhausted and numb and frustrated with their lives, it's not just them you're hurting, but everyone around them, everyone who loves them? When you make your profit calculations and your cost analyses, you know that a great measure of that cost is being paid in raw human dignity, right?

Right?

Bruce Eckel

STRONG TYPING VS. STRONG TESTING[1]

I remember when I was working on VBA at Microsoft we had lengthy debates about static vs. dynamic type checking.

"Static type checking" is when the compiler, at compile time, checks that all your variables are the right type. For example, if you have a function called log() that expects a number, and you call it thus: log("foo"), passing in a string, well, with static type checking, the compiler will say, "Wait a minute! You can't pass a string to that function because it expects a number," and your program won't compile.

This is the opposite of dynamic type checking in which the check is done at runtime. With dynamic type checking, log("foo") would compile fine, but at runtime it would raise an error. The disadvantage of this is that you may not find out about the bug until months later when somebody actually runs that line of code, especially if it's in a rarely used function.

In designing VBA, where the original goal was to provide a scripting language for Excel users, I was strongly in the "weak typing" camp, because it's demonstrably easier for nonprofessional programmers, who have enough trouble getting what a variable is, let alone what a type is.

On my side, I had the Smalltalk community, who, in those days, made the rather vague argument that "you're still going to find out

---

1. Bruce Eckel, "Strong Typing vs. Strong Testing," Thinking About Computing, Articles by Bruce Eckel on MindView.net (http://www.MindView.net), May 2, 2003. See http://mindview.net/WebLog/log-0025.

about the problem, you just find out about it a few seconds later..." Which is often true, but not always.

Eventually, I won the internal debate at Microsoft, and the "Variant" data type—a structure that can hold values of any type—was added to VBA and COM, and in fact later VBScript came along, which only supported variants, so it must have been a popular idea.

Yet, I always knew in the back of my mind that strong typing is a clever way to have the compiler check for many kinds of errors, and in fact, in C++, I always used the type system extensively to error-check for all kinds of things. For example, if you want to make absolutely sure that employees are never, ever, ever paid a bonus, you can create a type system with managers and employees and only managers have the PayBonus() method. Now, hey, presto, if your program compiles, you can be sure only the deserving and noble managers get bonuses, not the greedy employees.

The trouble is that creating types solely for the purpose of doing more tests at compile time is a little bit awkward. Types can only do one kind of test, i.e., "Can I do this thing to that object?" They can't test "Does this function actually return 2.12 when the input values are 1, 32, and 'aardvark'?"

Effectively, it's a puzzle for the programmer to come up with some kind of clever type scheme that can be used to check some small aspect of the program's correctness.

It turns out, if you want to ensure program correctness, we have a more straightforward and powerful tool: unit tests. So I was very intrigued by Bruce Eckel's idea of strong testing as a substitute for strong typing.

Now, before I turn you over to Bruce, I must warn you that dynamic typing has a serious downside in performance. Because types need to be evaluated and checked at runtime, dynamically typed languages will always be slower than statically typed languages. This may be OK or it may not, depending on the application. Python's obligatory dynamic typing makes it a very slow language. I use a spam filter written in Python that often makes me wait several seconds to flag a single message as spam, so when I need to mark 10 or 20 messages as spam I'm paying *something like a minute or two for this nice "dynamic typing" feature. If you're running a farm of web servers, using a dynamically typed language may mean that you need five or ten times as many servers to service the same number of customers, which can be very costly.*

So do use your own judgment about what kind of performance your application requires, but if your unit tests provide good code coverage, don't feel too paranoid about giving up compile-time type checking. – Ed.

~

In recent years my primary interest has become programmer productivity. Programmer cycles are expensive, CPU cycles are cheap, and I believe that we should no longer pay for the latter with the former.

How can we get maximal leverage on the problems we try to solve? Whenever a new tool (especially a programming language) appears, that tool provides some kind of abstraction that may or may not hide needless detail from the programmer. I have come, however, to always be on watch for a Faustian bargain, especially one that tries to convince me to ignore all the hoops I must jump through in order to achieve this abstraction. Perl is an excellent example of this—the immediacy of the language hides the meaningless details of building a program, but the unreadable syntax (based, I know, on backward-compatibility with Unix tools like awk, sed, and grep) is a counterproductive price to pay.

The last several years have clarified this Faustian bargain in terms of more traditional programming languages and their orientation toward static type checking. This began with a two-month love affair with Perl, which gave me productivity through rapid turnaround. (The affair was terminated because of Perl's reprehensible treatment of references and classes; only later did I see the real problems with the syntax.) Issues of static-vs.-dynamic typing were not visible with Perl, since you can't build projects large enough to see these issues and the syntax obscures everything in smaller programs.

After moving to Python (free at www.Python.org)—a language that *can* build large, complex systems—I began noticing that despite an apparent carelessness about type checking, Python programs seemed to work quite well without much effort, and without the kinds of problems you would expect from a language that doesn't have the static type checking that we've all come to "know" is the only correct way of solving the programming problem.

This was a puzzle: If static type checking is so important, why are people able to build big, complex Python programs (with much shorter time and effort than the static counterparts) without the disaster that I was so sure would ensue?

This shook my unquestioning acceptance of static type checking (acquired when moving from pre-ANSI C to C++, where the improvement was dramatic) enough that the next time I examined the issue of checked exceptions in Java,[2] I asked "why?" which produced a big discussion[3] wherein I was told that if I kept advocating unchecked exceptions, cities would fall and civilization as we know it would cease to exist. In *Thinking in Java, 3rd Edition* (Prentice Hall PTR, 2002), I went ahead and showed the use of RuntimeException as a wrapper class to "turn off" checked exceptions. Every time I do it now, it seems right (I note that Martin Fowler came up with the same idea at roughly the same time), but I still get the occasional email that warns me I am violating all that is right and true and probably the USA Patriot act as well (hi, all you guys from the FBI! Welcome to my weblog!).

But deciding that checked exceptions seem like more trouble than they're worth (the checking, not the exception—I believe that a single, consistent error reporting mechanism is essential) did not answer the question "Why does Python work so well, when conventional wisdom says it should produce massive failures?" Python and similar dynamically typed languages are very lazy about type checking. Instead of putting the strongest possible constraints on the type of objects, as early as possible (as Java does), languages like Ruby, Smalltalk, and Python put the *loosest* possible constraints on types, and evaluate types only if they have to.

---

2. Checked exceptions are a language feature where the compiler, at compile time, makes sure that every function has some code, somewhere, to either handle every possible exception or at least admit that it's not going to handle it so that someone else can be deemed responsible. – *Ed.*

3. See http://www.mindview.net/Etc/Discussions/CheckedExceptions.

This produces the idea of *latent typing* or *structural typing*, often casually called "duck typing" (as in "If it walks like a duck, and talks like a duck, we can just treat it like a duck"). This means that you can send any message to any object, and the language only cares that the object can accept the message. It doesn't require that the object be a particular type, as Java does. For example, if you have pets that can speak in Java, the code looks like this:

```
// Speaking pets in Java:
interface Pet {
  void speak();
}

class Cat implements Pet {
  public void speak() { System.out.println("meow!"); }
}

class Dog implements Pet {
  public void speak() { System.out.println("woof!"); }
}

public class PetSpeak {
  static void command(Pet p) { p.speak(); }
  public static void main(String[] args) {
    Pet[] pets = { new Cat(), new Dog() };
    for(int i = 0; i < pets.length; i++)
      command(pets[i]);
  }
}
```

Note that command() must know the exact type of argument it's going to accept—a Pet—and it will accept nothing else. Thus, I must create a hierarchy of Pet, and inherit Dog and Cat so that I can upcast them to the generic command() method.

For the longest time, I assumed that upcasting was an inherent part of object-oriented programming, and found the questions about same from ignorant Smalltalkers and the like to be annoying. But when I started working with Python I discovered the following curiosity. The above code can be translated directly into Python:

```python
# Speaking pets in Python:
class Pet:
    def speak(self): pass

class Cat(Pet):
    def speak(self):
        print "meow!"

class Dog(Pet):
    def speak(self):
        print "woof!"

def command(pet):
    pet.speak()

pets = [ Cat(), Dog() ]

for pet in pets:
    command(pet)
```

If you've never seen Python before, you'll notice that it redefines the meaning of a terse language, but in a very good way. You think C/C++ is terse? Let's throw away those curly braces—indentation already has meaning to the human mind, so we'll use that to indicate scope instead. Argument types and return types? Let the language sort it out! During class creation, base classes are indicated in parentheses. def means we are creating a function or method definition. On the other hand, Python is explicit about the this argument (called self by convention) for method definitions.

The pass keyword says "I'll define this later," so it's a variation on an abstract keyword.

Note that command(pet) just says that it takes some object called pet, but it doesn't give any information about what the type of that object must be. That's because it doesn't care, as long as you can call speak(), or whatever else your function or method wants to do. This is latent/duck typing, which we'll look at more closely in a minute.

Also, command(pet) is just an ordinary function, which is OK in Python. That is, Python doesn't insist that you make everything an object, since sometimes a function is what you want.

In Python, lists and dictionaries (a.k.a. maps or associative arrays) are both so important that they are built into the core of the language, so I don't need to import any special library to use them. You can see this here:

```
pets = [ Cat(), Dog() ]
```

A list is created containing two new objects of type Cat and Dog. The constructors are called, but no "new" is necessary (and now you'll go back to Java and realize that no "new" is necessary there, either—it's just a redundancy inherited from C++).

Iterating through a sequence is also important enough that it's a native operation in Python:

```
for pet in pets:
```

selects each item in the list into the variable pet. Much clearer and more straightforward than the Java approach, I think, even compared to the J2SE5 "foreach" syntax.

The output is the same as the Java version, and you can see why Python is often called "executable pseudocode." Not only is it simple enough to use as pseudocode, it has the wonderful attribute that it can actually be executed. This means you can quickly try out ideas in Python, and when you get one that works, you can rewrite it in Java/C++/C# or your language of choice. Or maybe you will realize that the problem is solved in Python, so why bother rewriting it? (That's usually as far as I get.) I've taken to giving exercise hints in Python during seminars, because then I'm not giving away the whole picture, but people can see the form that I'm looking for in a solution, so they can move ahead. And I'm able to verify that the pseudocode is correct by executing it.

But the interesting part is this: because the command(pet) method doesn't care about the type it's getting, *I don't have to upcast.* So I can rewrite the Python program without using base classes:

```python
# Speaking pets in Python, but without base classes:
class Cat:
    def speak(self):
        print "meow!"

class Dog:
    def speak(self):
        print "woof!"

class Bob:
    def bow(self):
        print "thank you, thank you!"
    def speak(self):
        print "hello, welcome to the neighborhood!"
    def drive(self):
        print "beep, beep!"

def command(pet):
    pet.speak()

pets = [ Cat(), Dog(), Bob() ]

for pet in pets:
    command(pet)
```

Since command(pet) only cares that it can send the speak() message to its argument, I've removed the base class Pet, and even added a totally non-pet class called Bob, which happens to have a speak() method, so it *also* works in the command(pet) function.

At this point, a statically typed language would be sputtering with rage, insisting that this kind of sloppiness will cause disaster and mayhem. Clearly, at some point the "wrong" type will be used with command() or will otherwise slip through the system. The benefit of simpler, clearer expression of concepts is simply not worth the danger—even if that benefit is a productivity increase of 5 to 10 times over that of Java or C++.

What happens when such a problem occurs in a Python program—an object somehow gets where it shouldn't be? Python reports all errors as exceptions, like Java and C# do and like C++ ought to do. So you *do* find out that there's a problem, but it's virtually always at runtime. "Aha!" you say, "There's your problem: you can't guarantee the correctness of your program because you don't have the necessary compile-time type checking."

When I wrote *Thinking in C++, 1st Edition* (Prentice Hall PTR, 1998), I incorporated a very crude form of testing: I wrote a program that would automatically extract all the code from the book (using comment markers placed in the code to find the beginning and ending of each listing), and then build makefiles that would compile all the code. This way I could guarantee that all the code in my books compiled and so, I reasoned, I could say, "If it's in the book, it's correct." I ignored the nagging voice that said, "Compiling doesn't mean it executes properly," because it was a big step to automate the code verification in the first place (as anyone who looks at programming books knows, many authors still don't put much effort into verifying code correctness). But naturally, some of the examples didn't run right, and when enough of these were reported over the years I began to realize I could no longer ignore the issue of testing. I came to feel so strongly about this that in the third edition of *Thinking in Java*, I wrote:

If it's not tested, it's broken.

That is to say, if a program compiles in a statically typed language, it just means that it has passed some tests. It means that the syntax is guaranteed to be correct (Python checks syntax at compile time as well—it just doesn't have as many syntax constraints). But there's no guarantee of correctness just because the compiler passes your code. If your code seems to run, that's also no guarantee of correctness.

The only guarantee of correctness, regardless of whether your language is statically or dynamically typed, is whether it passes all the tests that *define the correctness of your program*. And you have to write some of those tests yourself. These, of course, are unit tests, acceptance tests, etc. In *Thinking in Java, 3rd Edition*, I filled the book with a kind of unit test, and these tests paid off over and over again. Once you become "test infected," you can't go back.

It's very much like going from pre-ANSI C to C++. Suddenly, the compiler was performing many more tests for you and your code was getting right, faster. But those syntax tests can only go so far. The compiler cannot know how you expect the program to behave, so you must "extend" the compiler by adding unit tests (regardless of the language you're using). If you do this, you can make sweeping changes (refactoring code or modifying design) in a rapid manner because you know that your suite of tests will back you up, and immediately fail if there's a problem—just like a compilation fails when there's a syntax problem.

But without a full set of unit tests (at the very least), you can't guarantee the correctness of a program. To claim that the static type checking constraints in C++, Java, or C# will prevent you from writing broken programs is clearly an illusion (you know this from personal experience). In fact, what we need is:

Strong testing, not strong typing.

So this, I assert, is an aspect of why Python works. C++ tests happen at compile time (with a few minor special cases). Some Java tests happen at compile time (syntax checking), and some happen at runtime (array-bounds checking, for example). Most Python tests happen at runtime rather than at compile time, but they do happen, and that's the important thing (not when). And because I can get a Python program up and running in far less time than it takes you to write the equivalent C++/Java/C# program, I can start running the *real* tests sooner: unit tests, tests of my hypothesis, tests of alternate approaches, etc. And if a Python program has adequate unit tests, it can be as robust as a C++, Java, or C# program with adequate unit tests (although the tests in Python will be faster to write).

Robert Martin is one of the longtime inhabitants of the C++ community. He's written books and articles, consulted, taught, etc. A pretty hard-core, static type checking guy. Or so I would have thought, until I read a weblog entry he made (at http://www.artima.com/weblogs/viewpost.jsp?thread=4639 – *Ed.*). Robert came to more or less the same conclusion I have, but he did so by becoming "test infected" *first*, then realizing that the compiler was just one (incomplete) form of testing, then understanding that a dynamically typed language could be much more productive but create programs that are just as robust as those written in statically typed languages, by providing adequate testing.

Of course, Martin also received the usual "How can you possibly think this?" comments. Which is the very question that led me to begin struggling with the static/dynamic typing concepts in the first place. And certainly both of us began as static type checking advocates. It's interesting that it takes an earth-shaking experience—like becoming test infected or learning a different kind of language—to cause a reevaluation of beliefs.

Paul Ford

PROCESSING PROCESSING[1]

I've long been a fan of Paul Ford's website, Ftrain.com. So when Apress asked me to put together this book, I knew it had to include something of his.

Something about this article precisely captures the essence of what I consider to be "elegance" in software writing. The clarity and poetry in writing; the clean sparse lines of thought; the erudition; and the blockbuster, showstopper, mind-numbingly beautiful closing paragraph ... I think I'm going to faint; get me a chair.

Either that or it's really campy, but that's good too. – Ed.

~

Late-night thoughts on little computer languages, the Web as a form, and my own ignorance.

I've been fiddling with Processing,[2] a small computer language layered above Java. Processing makes it possible to quickly create hopefully interesting images and animations, like last week's Square/Sphere/Static[3] or yesterday's Red Rotator.[4] So far I've only dabbled with it, but the system is engaging, easy to learn, and pops up out of the zip file with a

---

1. Paul Ford, "Processing, Processing," Ftrain.com (http://www.ftrain.com), September 2, 2003. See http://www.ftrain.com/ProcessingProcessing.html.

2. See http://processing.org/.

3. See http://www.ftrain.com/SquareSphereStatic.html#ProcessingProcessing.

4. See http://www.ftrain.com/RotatingSquares.html#ProcessingProcessing.

bare-bones but clever IDE that allows you to click "play" to compile your applet.

Processing's programming constructs are consistent and well thought out—essentially simplified Java, although "simplified" is the wrong word; it might be better to say "elegantized," because the authors of Processing have identified a target audience—geeky artists—and have created something out of Java's baroque environment that geeky artists can learn quickly and explore immediately; they've whittled down Java's carved-oak throne into a slick, Swiss sling-back chair on an aluminum frame.

Why am I discussing this here? I have a passion, which I do not discuss in polite or easily bored company,[5] for languages like Processing—computer languages that compile not to executable code but to aesthetic objects, whether pictures, songs, demos, or websites. Domain-specific languages like this include CSound, which compiles to sound files; POV-Ray, which compiles to 3D images; TeX, which compiles to typographically consistent manuscripts; or SVG (Scalable Vector Graphics), an XML schema that creates vector graphics.

There are more general-purpose languages that are focused on meeting the needs of a particular kind of programmer: ActionScript undergirds Macromedia's Flash, and is ubiquitous across the Web; Graham Nelson's Inform, with its large library of community-developed enhancements, compiles to interactive text adventures. At the far end of the spectrum are totally general languages like C, Java, Perl, and Python, languages that are intended to let you do anything a computer can do.

Processing lives somewhere between the former and the latter kinds of languages—it is, in one way, a general-purpose programming language (particularly as it can call any Java function), but it is also constrained by a very small set of primitives—points, spheres, rectangles, etc.—and a straightforward model of 3D space, and it compiles to a very specific kind of object: an interactive graphical widget. Processing is most like Inform in its focus on a specific goal: Inform would not be useful if you wanted to write a word processor, nor would Processing. But if you want to create a text adventure, Inform is a solid choice, much better than raw C, and if you want to create a 200×200 clickable thingy, Processing is a pretty good bet.

---

5. Now you know how I see my audience.

Languages like those mentioned previously reward study because they represent the place where aesthetics touches computation—in CSound, for instance, there is a score file and an orchestra file; the orchestra contains a set of instruments, which are made up of oscillators, sound samples, and all manner of other time-bounded constructs: signals, lines, and waves. The score file is a collection of beats and variables that are fed to the instruments. There is a great deal to learn from such a language; it represents a very focused attempt to identify a creative grammar that is constrained by three things: (1) the computer's power to effectively manipulate only certain kinds of data, (2) the language developers' biases and understanding of their chosen discipline, and (3) the willingness of regular programmers to work within the limits of (1) and (2). I'm not suggesting that everyone learn these languages, but if, like me, you're interested in understanding what computers can do with media, and the cultural factors that go into building tools that create media on computers, you'll find that these languages are fascinating objects to study.

CSound was the first programming language I learned, in 1996, using online documentation of such spotty quality that I was sent to the library to better understand oscillator theory and the differences between additive, subtractive, and granular syntheses, finally building a homegrown oscilloscope out of an old TV in order to see the patterns of energy inherent in the sound, trying to understand why a camel-backed sine wave sounded so different from a sawtooth wave's Matterhorn. One CSound file I compiled took 20 hours to build, because there were tens of thousands of interacting instruments, manipulating each other, reverbrating all over the spectrum of audible sound. It sounded dreadful; I am not a good musician. But it was fascinating to look inside sound through that small language.

When I look at Processing, I see much that I learned from CSound translated to the visual realm (Processing supports sound, but only minimally). The oscillator in CSound is like a "for" loop in Processing; in the code I posted yesterday, squares rotate around a fixed point, each frame moving the squares forward a few pixels. In CSound I might define a series of oscillators that modulated one another; one oscillator's changing values might add tremolo to another oscillator's noisy chord. In Processing, looping values can be added to one another (with some data inserted from the mouse or other sources) that, instead of adding some tremor to the sound of a synthesizer, push red squares around in a circle. But the idea is the same: values change over time, rising and falling, and this regular change in value can be useful in making something interesting, or pretty, making it move or change frequency. It works because humans happen to like shiny moving patterns, and sounds that change frequency and amplitude in regular intervals over time.

Processing has taken me back to age 14, when I played with Deluxe Paint's animation mode on the Amiga, learning to spin text along the X, Y, and Z axes, spending hours learning, by accident and because it was fun, about perspective and geometry; I've been looking for a replacement for that sense of visual flexibility for years, and Processing finally fills the need.

$\sim$

Rereading the above, I am left with a question: if there are languages for defining instruments and oscillators, lines and splines, and even languages like TeX for implementing the ideas of typography, why is there no consistent system for web publishing that is widely accepted?

I know that there are thousands of content management systems, from Midgard to Movable Type, and each of these represents a specific way of seeing the world of content. They use databases; they sort things by date and time, by author and category; they incorporate XML tags, schemas, and DTDs. But there is no unified way to speak of them. There is no consistent framework. I made this point in Web Pidgin,[6] but to explore it a little further: Ftrain is built using a custom XML schema, XSLT (which is actually two languages, the transformation language XSLT [Extensible Stylesheet Language Transformations] and the document-tree-access language XPath); a Makefile; XHTML1.1, which defines the structure of a given page; CSS, which defines the appearance of the XHTML1.1; and JavaScript, which defines some of the interactive features of the page. It will eventually export to RSS0.91, RSS1.0, RSS2.0, and Atom, and an entire copy of the site will be output in RDF (Resource Description Framework). It contains Java applets, sound files in RealAudio and MP3 format, JPEGs, GIFs, PNG files, text files, Python scripts, Perl scripts, PHP pages, and a search engine.

---

6. See http://www.ftrain.com/WebPidgin.html#ProcessingProcessing.

That's one website, for one person. Too much.

TeX is extraordinarily flexible in what it defines a book to be, and what might go into a book, and it has been used to publish thousands of works. But it's ultimately two small, homely languages: TeX for the layout and MetaFont for the glyphs, with a variety of sublanguages and libraries available to extend it. Suites like Adobe's InDesign, Photoshop, and Illustrator combo seem to address a similar problem: they provide a consistent environment, in this case one where you point and click instead of programming, for doing work. A problem is solved in one place, in one environment, with one set of tools.

Websites are not any more complicated to produce than books—and in fact are much less complicated in many ways—but the book production process is codified and clearly established; there are norms, a clear division of labor, and an understanding of what comes next at each point. Read a few manuals of typography and visit a publishing plant, look at a Heidelberg press, then talk to an editor at a large publishing house. If you cut your teeth on the Web, the process will seem agonizingly slow and inflexible—for example, the demand for the latest Harry Potter pushed back dozens of other books so that the multimillion-copy first edition of Rowling's book could be shipped. On the Internet, you can simply snap a few new servers into place, buy more bandwidth, and meet demand.

But you'd have to figure out who to call first, and figure out all manner of switchover and high-availability processes before you could do this; it's possible, but not easy. So, all right, in the publishing world there's less flexibility, but less sobbing in terror. Because the web development process is horrifying. There is no point where you can say with total confidence, "I'm done." Right now I am fielding steady complaints concerning this website from users of Macintosh Internet Explorer 5.2. I've done about 10 different things to make this site passable in their browser of choice, but with no luck.[7] The drawing board continually beckons, as does the possibility of failure—because some problems genuinely cannot be solved, not without resources, time, and research, and all three are in short supply for those who must get the site up by 9 p.m. Sunday night.

I think part of the problem is that the web folks are still riding high on the new economy hubris, believing that they have some special

---

7. This site is, in truth, the dumbest possible hobby I could ever choose.

genius, some deep wisdom that transcends every thought process that came before, that they are the fulfillment of the Macluhanist prophecy. Except there are an awful lot of amazingly smart people who never gave a damn about Cascading Style Sheets, working for nonprofits, selling things, building things. And many of them, unlike many of us, still have jobs doing what they love. You have to wonder how great the Web really is, if so many of its staunchest advocates can't make a living working to improve it. I think it's time to step back and say, "Is all this really worth all the fuss?" Of *course* you can guess my answer,[8] but I think it's still an important question to ask.

Looking at Processing, I find myself thinking: I wish the Web worked like this. I don't wish the Web was a collection of little clickable graphics, but rather I wish that people would take a step back and look at everything we've done and "elegantize" the Web as a construct, define a set of core goals that web developers want to solve, and create as small a language as possible, based on the smallest possible set of principles, that will help them meet those goals. At this point in my life as a web developer, I don't want tutorials on hacking my CSS so it looks good in IE 5.2 for the Macintosh (I'm about to give up on that very thing, in fact, after dozens of hours); rather, I want an answer to the question "What is a link?" I don't want someone to make it easier, another Dreamweaver or FrontPage, I want it to be *elegant,* like the computer language Scheme is elegant. I want to know:

1. What is a web page? Where does it begin and end? Is such a concept useful, or should we see the web page as a single view of a much larger database of interlinked documents?

2. Is the browser the right way to navigate the Web? It's okay for viewing HTML pages, but I'd much rather have a smart database/spreadsheet that lets me search the Web and my local files, and pops up a browser when I want one. That is, like Google, but inside Excel. A huge portion of web content is metadata—search boxes, tables of contents, navigation, most recently added. Just as sites can have a single, tiny icon that appears in the URI navigation bar, wouldn't it be useful for them to have a single navigation system that is available at the top of the site?

---

8. I've written the world's only 200-megabyte personal ad in the form of a website.

3. Why is *em* better than *i*? When I'm publishing content from 1901 and it's in italics, it's in *italics,* not emphasized. Typography has a semantics that is subtle, changing, and deeply informed by history. The current state of the Web ignores this more or less completely, and repeatedly seeks to encode typographic standards and ideas into tree-based data structures, like in a <q> (quote) tag.

4. Why are some semantic constructs more privileged than others? Why are the blockquote, em, strong, and q tags more essential than the nonexistent event, note, footnote, or fact tags? Because HTML tried to inherit the implied semantics of typography, that's why! And those semantics are far more subtle and complex than most people (outside of the TEI folks, and their text-aware kind) will acknowledge. But sticking with them means we have a typographically *and* semantically immature Web. . . oh, it is madness, madness.

5. How can content truly be reused? I don't mean turning DocBook XML into either a book or a set of web pages, but taking individual sentences and phrases and flowing them into timelines, automatically extracting plays from short stories, that sort of thing.

6. If links are to be given semantics, so that you don't just say, "Link to this page," but "This page is a broadening of that page," or "The author of this page is a resource named X," what do we do with that? I mean, what does that actually *get* us, really?

7. Why bother with a browser at all? Recently I found a huge database of scanned-in magazines from 1800 to 1900, all rather painfully listed in big tables of contents that I did not enjoy browsing. So I spidered that database and made my own table of contents, which I dropped into a database (and which my friend Kendall Clark converted to RDF, so that it can be used in Semantic Web applications; I'll try to release it before long).

The last three questions are loaded for me, because I've been working hard over the last two months to solve them here. I've come up with several solutions, which I'll describe in a near-future essay. But I doubt my solutions are very good; they're just necessary so that I can do what I want to do. The one thing that might be fun for others is that I'm going to distribute the entire site (edging on 1,000,000 words before long) in a straight RDF format, with an attached fact base of quotes, events, and suchlike culled from the content. This way, if anyone wants to browse Ftrain (or an Ftrain-like site) in some other format, they can simply write the best interface for themselves. I plan to move asset management to a spreadsheet. And I'm going to buy some really nice socks, and a bell for my bicycle.

~

So I'm up late wondering if it's possible to create a CSound or Processing for the Web. Something that understands links and the very specific needs of designers, information architects, and readers/users of a site, and something that is not bound by competing traditions from interface design, publishing, journalism, and typography. Something that would allow us to see the Web as a unified space, rather than as a set of design interfaces (CSS), transformation languages (XSLT), data structure addressing mechanisms (DOM, XPath), interface specifiers (JavaScript), and markup approaches (XHTML).

One way things might go can be seen in REST (Representational State Transfer). The REST architecture for the Web is an "elegantizing" of something that, prior to its formal description, was quite ad hoc and inconvenient. REST is a way to describe what URIs (like http:// ftrain.com) mean, how they can be used to generate queries across the network, and how the entire Web can be seen as a collection not of pages but of connectable programs that are accessed by URIs. Compare REST, which is simple and already works, to web services, which add a layer of complexity to the existing Web, exist in parallel to the content-based Web, and are grounded in a collection of ideas about distributed objects and network computing that arrived before the Web.

Both approaches try to do roughly the same thing. But I'd argue that what makes REST a success and web services less of a success is that REST is truly grounded in the Web. It kept what worked and then made it more elegant: easier to understand in a formal way, easier to teach. Elegance is not just some sort of prissy foolishness; it's a way to describe ideas and solutions that have staying power, that appeal to something outside of the moment, that can contribute to a discipline and be built upon, rather than simply being applied to the problem at hand and forgotten. REST has these qualities: it made what was there better.

The same issue comes up with the Semantic Web. The Semantic Web framework addresses problems of importance to the artificial intelligence research community, but of less importance to everyone else. Less robust but more web-like alternatives like SHOE (Simple HTML Ontology Extensions), which allowed you to embed logical data inside of HTML, have been put aside in order to create something that can solve a much larger set of problems: the RDF/RDFS/OWL combination. But a serious problem sometimes arises when a community that is heavily invested in a set of ideas and practices (in this case, the knowledge representation research community) defines the standard: they solve problems most people don't care about; they build general systems that incorporate decades of research and anticipate hundreds of complex problems no one else knows exists.

There's nothing wrong with this, but it leads to strange dialogues between the standards-makers and the wider world. In the case of the Semantic Web, the dialogue is like this:

World: I'd love to make my website smarter, link things together more intelligently.

Semantic Web Research Community: Sure! You need a generalized framework for ontology development.

World: Okay. That'll help me link things together more easily?

SWRC: Even better, it will lead to a giant throbbing robot world-brain that arranges dentist appointments for you! Just read the *Scientific American* article.

World: Will that be a lot of work?

SWRC: No. But even if it is, we will blame you for being too stupid to understand why you need it.

World: Huh. I guess so. But I don't understand why I need it, exactly.

SWRC: That is because you are too stupid. It's fine, we have your best interests in mind.

World: I don't want to nag, but while I read a book on set theory, how about those fancy links?

SWRC: Well, if you insist, and can't wait, there's always XLink.

World: Aha. That looks handy... except, oh, there's no easily available implementation. And I'm not really sure what it's supposed to do.

SWRC: That is because you are lazy *and* stupid.

World: Ah well. Do you think I should apply for grants for the development of my little website Ftrain.com? Just enough for a monthly unlimited Metrocard would be a help.

SWRC: We will have all the grants! Be gone with your bachelor's degree from a second-tier private liberal arts college! And where is your RSS feed?

World: Sorry.

SWRC: Slacker! Bring me more graduate students, I am hungry!

Anyway, the way the Semantic Web works may incorporate XML and be transmitted over HTTP, but it's only a little bit like the current web framework of HTML pages and suchlike. It took me about 15 minutes to fully understand SHOE, which was embedded inside of HTML. It's taken me two years to understand RDF.[9] I lack anything like genius, but I do score better on standardized tests than a box of hammers, and two years is too long. (By the way, the secret to understanding RDF is to read a tutorial for the language Prolog; the concepts are all the same, and not that difficult to fathom, and then the opaque, nefarious RDF spec comes right into focus.)

In any case, I did not come to slam RDF—I use it and have come to like it, believe in it as a fundamental technology for data interchange, and have a billion ideas for using it here on Ftrain. But I'd also like to see it defined in terms of an "elegantization" of the existing Web before I leap up and down to praise it. In fact, I'd love to see all the standards at the W3C and elsewhere defined in this abstract, indistinct way, even though that will never happen: "This schema or standard makes things more elegant and beautiful because. . ." Had this simple test been applied, XML Schema would never have existed, SOAP (Simple Object Access Protocol) would be eyed with deep suspicion, and REST and RelaxNG would be placed in the pantheon of useful standards.

---

9. This reminds me of my rule: if you can't understand the spec for a new technology, don't worry: nobody else will understand it either, and the technology won't be that important. – *Ed.*

I care about all this because, you know, it can be beautiful. It isn't, right now. After countless hours setting up databases, tweaking CSS, and defining schemas, learning RDF so that I can borrow ideas from it, and thinking about what a link actually is, I can say with confidence that the Web is not beautiful. In terms of the maturity of a technology, which can be measured as being a technology's ability to reflect the actual skills and awareness of the individuals it seeks to serve, the Web is about equivalent to a IBM PC Jr. The equivalent in interface abstraction of a windowing interface has not yet come to this space. When you look at your information architecture books, and your how-to-build-websites books about 15 years from now, they'll seem as relevant and ridiculous as a manual for an Epson dot-matrix printer in these days of PostScript. I don't know what will take their place, but I'd place money on obsolescence (as would everyone else, of course; this isn't exactly a big idea).

The next-big-thing tends to come out of small groups of individuals thinking very hard. Take windowing: you needed a Xerox Palo Alto Research Center (PARC)-style facility to create the new unified way of working on things, a collection of slightly unscrupulous businesspeople looking to infringe on one another's patents at Apple and Microsoft, and a core of genius engineers who could be beaten and abused into absolute exhaustion who were pushed to commodify the technology, to make it cheaper and more accessible. Take those ingredients, a few million dollars, and bam: you had it, the computer that would change the world, the Apple Lisa.

And also the Macintosh soon after, when no one wanted to spend $8 trillion on the Lisa (and the Apple II GS, and GEOS for the Commodore 64, which retrofitted old computers with new windows). The idea stuck. The Mac is still here, along with its half-witted brother Windows, and their friend X Windows, which suffers from multiple personality disorder. So it'll be interesting to see where it comes from for the Web: who helps focus the ideas, and which manic-depressive lunatic CEO is able to turn it into a big, marketable, virus-like idea.

~

Maybe this is the question: if we can say that a website is a *form*, then maybe we can create a language like Processing to help people build websites; instead of new standards you could have libraries that would plug into your development framework, like TeX does. That would beat the 30-some standards that we juggle now, all of which overlap terribly.

I'm not talking about what will work, or what will happen, but what could be elegant—what could allow people to create beautiful websites. I have a few ideas that I've worked into Ftrain: I got rid of all internal structures for the site, like sections, chapters, authors, and descriptions, and instead express that data in an RDF-like syntax that is backed by a (pseudo) ontology. This way, when someone wants to see all the stories on the site, it can produce all the fictional stories as well as all the non-fiction stories, and if they want to see just the fictional stories, well, we can do that too. This is a very different way of thinking about a site, and I'm not sure I understand it yet. But having an internal ontology of content structures does give me an awful lot of new ideas about navigation, reading, and suchlike.

I got rid of markup-level arbitrary semantic boundaries like quotes and blockquotes, which were evil, and use URI-addressable unique nodes instead. So every event, quote, fact, lie, or so forth is totally unique. I included conditional text, so that a quote can appear one way inside, say, a newspaper article, and in a different way inside a collection of quotes somewhere else; an article might have the line: "I dropped the dog," President Bush said, "oh my God, I dropped the dog." But on the George Bush page, you want the quote to read: I dropped the dog, oh my God, I dropped the dog. George W. Bush. Using one source to create both views is not as simple as it might look, at least not to a dullard with an English degree. And it should be possible to grab one big Ftrain RDF file, and an RDF file from someone using the same site kit, and merge them into one big shared-ontology content base and *browse them like crazy*. I'm over here working hard on that, alone and in total confusion (while receiving dozens of messages asking where my RSS file is; my priorities are obviously backwards).

Why bother with all this? Because it's fun, and just as CSound helped me understand what sound is, building my own system is a good way to learn what text really is, what typography is, what narrative is in the context of the Web. It's a way to resolve the age-old tension between the rhetorical tradition of the Sophists and the Aristotelian rhetorical tradition. The text that appears on the screen is straight prose, designed to go down smoothly, smoothed and buffed to a rhetorical sheen. But the links and the data used to manage the content are simple, logical statements:

Men are mortal. Socrates is a man. Therefore Socrates is mortal. Paul Ford wrote this essay. Therefore Paul Ford is a writer. This page is related to that page.

You're reading something constructed using a rhetorical practice, something informed both directly and indirectly by the entire history of composition up until this point, from the Sophists to Derrida. But you're navigating it using pure logical statements, using spans of text or images that, when clicked or selected, get other files and display them on your screen. The text is based in the rhetorical tradition; the links are based in the logical tradition; and somewhere in there is something worth figuring out (and steps have been taken by people like Richard Lanham, the people who developed the PLINTH system, and others).

A historian of rhetoric, Lanham points out that the entire history of Western pedagogical understanding can be understood as an oscillation between these two traditions, between the tradition rhetoric as a means for obtaining (or critiqueing) power—language as a collection of interconnected signifiers co-relating, outside of morality and without a grounding in "truth," and the tradition of seeking truth, of searching for a fundamental, logical underpinning for the universe, using ideas like the platonic solids or Boolean logic, or tools like expert systems and particle accelerators. Rather than one of these traditions being correct, Lanham writes in *The Electronic Word*, it's the tension between the two that characterizes the history of discourse; the oscillation is built into Western culture, and often discussed as the concept *sprezzatura* (the art of making it look easy). And hence this site, which lets me work out that problem in practice: what is the relationship between narratives and logic? What is *sprezzatura* for the Web?

Hell if I know. My way of figuring it all out is to build the system and write inside it, because I'm too dense to work out theories. I have absolutely no idea what I'm doing, and most of it is done with a sense of hopelessness, as when, like tonight, I produce nearly 4,500 words in a sitting that represent the absolute best of my thinking, but those words are as solid as cottage cheese, as filled with holes as swiss cheese, as stinky as limburger, as tasty as a nice brie, as spreadable as Velveeta, as covered in wax as a Gouda, as sharp as a mild cheddar from Cracker Barrel, as metaphorically overextended as a cheese log.

Obviously it is late, and we are all tired. There are many people much smarter than I will ever, ever be working in language, in the semiotics of fiction, breaking down language into its component parts, defining, like Saul Kripke, what a *name* actually is. They use equations, and seek the truth. I'm looking for a way to tell a story that works within the boundaries established by these machines. I seek to entertain, amuse, and evoke. I'm too gullible to believe in the idea of truth. Which means that I look on, in profound, gap-jawed stupidity, at the artificial intelligence community, the specialists in linguistics, the algorithm experts, the standard-writers, the algorithm specialists, the set theory specialists, the textual critics and other hermenauts, and the statisticians, but I don't look on in jealousy, but in a kind of depression, like being a three-chord guitarist missing a few fingers, trying to play a cover of *Le Sacre du Printemps*. As much as I want to fathom it all, any sort of understanding that might be complete eludes me. I've met the people who can think in thoughts longer than a few pages—and I am not of them.

That said, I have my good points. And as of now, the world has 4,500 more words in it.[10] That's worth something; even if they're lousy words, they might be a useful bad example to someone. Perhaps, for all their jargon, they managed to entertain, amuse, or evoke. And I do have a content management system that is beginning to work for me, that is showing me the limits in my prose, paving the way for future work, and letting me do some of the things with words that I could not do before, and doing it in such a way that it is invisible to most readers, creating an experience that is focused on the author's ideas, and not on the medium in which I work.

That is what is most painful about a new medium: how much the work is about the medium itself. Weblogs are a pure example: there is a significant percentage of weblogging that is *about* weblogging, as people figure out what to do with the new forms, much as when people, faced with a microphone, will say, "I am talking into the microphone, hello, on the microphone, me, hey, microphone. Microphone. Hey. Me. I'm here. Talking. Hi there, on the microphone. That's me, talking. Please check out my blog." As any toddler's parents will tell you, narcissistic self-consciousness is a part of early growth, and it will take years before we get it out of our collective systems, but eventually people will realize the value of saying something besides "I am saying something," and we can go from there. The medium may be the message, but the *message* is also the message.

---

10. More like 5,600. – *Ed.*

Me, I figure I can keep working in this vein (until I go broke), suffer-ing from the same navel-gazing as everyone else, figuring out how to broadcast my signal without getting too bogged down in the machinery for the broadcasting, without whipping myself over my own ignorance more than a few hours a day. I'll always be stupid, given the scope of human thought, but I can try to avoid making a botched job of it, and it's not like I could ever stop with so many things to figure through. Like the fool says: you know, it can be beautiful.

Paul Graham

GREAT HACKERS[1]

There's no doubt that a software project won't succeed without the right programming superstars. Paul Graham calls those superstars hackers and has been thinking about what hackers have in common.

When this article first appeared, it was enormously controversial, mainly because Paul implies that anyone who programs in Java or who writes code for Windows could not possibly be a good hacker. I disagree with that observation strongly; I guess Paul doesn't know the same people I know. The great hackers I know are also the smartest students, so they go to top schools, where they learn Unix, which they tend to prefer out of familiarity. And many people use Visual Basic or Java because they're not great hackers and those languages let regular people get workable programs written.

But the really great hackers aren't prima donnas about their tools, and they will use the tool that solves the problem at hand. I'm far more impressed by someone who does something brilliant with a terrible programming environment than someone who won't work on the problems that need to be solved because the solution cannot be expressed in Python.

Anyway, don't let that distract you from paying attention to what is otherwise a very important essay by one of the great writers about software development today. – Ed.

---

1. Paul Graham, "Great Hackers," July 2004. See http://paulgraham.com/gh.html.

~

(THIS ESSAY IS DERIVED FROM A KEYNOTE TALK AT OSCON 2004.)

A few months ago I finished a new book, and in reviews I keep notic-ing words like "provocative" and "controversial." To say nothing of "idiotic." I didn't mean to make the book controversial. I was trying to make it efficient. I didn't want to waste people's time telling them things they already knew. It's more efficient just to give them the diffs.[2] But I suppose that's bound to yield an alarming book.

~

Edisons

There's no controversy about which idea is most controversial: the sug-gestion that variation in wealth might not be as big a problem as we think.

I didn't say in the book that variation in wealth was in itself a good thing. I said in some situations it might be a sign of good things. A throb-bing headache is not a good thing, but it can be a sign of a good thing—for example, that you're recovering consciousness after being hit on the head.

Variation in wealth can be a sign of variation in productivity. (In a society of one, they're identical.) And that is almost certainly a good thing: if your society has no variation in productivity, it's probably not because everyone is Thomas Edison. It's probably because you have no Thomas Edisons.

In a low-tech society you don't see much variation in productivity. If you have a tribe of nomads collecting sticks for a fire, how much more productive is the best stick gatherer going to be than the worst? A factor of two? Whereas when you hand people a complex tool like a computer, the variation in what they can do with it is enormous.

---

2. "Diffs" are the lines of code that have changed from one version of a program to the next. – *Ed.*

That's not a new idea. Fred Brooks wrote about it in 1974,[3] and the study he quoted was published in 1968. But I think he underestimated the variation between programmers. He wrote about productivity in lines of code: the best programmers can solve a given problem in a tenth of the time. But what if the problem isn't given? In programming, as in many fields, the hard part isn't solving problems, but deciding what problems to solve. Imagination is hard to measure, but in practice it dominates the kind of productivity that's measured in lines of code.

Productivity varies in any field, but there are few in which it varies so much. The variation between programmers is so great that it becomes a difference in kind. I don't think this is something intrinsic to programming, though. In every field, technology magnifies differences in productivity. I think what's happening in programming is just that we have a lot of technological leverage. But in every field the lever is getting longer, so the variation we see is something that more and more fields will see as time goes on. And the success of companies, and countries, will depend increasingly on how they deal with it.

If variation in productivity increases with technology, then the contribution of the most productive individuals will not only be disproportionately large but will actually grow with time. When you reach the point where 90% of a group's output is created by 1% of its members, you lose big if something (whether Viking raids, or central planning) drags their productivity down to the average.

If we want to get the most out of them, we need to understand these especially productive people. What motivates them? What do they need to do their jobs? How do you recognize them? How do you get them to come and work for you? And then of course there's the question, how do you become one?

~

More than Money

I know a handful of super-hackers, so I sat down and thought about what they have in common. Their defining quality is probably that they

---

3. . . . in his book *The Mythical Man Month.* – Ed.

really love to program. Ordinary programmers write code to pay the bills. Great hackers think of it as something they do for fun, and which they're delighted to find people will pay them for.

Great programmers are sometimes said to be indifferent to money. This isn't quite true. It is true that all they really care about is doing interesting work. But if you make enough money, you get to work on whatever you want, and for that reason hackers are attracted by the idea of making really large amounts of money. But as long as they still have to show up for work every day, they care more about what they do there than how much they get paid for it.

Economically, this is a fact of the greatest importance, because it means you don't have to pay great hackers anything like what they're worth. A great programmer might be ten or a hundred times as productive as an ordinary one, but he'll consider himself lucky to get paid three times as much. As I'll explain later, this is partly because great hackers don't know how good they are. But it's also because money is not the main thing they want.

What do hackers want? Like all craftsmen, hackers like good tools. In fact, that's an understatement. Good hackers find it unbearable to use bad tools. They'll simply refuse to work on projects with the wrong infrastructure.

At a startup I once worked for, one of the things pinned up on our bulletin board was an ad from IBM. It was a picture of an AS400,[4] and the headline read "despised by hackers."[5]

When you decide what infrastructure to use for a project, you're not just making a technical decision. You're also making a social decision, and this may be the more important of the two. For example, if your company wants to write some software, it might seem a prudent choice to write it in Java. But when you choose a language, you're also choosing a community. The programmers you'll be able to hire to work on a Java project won't be as smart as the ones you could get to work on a project written in Python. And the quality of your hackers probably

---

4. A smaller version of the IBM mainframe, designed to run the same programs that mainframes run on less expensive hardware. Almost entirely used by businesses for boring business stuff. – *Ed.*

5. In fairness, I have to say that IBM makes decent hardware. I wrote this on an IBM laptop.

matters more than the language you choose. Though, frankly, the fact that good hackers prefer Python to Java should tell you something about the relative merits of those languages.

Business types prefer the most popular languages because they view languages as standards. They don't want to bet the company on Betamax. The thing about languages, though, is that they're not just standards. If you have to move bits over a network, by all means use TCP/IP. But a programming language isn't just a format. A programming language is a medium of expression.

I've read that Java has just overtaken Cobol as the most popular language. As a standard, you couldn't wish for more. But as a medium of expression, you could do a lot better. Of all the great programmers I can think of, I know of only one who would voluntarily program in Java. And of all the great programmers I can think of who don't work for Sun, on Java, I know of zero.

Great hackers also generally insist on using open source software. Not just because it's better, but because it gives them more control. Good hackers insist on control. This is part of what makes them good hackers: when something's broken, they need to fix it. You want them to feel this way about the software they're writing for you. You shouldn't be surprised when they feel the same way about the operating system.

A couple years ago a venture capitalist friend told me about a new startup he was involved with. It sounded promising. But the next time I talked to him, he said they'd decided to build their software on Windows NT, and had just hired a very experienced NT developer to be their chief technical officer. When I heard this, I thought, these guys are doomed. One, the CTO couldn't be a first-rate hacker, because to become an eminent NT developer he would have had to use NT voluntarily, multiple times, and I couldn't imagine a great hacker doing that; and two, even if he was good, he'd have a hard time hiring anyone good to work for him if the project had to be built on NT.[6]

---

6. They did turn out to be doomed. They shut down a few months later.

~

The Final Frontier

After software, the most important tool to a hacker is probably his office. Big companies think the function of office space is to express rank. But hackers use their offices for more than that: they use their office as a place to think in. And if you're a technology company, their thoughts are your product. So making hackers work in a noisy, distracting environment is like having a paint factory where the air is full of soot.

The cartoon strip Dilbert has a lot to say about cubicles, and with good reason. All the hackers I know despise them. The mere prospect of being interrupted is enough to prevent hackers from working on hard problems. If you want to get real work done in an office with cubicles, you have two options: work at home, or come in early or late or on a weekend, when no one else is there. Don't companies realize this is a sign that something is broken? An office environment is supposed to be something you work in, not something you work despite.

Companies like Cisco are proud that everyone there has a cubicle, even the CEO. But they're not so advanced as they think; obviously they still view office space as a badge of rank. Note too that Cisco is famous for doing very little product development in house. They get new technology by buying the startups that created it—where presumably the hackers did have somewhere quiet to work.

One big company that understands what hackers need is Microsoft. I once saw a recruiting ad for Microsoft with a big picture of a door. Work for us, the premise was, and we'll give you a place to work where you can actually get work done. And you know, Microsoft is remarkable among big companies in that they are able to develop software in house. Not well, perhaps, but well enough.

If companies want hackers to be productive, they should look at what they do at home. At home, hackers can arrange things themselves so they can get the most done. And when they work at home, hackers don't work in noisy, open spaces; they work in rooms with doors. They work in cozy, neighborhoody places with people around and somewhere to walk when they need to mull something over, instead of in glass boxes set in acres of parking lots. They have a sofa they can take a nap on when they feel tired, instead of sitting in a coma at their desk, pretending to work. There's no crew of people with vacuum cleaners that roars through every evening during the prime hacking hours. There are no meetings or, God forbid, corporate retreats or team-building exercises. And when you look at what they're doing on that computer, you'll find it reinforces what I said earlier about tools. They may have to use Java and Windows at work, but at home, where they can choose for themselves, you're more likely to find them using Perl and Linux.

Indeed, these statistics about Cobol or Java being the most popular language can be misleading. What we ought to look at, if we want to know what tools are best, is what hackers choose when they can choose freely—that is, in projects of their own. When you ask that question, you find that open source operating systems already have a dominant market share, and the number one language is probably Perl.

~

Interesting

Along with good tools, hackers want interesting projects. What makes a project interesting? Well, obviously overtly sexy applications like stealth planes or special effects software would be interesting to work on. But any application can be interesting if it poses novel technical challenges. So it's hard to predict which problems hackers will like, because some become interesting only when the people working on them discover a new kind of solution. Before ITA (who wrote the software inside Orbitz), the people working on airline fare searches probably thought it was one of the most boring applications imaginable. But ITA made it interesting by redefining the problem in a more ambitious way.

I think the same thing happened at Google. When Google was founded, the conventional wisdom among the so-called portals was that search was boring and unimportant. But the guys at Google didn't think search was boring, and that's why they do it so well.

This is an area where managers can make a difference. Like a parent saying to a child, I bet you can't clean up your whole room in ten minutes, a good manager can sometimes redefine a problem as a more interesting one. Steve Jobs seems to be particularly good at this, in part simply by having high standards. There were a lot of small, inexpensive computers before the Mac. He redefined the problem as: make one that's beautiful. And that probably drove the developers harder than any carrot or stick could.

They certainly delivered. When the Mac first appeared, you didn't even have to turn it on to know it would be good; you could tell from the case. A few weeks ago I was walking along the street in Cambridge, and in someone's trash I saw what appeared to be a Mac carrying case. I looked inside, and there was a Mac SE. I carried it home and plugged it in, and it booted. The happy Macintosh face, and then the finder. My God, it was so simple. It was just like ... Google.

Hackers like to work for people with high standards. But it's not enough just to be exacting. You have to insist on the right things. Which usually means that you have to be a hacker yourself. I've seen occasional articles about how to manage programmers. Really there should be two articles: one about what to do if you are yourself a programmer, and one about what to do if you're not. And the second could probably be condensed into two words: give up.

The problem is not so much the day-to-day management. Really good hackers are practically self-managing. The problem is, if you're not a hacker, you can't tell who the good hackers are. A similar problem explains why American cars are so ugly. I call it the design paradox. You might think that you could make your products beautiful just by hiring a great designer to design them. But if you yourself don't have good taste, how are you going to recognize a good designer? By definition you can't tell from his portfolio. And you can't go by the awards he's won or the jobs he's had, because in design, as in most fields, those tend to be driven by fashion and schmoozing, with actual ability a distant third. There's no way around it: you can't manage a process intended to produce beautiful things without knowing what beautiful is. American cars are ugly because American car companies are run by people with bad taste.

Many people in this country think of taste as something elusive, or even frivolous. It is neither. To drive design, a manager must be the most demanding user of a company's products. And if you have really good taste, you can, as Steve Jobs does, make satisfying you the kind of problem that good people like to work on.

~

Nasty Little Problems

It's pretty easy to say what kinds of problems are not interesting: those where instead of solving a few big, clear, problems, you have to solve a lot of nasty little ones. One of the worst kinds of projects is writing an interface to a piece of software that's full of bugs. Another is when you have to customize something for an individual client's complex and ill-defined needs. To hackers these kinds of projects are the death of a thousand cuts.

The distinguishing feature of nasty little problems is that you don't learn anything from them. Writing a compiler is interesting because it teaches you what a compiler is. But writing an interface to a buggy piece of software doesn't teach you anything, because the bugs are random.[7] So it's not just fastidiousness that makes good hackers avoid nasty little problems. It's more a question of self-preservation. Working on nasty little problems makes you stupid. Good hackers avoid it for the same reason models avoid cheeseburgers.

Of course some problems inherently have this character. And because of supply and demand, they pay especially well. So a company that found a way to get great hackers to work on tedious problems would be very successful. How would you do it?

One place this happens is in startups. At our startup we had Robert Morris working as a system administrator.[8] That's like having the Rolling Stones play at a bar mitzvah. You can't hire that kind of talent. But people will do any amount of drudgery for companies of which they're the founders.[9]

---

7. I think this is what people mean when they talk about the "meaning of life." On the face of it, this seems an odd idea. Life isn't an expression; how could it have meaning? But it can have a quality that feels a lot like meaning. In a project like a compiler, you have to solve a lot of problems, but the problems all fall into a pattern, as in a signal. Whereas when the problems you have to solve are random, they seem like noise.

8. Robert Morris is one of the leading experts on Unix networking. He is now a professor at MIT. – *Ed.*

9. Einstein at one point worked designing refrigerators. (He had equity.)

Bigger companies solve the problem by partitioning the company. They get smart people to work for them by establishing a separate R&D department where employees don't have to work directly on customers' nasty little problems.[10] In this model, the research department functions like a mine. They produce new ideas; maybe the rest of the company will be able to use them.

You may not have to go to this extreme. Bottom-up programming suggests another way to partition the company: have the smart people work as toolmakers. If your company makes software to do x, have one group that builds tools for writing software of that type, and another that uses these tools to write the applications. This way you might be able to get smart people to write 99% of your code, but still keep them almost as insulated from users as they would be in a traditional research department. The toolmakers would have users, but they'd only be the company's own developers.[11]

If Microsoft used this approach, their software wouldn't be so full of security holes, because the less-smart people writing the actual applications wouldn't be doing low-level stuff like allocating memory. Instead of writing Word directly in C, they'd be plugging together big Lego blocks of Word-language. (Duplo, I believe, is the technical term.)

~

Clumping

Along with interesting problems, what good hackers like is other good hackers. Great hackers tend to clump together—sometimes spectacularly so, as at Xerox Parc. So you won't attract good hackers in linear proportion to how good an environment you create for them. The tendency to

---

10. It's hard to say exactly what constitutes research in the computer world, but as a first approximation, it's software that doesn't have users.

11. Something similar has been happening for a long time in the construction industry. When you had a house built a couple hundred years ago, the local builders built everything in it. But increasingly what builders do is assemble components designed and manufactured by someone else. This has, like the arrival of desktop publishing, given people the freedom to experiment in disastrous ways, but it is certainly more efficient.

clump means it's more like the square of the environment. So it's winner take all. At any given time, there are only about ten or twenty places where hackers most want to work, and if you aren't one of them, you won't just have fewer great hackers, you'll have zero.

Having great hackers is not, by itself, enough to make a company successful. It works well for Google and ITA, which are two of the hot spots right now, but it didn't help Thinking Machines or Xerox. Sun had a good run for a while, but their business model is a down elevator. In that situation, even the best hackers can't save you.

I think, though, that all other things being equal, a company that can attract great hackers will have a huge advantage. There are people who would disagree with this. When we were making the rounds of venture capital firms in the 1990s, several told us that software companies didn't win by writing great software, but through brand, and dominating channels, and doing the right deals.

They really seemed to believe this, and I think I know why. I think what a lot of VCs are looking for, at least unconsciously, is the next Microsoft. And of course if Microsoft is your model, you shouldn't be looking for companies that hope to win by writing great software. But VCs are mistaken to look for the next Microsoft, because no startup can be the next Microsoft unless some other company is prepared to bend over at just the right moment and be the next IBM.

It's a mistake to use Microsoft as a model, because their whole culture derives from that one lucky break. Microsoft is a bad data point. If you throw them out, you find that good products do tend to win in the market. What VCs should be looking for is the next Apple, or the next Google.

I think Bill Gates knows this. What worries him about Google is not the power of their brand, but the fact that they have better hackers.[12]

---

12. Google is much more dangerous to Microsoft than Netscape was. Probably more dangerous than any other company has ever been. Not least because they're determined to fight. On their job listing page, they say that one of their "core values" is "Don't be evil." From a company selling soybean oil or mining equipment, such a statement would merely be eccentric. But I think all of us in the computer world recognize who that is a declaration of war on.

~

Recognition

So who are the great hackers? How do you know when you meet one? That turns out to be very hard. Even hackers can't tell. I'm pretty sure now that my friend Trevor Blackwell is a great hacker. You may have read on Slashdot how he made his own Segway. The remarkable thing about this project was that he wrote all the software in one day (in Python, incidentally).

For Trevor, that's par for the course. But when I first met him, I thought he was a complete idiot. He was standing in Robert Morris's office babbling at him about something or other, and I remember standing behind him making frantic gestures at Robert to shoo this nut out of his office so we could go to lunch. Robert says he misjudged Trevor at first too. Apparently when Robert first met him, Trevor had just begun a new scheme that involved writing down everything about every aspect of his life on a stack of index cards, which he carried with him everywhere. He'd also just arrived from Canada, and had a strong Canadian accent and a mullet.

The problem is compounded by the fact that hackers, despite their reputation for social obliviousness, sometimes put a good deal of effort into seeming smart. When I was in grad school I used to hang around the MIT AI Lab occasionally. It was kind of intimidating at first. Everyone there spoke so fast. But after a while I learned the trick of speaking fast. You don't have to think any faster; just use twice as many words to say everything.

With this amount of noise in the signal, it's hard to tell good hackers when you meet them. I can't tell, even now. You also can't tell from their resumes. It seems like the only way to judge a hacker is to work with him on something.

And this is the reason that high-tech areas only happen around universities. The active ingredient here is not so much the professors as the students. Startups grow up around universities because universities bring together promising young people and make them work on the same projects. The smart ones learn who the other smart ones are, and together they cook up new projects of their own.

Because you can't tell a great hacker except by working with him, hackers themselves can't tell how good they are. This is true to a degree in most fields. I've found that people who are great at something are not so much convinced of their own greatness as mystified at why everyone else seems so incompetent.

But it's particularly hard for hackers to know how good they are, because it's hard to compare their work. This is easier in most other fields. In the hundred meters, you know in 10 seconds who's fastest. Even in math there seems to be a general consensus about which problems are hard to solve, and what constitutes a good solution. But hacking is like writing. Who can say which of two novels is better? Certainly not the authors.

With hackers, at least, other hackers can tell. That's because, unlike novelists, hackers collaborate on projects. When you get to hit a few difficult problems over the net at someone, you learn pretty quickly how hard they hit them back. But hackers can't watch themselves at work. So if you ask a great hacker how good he is, he's almost certain to reply, I don't know. He's not just being modest. He really doesn't know.

And none of us know, except about people we've actually worked with. Which puts us in a weird situation: we don't know who our heroes should be. The hackers who become famous tend to become famous by random accidents of PR. Occasionally I need to give an example of a great hacker, and I never know who to use. The first names that come to mind always tend to be people I know personally, but it seems lame to use them. So, I think, maybe I should say Richard Stallman, or Linus Torvalds, or Alan Kay, or someone famous like that. But I have no idea if these guys are great hackers. I've never worked with them on anything.

If there is a Michael Jordan of hacking, no one knows, including him.

～

Cultivation

Finally, the question the hackers have all been wondering about: how do you become a great hacker? I don't know if it's possible to make yourself into one. But it's certainly possible to do things that make you stupid, and if you can make yourself stupid, you can probably make yourself smart too.

The key to being a good hacker may be to work on what you like. When I think about the great hackers I know, one thing they have in common is the extreme difficulty of making them work on anything they don't want to. I don't know if this is cause or effect; it may be both.

To do something well you have to love it. So to the extent you can preserve hacking as something you love, you're likely to do it well. Try to keep the sense of wonder you had about programming at age 14. If you're worried that your current job is rotting your brain, it probably is.

The best hackers tend to be smart, of course, but that's true in a lot of fields. Is there some quality that's unique to hackers? I asked some friends, and the number one thing they mentioned was curiosity. I'd always supposed that all smart people were curious—that curiosity was simply the first derivative of knowledge. But apparently hackers are particularly curious, especially about how things work. That makes sense, because programs are in effect giant descriptions of how things work.

Several friends mentioned hackers' ability to concentrate—their ability, as one put it, to "tune out everything outside their own heads." I've certainly noticed this. And I've heard several hackers say that after drinking even half a beer they can't program at all. So maybe hacking does require some special ability to focus. Perhaps great hackers can load a large amount of context into their head, so that when they look at a line of code, they see not just that line but the whole program around it. John McPhee wrote that Bill Bradley's success as a basketball player was due partly to his extraordinary peripheral vision. "Perfect" eyesight means about 47 degrees of vertical peripheral vision. Bill Bradley had 70; he could see the basket when he was looking at the floor. Maybe great hackers have some similar inborn ability. (I cheat by using a very dense language, which shrinks the court.)

This could explain the disconnect over cubicles. Maybe the people in charge of facilities, not having any concentration to shatter, have no idea that working in a cubicle feels to a hacker like having one's brain in a blender. (Whereas Bill, if the rumors of autism are true, knows all too well.)

One difference I've noticed between great hackers and smart people in general is that hackers are more politically incorrect. To the extent there is a secret handshake among good hackers, it's when they know one another well enough to express opinions that would get them stoned to death by the general public. And I can see why political incorrectness would be a useful quality in programming. Programs are very complex and, at least in the hands of good programmers, very fluid. In such situations it's helpful to have a habit of questioning assumptions.

Can you cultivate these qualities? I don't know. But you can at least not repress them. So here is my best shot at a recipe. If it is possible to make yourself into a great hacker, the way to do it may be to make the following deal with yourself: you never have to work on boring projects (unless your family will starve otherwise), and in return, you'll never allow yourself to do a half-assed job. All the great hackers I know seem to have made that deal, though perhaps none of them had any choice in the matter.

Thanks to Jessica Livingston, Robert Morris, and Sarah Harlin for reading earlier versions of this talk.

John Gruber

THE LOCATION FIELD IS THE NEW COMMAND LINE[1]

I used to hate the idea that application development was moving to the Web. Web browser–based interfaces, to me, were a huge step backward, hailing back to the generation of mainframes with their awful CICS interfaces. You get a form, you fill it out, you press Enter, and you wait a few seconds while a mainframe in Dubuque decides what form you get to fill out next.

Gaaaaaaaah!

But I'm coming around. Browsers have gotten a lot better, everybody has upgraded, and the web development community has stopped worrying about poor old Aunt Marge still running Netscape 0.9. Creative programmers have shown us breathtakingly interactive user interfaces built on the Web, like Flickr (`http://www.flickr.com`*) and Google Maps (*`http://maps.google.com`*), using Flash or Ajax[2] to create a web page you can interact with in ways other than submitting a form and waiting for a whole new web page to arrive.*

In terms of interactivity, it turns out drag and drop and fast keyboard interfaces weren't that important after all. Drag and drop was completely nondiscoverable and required 25 minutes of window arrangement before you could begin. Aunt Marge really just wanted to click on a menu instead of memorizing keyboard

---

1. John Gruber, "The Location Field Is the New Command Line," Daring (`http://daringfireball.net`), June 22, 2004. See `http://daringfirel` `2004/06/location_field`.

2. Asynchronous JavaScript and XmlHttpRequest

shortcuts. And the web-based applications turned out to be far more popular than the—seemingly more ergonomic—Windows user interfaces.

This does not bode well for Microsoft. To their credit, they saw this coming long before anyone else, back when Marc Andreessen was calling Windows "a set of poorly debugged device drivers" and nobody else got what that meant. And their strategy for combating it was surprisingly brave, the equivalent of sacrificing a queen in chess: they had to make their own web browser, make it so much better that everybody used it and the competition was wiped out, but not efficient enough that it could replace Windows for rich application development. That was a very brave move that worked for about three years, but ultimately, you can't beat back the tide with a stick, and programmers got creative; that XmlHttpRequest thing got in there somehow, and Microsoft overestimated how much the average user appreciated the little niceties of the Windows user interface. – Ed.

~

When you publish your opinions on a regular basis, it's hard to resist the urge to gloat after you've been proven correct. It's also rather easy to ignore the times when you've been proven wrong.

It's a good thing I wasn't publishing essays on software back in the mid-to-late '90s, because if I had been, I'd currently be eating an awful lot of crow with regard to what I would have written about the Web's potential as an application platform.

At that time, at the peak of the Netscape–Microsoft browser war, the conventional wisdom was that the Web was the future of application development. The technology certainly didn't yet exist, but the idea was that Netscape's web browser posed a serious threat to Microsoft's Windows monopoly—that at some point in the future, user applications would be written to run within the browser.

Thus, Microsoft's incredible change of course, going from more or less ignoring the Internet to completely dominating it within a few years. The idea was that Microsoft killed Netscape because Microsoft saw ˜m as a threat to Windows.

Me, however, I just didn't buy it. I completely saw the potential of the Web as a *publishing* medium, but I just didn't see how the Web was ever going to serve as a high-quality application development environment. The way I saw it, Microsoft killed Netscape not because it was a threat to Windows, but simply because they (Microsoft) wanted control over this new publishing medium.

I simply couldn't have been more wrong. The conventional wisdom was in fact correct—the Web *has* turned into a popular application development environment. Where I'd gone wrong was in getting hung up on the idea of it needing to be high quality before it could become popular.

I was thinking in terms of the apps that I used every day, circa 1996: BBEdit, QuarkXPress, Photoshop, Eudora. There was simply no way that a "web app" could ever provide the same quality experience as the "real" apps I was already using. And I was right about that—the user experience of any app running in a web browser is crippled.

What I'd overlooked is that most people don't use advanced text editors or desktop publishing software; and more important, most people simply don't care about the quality of an app's user experience. Not at all. They just want it to work, and to be "easy."

My saying that web apps would never become popular was like a theater critic in the early 1950s dismissing television.

The user-experience limitations of a web app are glaringly obvious. They simply don't look or act like normal desktop apps. The browser in which they're running—*that's* a normal app. But the web apps running within the browser aren't. They don't have menu bars or keyboard shortcuts. (The browser itself does.) This isn't about being "Mac-like"— it applies equally to Windows and open source desktop platforms. Instead of looking and feeling like real Mac/Windows/Linux desktop apps, web apps look and feel like web pages.

The persnickety little UI details I obsess over—these are nothing compared to the massive deficiencies of even the best web app. But most people don't care, because web apps are just so damned easy to use. What's interesting is that web apps are "easy" despite their glaring user-experience limitations.

What they've got going for them in the ease-of-use department is that they don't need to be installed, and they free you from worrying about where and how your data is stored. Exhibit A: web-based email apps.

In terms of features, especially comfort features such as a polished UI, drag and drop, and a rich set of keyboard shortcuts, web-based email clients just can't compare to desktop email clients.

But . . .

With web-based email, you can get your email from any browser on any computer on the Internet. "Installation" consists of typing a URL into the browser's location field. The location field is the new command line.

Google's Gmail has turned the competition up a notch by providing a few features that actually do compare well against desktop email clients—fast, accurate search (of course), and a very nice threaded display for discussions. Gmail also offers a bunch of keyboard shortcuts, implemented in JavaScript, but as Mark Pilgrim described them in his Gmail review,[3] they "[appear] to have been designed by vi[4] users (j moves down, k moves up, and we are expected to memorize multi-key sequences for navigation)."

Gmail's threading and searching are indeed nice, but its overall look and feel is far inferior to that of a real desktop mail client. What it has going for it is what all webmail apps have—zero installation, zero maintenance, access from any computer, anywhere (including from work, a major factor for personal email). Gmail is simply better than the other major web-based mail apps; but Yahoo and Hotmail and the others are still ragingly popular.

What I neglected to realize when I dismissed them a decade ago is that web apps don't need to beat desktop apps on the same terms. What's happened is that they're beating them on an entirely different set of terms. It's all about the fact that you just type the URL and there's your email.

---

3. See http://diveintomark.org/archives/2004/04/10/gmail-accessibility.

4. An ancient Unix text editor designed before arrow keys on the keyboard were widely available – *Ed.*

~

Who Loses As Web Apps Win?

What got me thinking about this was Joel Spolsky's "How Microsoft Lost the API War,"[5] a terrific essay published last week. The gist of Spolsky's argument is that Microsoft's crown jewel is the Win32 API— the set of programming interfaces that developers use to write desktop Windows software—and that web app development is gaining momentum, at the direct expense of Win32 development.

The reason the Win32 API is so important to Microsoft's Windows monopoly is dependence: if your company relies on Win32 software, then it also relies on Windows. And conversely, as a developer, writing against the Win32 APIs allows your software to run on over 90 percent of the computers in the world. That's the cycle that built a $50 billion pile of cash—customers use Windows because that's where the software is, and developers write Windows software because that's where the customers are.

Switching to, say, Mac OS X is an expensive proposition for a large corporation. Not only do you need all-new hardware, but you also need all-new software. And we're not just talking about buying new licenses—for large corporations, we're also talking about custom apps written in-house (what do you think all those Visual Basic developers have been writing all these years?).

Switching to open source desktops—KDE or Gnome or what have you—is also expensive. No, you don't need new hardware, but you still run into the same situation with regard to software. (Yes, I know—you can run Win32 apps on Linux using the Wine Win32 emulator,[6] or with Virtual PC for Macs, but these are second-class Win32 environments. I'm not saying it can't be done, just that it's unappealing.)

---

5. From *Joel on Software*, Apress 2004. Also online at http://www.joelonsoftware.com/articles/APIWar.html.

6. See http://www.winehq.com/.

Switching to web applications, however—well, that's different. It can be done gradually, because you can switch one app at a time while still running Windows, and thus while still running all your other Win32 software.

It's not so much that switching to web apps is cheap as that it's easy. In fact, in many ways, switching your employees to web apps is even easier than upgrading the Win32 apps they're already using. That is, it's easier for corporations to migrate to web apps than it is for them to stay Windows only.

Web apps are easier to deploy. No need to install software on each client machine; there's just one instance of the app, on a web server. Every user gets the latest version of the software, automatically.

Custom web apps are easier to develop than custom desktop apps. That's not to say it's easy to make a web app that looks and feels like a desktop app—that's not really even possible. But it's easy to write a web app that looks and feels like a web page, which is apparently good enough for most purposes, especially data-entry and data-retrieval apps that tie into server-hosted SQL databases.

And if you think the 90 percent market share of computers that can run Win32 software is huge—how many computers do you think run a typical web app?

Most email web apps (e.g., Gmail and Yahoo Mail) run on any computer with Internet Explorer, Safari, or any Mozilla-derived browser. Most weblog web apps (e.g., Blogger, Movable Type, WordPress, and Textpattern) run in every browser I've ever tried. These apps are effectively usable from any Internet-connected computer in the world.

I've been thinking about the rise of the Web as an application platform for a while. But what hadn't occurred to me until I read Spolsky's essay last week is this, which I think is quite remarkable: Microsoft totally screwed up when they took aim at Netscape. It wasn't *Netscape* that was a threat to Windows as an application platform—it was the Web itself.

They spent all that time, money, and development effort on IE, building a browser monopoly and crushing Netscape—but to what avail? Here we are, and the Web is still gaining developer mindshare at the expense of Win32.

There are certainly exceptions—banking sites come to mind—but for the most part, web apps are being built to run in any modern browser, not just IE.

I think Spolsky is very much correct that Microsoft is losing the API war. But what's ironic is that they're losing this war despite the fact that they won the browser war. Winning the browser war—destroying Netscape—was supposed to prevent there ever even being an API war.

Gregor Hohpe

STARBUCKS DOES NOT USE TWO-PHASE COMMIT [1]

Many years ago, I was working at an ISP that was rolling out a new DSL service. Of course, they could not possibly have actually provided the DSL service themselves. That would have required vans and technicians and splicing wires and yucky stuff like that. Ick. They were simply reselling DSL service provided by a company called Covad, which, in turn, was depending heavily on cooperation from the local incumbent phone companies, who in turn really wanted nothing more than to see Covad die, die, die!

Anyway, what struck me was that the procedure for signing up for DSL was immensely complicated. Our customer service folks had come up this huge poster with a gigantic, immensely complicated flowchart, and as I looked at the flowchart from a programmer's perspective, I found many obvious flaws. Bugs, we would call them, to use a little programming "jargon." The customer service people designing the sign-up procedure were quite nice people, but not programmers. And they didn't have training in exception handling, and asynchronous processing, and two-phase commit, and multithreading, and even the basic "if" statement.

The title of this essay immediately drew my rapt attention. As a programmer I find myself constantly evaluating everyday life scenarios in terms of programming and software architecture metaphors.

---

1. Gregor Hohpe, "Starbucks Does Not Use Two-Phase Commit," Gregor's Ramblings on Enterprise Integration (http://www.eaipatterns.com), November 19, 2004. See www.eaipatterns.com/ramblings/18_starbucks.html.

In fact, I think that more attention needs to be drawn to the parallels between business process design and software architecture. I think that modern businesses are so complex that you basically have to have the skills of a software architect to get them right. In particular, it's clear to me that the reason so many airlines and cellphone companies have ghastly and horrible customer service can be attributed directly to the fact that the people who designed the procedures for helping customers simply do not understand the concept of two-phase commit. So you wait on hold for 15 minutes, spend 25 minutes with a low-level dolt who doesn't help you with your problem, and then he finally agrees to transfer you to a supervisor and . . . click, dial tone. Whoever designed the Transfer You To A Supervisor procedure wouldn't understand two-phase commit if it bit him in the butt. – Ed.

~

Hotto Cocoa o Kudasai

I just returned from a 2-week trip to Japan. One of the more familiar sights was the enormous number of Starbucks® (スターバックス)[2] coffee shops, especially around Shinjuku and Roppongi.[3] While waiting for my "Hotto Cocoa," I started to think about how Starbucks processes drink orders. Starbucks, like most other businesses, is primarily interested in maximizing throughput of orders because more fulfilled orders equals more revenue. That's why they use asynchronous processing: when you place your order, the cashier marks a coffee cup with your order and places it into the queue. The queue is quite literally a line of coffee cups

---

2. Starbucks is a registered trademark of Starbucks U.S. Brands, LLC.

3. If you've somehow managed to never go to a Starbucks coffee shop, here's how it works. You go in and wait in line for the cashier. You describe the exact coffee drink you want to the cashier. There are millions upon millions of possible combinations of coffee drinks, and you can customize anything you want about your coffee, which is part of the appeal. The cashier rephrases your order in standard Starbucks terminology (for example, you may refer to a "small" size but they like to call this a "tall") and calls it out to the barista, that is, the person making the coffee. The barista grabs the appropriate size cup and writes the order on the cup, or, if the barista is very busy, the cashier will do this. You pay the cashier and go wait for the barista to make your drink. The barista sets the drink on the counter and either calls out your name or a description of the drink. – Ed.

on top of the espresso machine. This queue decouples cashier and barista, and allows the cashier to keep taking orders even if the barista is backed up for a moment. It also allows them to deploy multiple baristas in a "Competing Consumer"[4] scenario if the store gets busy.

~

Correlation

By taking advantage of an asynchronous approach, Starbucks also has to deal with the same challenges that asynchrony inherently brings. Take, for example, correlation. Drink orders are not necessarily completed in the order they were placed. This can happen for two reasons. First, multiple baristas may be processing orders using different equipment. For example, blended drinks may take longer than a drip coffee. Second, baristas may make multiple drinks in one batch to optimize processing time. As a result, Starbucks has a correlation problem. Drinks are delivered out of sequence and need to be matched up to the correct customer. Starbucks solves the problem with the same "pattern" we use in messaging architectures—they use a Correlation Identifier.[5] In the United States, most Starbucks use an explicit correlation identifier by writing your name on the cup and calling it out when the drink is complete. In other countries, you typically have to correlate by the type of drink.

~

Exception Handling

Exception handling in asynchronous messaging scenarios can be difficult. If the real world writes the best stories, maybe we can learn something by watching how Starbucks deals with exceptions. What do they do if you can't pay? They will toss the drink if it has already been

---

4. See http://www.eaipatterns.com/CompetingConsumers.html.

5. See http://www.eaipatterns.com/CorrelationIdentifier.html.

made or otherwise pull your cup from the "queue." If they deliver you a drink that is incorrect or nonsatisfactory, they will remake it. If the machine breaks down and they cannot make your drink, they will refund your money. Each of these scenarios describes a different but common error-handling strategy:

> **Write-off.** This error-handling strategy is the simplest of all: do nothing, or discard what you have done. This might seem like a bad plan, but in the reality of business this option might be acceptable. If the loss is small, it might be more expensive to build an error-correction solution than to just let things be. For example, I worked for a number of ISP providers who would choose this approach when there was an inconsistency in the billing/provisioning cycle. As a result, a customer might end up with active service without being billed. The revenue loss was small enough to allow the business to operate in this way. Periodically, they would run reconciliation reports to detect the "free" accounts and close them.

> **Retry.** When some operations of a larger set (i.e., "transaction") fail, we have essentially two choices: undo the ones that are already done or retry the ones that failed. Retry is a plausible option if there is a realistic chance that the retry will actually succeed. For example, if a business rule is violated, it is unlikely a retry will succeed. However, if an external system is not available, a retry might well be successful. A special case is a retry with an Idempotent Receiver.[6] In this case, we can simply retry all operations since the successful receivers will ignore duplicate messages.

> **Compensating action.** The last option is to undo operations that were already completed to put the system back into a consistent state. Such "compensating actions" work well, for example, if we deal with monetary systems where we can re-credit money that has been debited.

---

6. See http://www.eaipatterns.com/IdempotentReceiver.html.

All of these strategies are different than a two-phase commit that relies on separate prepare and execute steps. In the Starbucks example, a two-phase commit would equate to waiting at the cashier with the receipt and the money on the table until the drink is finished. Then, the drink would be added to the mix. Finally the money, receipt, and drink would change hands in one swoop. Neither the cashier nor the customer would be able to leave until the "transaction" is completed. Using such a two-phase-commit approach would certainly kill Starbucks' business because the number of customers they can serve within a certain time interval would decrease dramatically. This is a good reminder that although a two-phase commit can make life a lot simpler it can also hurt the free flow of messages (and therefore the scalability) because it has to maintain stateful transaction resources across the flow of multiple, asynchronous actions.

~

Conversations

The coffee shop interaction is also a good example of a simple but common conversation pattern.[7] The interaction between two parties (customer and coffee shop) consists of a short synchronous interaction (ordering and paying) and a longer, asynchronous interaction (making and receiving the drink). This type of conversation is quite common in purchasing scenarios. For example, when you place an order on Amazon, the short synchronous interaction assigns an order number and all subsequent steps (charging credit card, packaging, shipping) are done asynchronously. You are notified via email (asynchronous) when the additional steps complete. If anything goes wrong, Amazon usually compensates (refunds to credit card) or retries (re-sends lost goods).

---

7. See http://www.eaipatterns.com/ramblings/09_correlation.html.

Real Life Architecture

In summary we can see that the real world is often asynchronous. Our daily lives consist of many coordinated but asynchronous interactions (reading and replying to email, buying coffee, etc.). This means that an asynchronous messaging architecture can often be a natural way to model these types of interactions. It also means that often we can look at daily life to help design successful messaging solutions. *Domo arigato gozaimasu*!

Ron Jeffries

PASSION[1]

I work in software development because it's fun, and I love it, not because it pays particularly well or to fill time between now and when I die. I loved Ron Jeffries' piece about the early excitement around Extreme Programming.

Much of that excitement has worn off by now, I think. Extreme Programming has become an industry, with its band of expensive consultants, speakers, and books coming out every month. It has also ossified: what started as a quest for the truth with a bunch of ideas, some good, some not so good, has become a rigid canon of required practices, some good, some dangerously bad. Today many programmers who claim to be practicing Extreme Programming really treat it as a menu of delightful offerings, and they pick the items off the menu they like (no documentation! Yay!) while ignoring the items they don't (test-driven development, pair programming), resulting in something that we traditionally call Shoot From The Hip Programming—which everyone agrees Will Not Work.

1. Ron Jeffries, "Passion," XProgramming.com (http://www.xprogramming.com), October 4, 2004. See http://www.xprogramming.com/xpmag/jatPassion.htm.

Still, it's nice to think back to the good ol' days, to the early spring of the revolution, and I salute Ron for capturing the elusive feeling of excitement and passion around programming. – Ed.

~

Brian Marick, in a blog entry[2] that is quite interesting on its own, points to a very provocative article about group think, German philosophy, and the old Saturday Night Live gang.[3] It got me thinking about Extreme Programming and the "Agile" methods. Have I mentioned passion lately?

Grampa Speaks

I remember way back when Extreme Programming and all this Agile stuff was new and edgy. At the same time, it hearkened further back, to times when we had all written great software, responding to our customers' needs with some fantastic kind of creativity and team spirit. All the good things from our best days were there, and there were new things as well, to cancel out some of the bad things that had always seemed to be a necessary part of the good.

A number of us were writing about these ideas. We used to get together to talk, argue, and think about what was going on and how it could change the world. For a time, there was even a book in our mind's eye, to be written by Kent Beck, Ward Cunningham, Martin Fowler, and Ken Auer. They were even going to let me be part of it.

We met and corresponded with all the current names in Agile, and with many more people who were interested and excited. New names arrived, contributed, explained, questioned, and built on to the ideas.

There was the famous Snowbird meeting where we wrote the Agile Manifesto.[4] Look at that list of names, all together in one room for a few days, hammering out an understanding of what we were about. We built on one another, argued with one another. It was marvelous.

---

2. See http://www.testing.com/cgi-bin/blog/2004/10/03#testing-metaphor.
3. See http://www.gladwell.com/2002/2002_12_02_a_snl.htm.
4. See http://www.agilemanifesto.org.

Quickly, what we were doing polarized the development world. Great contributors came out of the woodwork, some of whom came to Snowbird, and some of whom came along later. The movement spawned books, sessions at major conferences, and international conferences of its own. We had news groups, mailing lists. We even had serious detractors who were there to explain that the ideas were too radical, couldn't possibly work, that we were deranged if not evil. Strange days, indeed. Most peculiar, mama.

It was great! We had a fire and an energy that was exciting, uplifting, energetic, all good things. We had a mission and a piece of the truth.

~

Born for Passion

I was born for passion: passion in my work and the people relating to it. I have great success in building teams with a mission and getting things done, and some great failures in the trying. I've had people love me and had people hate me, and while I prefer the love by a wide margin, I kind of prefer either to indifference. Because I'm not about making *in*difference; I'm about making *a* difference.

That's what I think this movement is about: making a difference. That's what I want it to be about: making a difference.

Here's what I try to be, and what I like to find in those around me:

- I want to stay the course with the people who converse with me, not just drift away as if no longer interested.

- I want to argue passionately without rancor, let you call me names in the morning and drink in peace and affection with me that night.

- I want to hold others in the true respect that allows them to be what they are, act like they will, while working as hard as possible to influence them to try other things.

- I want to give my ideas away, confident that my little gift will come back to me manyfold.

- I want to try every way I can to communicate with my colleagues, to get my ideas across and to get their ideas back in return.

- I want to honor the passion that people feel, to honor the strongly held beliefs and ideas of others as much as I honor my own.

- I want to crash-test those beliefs and ideas hard against each other, confident that even better ideas will come out of the testing.

- I want to assume that we do this from love, that we care about each other, and that we welcome the crackle of real passion, real work, the real interaction of ideas.

I do my best to be that kind of person. And I want to be with other people like that. Thanks for being around.

Eric Johnson

C++—THE FORGOTTEN TROJAN HORSE[1]

I know programmers who started using C++ solely to get the ability to use "//" as a comment delimiter. C++ definitely owes a lot of its popularity to the fact that any legal ANSI-C program was also a C++ program that pretty much did the same thing. – Ed.

~

I find C++ interesting. No, not because my compiler can spit out an incoherent set of errors if I fail to include all of the right headers to appease the angry STL gods. And, no, not because its population of practitioners has reached a steady state and is now beginning a slow decline.

I find it interesting because there's a lesson to be learned about how it conquered an existing community. The tactic it took was deceptively simple yet it's one that technologists, especially the "system architects," rarely learn.

To understand what happened, we need to fire up the way-back machine. Before P2P, before spam, before the Web, before the Internet was even close to being mainstream, we need to go back to a time when the Macintosh was still running on those old-school 68000 Motorola chips.

C++ was born in a world that was clearly on its way to being dominated by C. In the late 1980s, C had become the language of choice for

1. Eric Johnson, "C++—The Forgotten Trojan Horse," Parity Check: Opinions on software development (http://ejohnson.blogs.com), November 20, 2004. See http://ejohnson.blogs.com/software/2004/11/i_find_c_intere.html.

many computer science graduates. It was just respectable enough to be taught at the collegiate level, and fast enough to be usable for that degrading domain of problems known as "the real world."

The only real competition that C had faced was from such powerful threats as Pascal, Basic, FORTRAN, and Cobol. Pascal briefly flirted with fame but flamed out. Basic won its market share, but could never shake the stink of its backwater roots, undeserved as it may be.

With that, we were left with the only two real contenders. FORTRAN was for the slide ruler crowd and Cobol was, well, it was Cobol. C found the then-perfect balance between respectable programming language and reasonable business tool. From there, it took over the development scene.

Now, of course I'm aware that there are many other languages out there. There was Ada, but it had all the sex appeal of an 800-page requirements document from the U.S. Department of Defense. The rest of the plausible contenders—Modula, CLU, Smalltalk, Prolog—couldn't find their tipping point because they overlooked the needs of their core audience: the undergrad student. The language couldn't have fit into their dorm-room PCs let alone their brains.

Across the industry, nothing was as entrenched as FORTRAN, Cobol, and Basic over such a large swath of development arenas.

In any given system that used these classic programming languages, one could achieve a semi-plausible détente between most of them. Interoperability between any of them was never perfect, but it was certainly doable. Depending on your operating system, FORTRAN could call into Cobol or even Basic into FORTRAN. Link-level compatibility was possible.

The power of this détente did more than mitigate the debates among the communities. It meant that the high-priced business consultants writing in Cobol had half a chance at repurposing a statistical package written in FORTRAN. Never pretty, but most real-world integration efforts rarely are. If anything, the groups got to leverage each other through the level playing field that was the linker in most environments.

Let's not forget that the Mac had an early academic love affair with the Pascal community that resulted in its Pascal calling convention and predilection toward Pascal strings. Fortunately, the Mac was cured of that silliness. Despite the awkward nature, C and FORTRAN still interoperated with the Mac.

The C programming language fit very naturally into this small, tranquil world. On most systems, C functions could call into FORTRAN and vice versa. In any given system, C could be the dominant, the subordinate, or the equal with its peers in a development context.

Why is this so important? Because for any new technology to take root, it must successfully leverage existing legacy into which the contender wants to take over. That's just a fancy way of saying that it can't require an organization to rewrite everything from scratch. Leverage what's already there, and you're a helpful contributor.

So C comes as a helper. What makes C++ so fascinating is that it first emerges as a helper, but with enough encouragement, it's transformed into the conqueror and eventually the new master to which all must yield.

The C++ language was purposefully designed to subsume as much of the existing C language as possible. Only the most observant C++ language lawyer can articulate the areas in which C compatibility was not kept.

So what does such "subsumption" get you?

Existing C developers could be dropped, almost entirely unaware, into a C++ compiler. Yes, there were performance differences in those early days, and yes, C++ compilers have a cranky streak to them.

Most C developers could be guilted into accepting such pedantic warnings. Those random warnings about undeclared functions always gnawed away at their conscience late at night anyway. And if that didn't get them, the high-falutin' talk of the wondrous powers of object-oriented programming shamed them into using the compiler.

But in reality, all this meant was that existing C developers would continue to write C and merely append a few more letters to their compiler invocations and their world wasn't different. Not yet. But the trap was set.

C++ made the switching easier since it easily consumed all of the functionality in an existing C domain. There was nothing to rewrite. The only real code change to make was to declare those old-school functions with their "extern C" magic and C++ could easily consume them.

In years before, interoperability between a C function and a FORTRAN function required a little bit of thought and some understanding of how the two worlds work. How would floating-point values be passed? Is it pass by value or pass by reference? How do Boolean return values map between the two? C++ worked differently. Heck, it just worked.

This gave considerable power to the C++ advocates who would arrive in an existing C organization. They could easily develop new functionality by leveraging the existing code base. They could co-opt the system. They were merely adding a new layer onto the existing edifice.

On top of this, C++ at least made it feasible to declare functions such that the old-school C geezers could still consume them. Of course, the old C school couldn't get access to the newfangled classes or templates, but that was OK by both parties. Those mangled names that the C++ compiler brought into the world were mildly freakish.

The geezers weren't entirely threatened by the C++ upstarts. And if the organization was growing, those old-timers were headed for management real soon anyway, so it was just a matter of time before their protestations for a kinder, gentler world would no longer be heard.

It's at this point in the transformation that C++ flexes its muscles. This is the tipping point. Not only does it leverage the features of the existing code base, but it also offers a potpourri, a smorgasbord, a veritable endless supply of doodads and useful features that the willing and intelligent developer is able to use.

The C++ language never rammed any features down your throat. Let's not confuse the languages stance with that of the zealots in that community. You never had to use those OO features if you didn't want to.

But they were so tempting, weren't they? They glistened like gold and were so much fun to use. You were young. You didn't know any better. You needed the money. And it was fun too. C++ looked like it could fulfill the dreams of programming in the large.

At first, the changes start in small ways. The comment style changes. /* */ evolves into //. Shortly thereafter variable declarations are sprinkled liberally in the middle of functions. Small and simple. Yet it hit a relevant sweet spot with many developers.

Then the inevitable happens. References find their way into function declarations. The inexperienced developer begins to dabble with function overloading, which results in the requisite name mangling. Now the peer programming languages from the past have a huge barrier to cross.

Structs turn into classes with virtual functions. Classes pick up non-trivial constructors, and critical high-level functions start throwing exceptions. Then comes the mind-bending multiple inheritance designs. When this phase appears, the old-school programming languages have no hope of participating.

By the time the metamorphosis is complete, it's too late. There's no turning back. The beauty of this evolutionary process is that as the code base becomes more entrenched with C++-specific features, it becomes harder to get out. The code begets further C++. Its existence serves as the accelerant in the process.

Given the difficulties created by the linkers on most modern operating systems, C++ has to go through extraordinary gyrations to make its function overloading available to mere mortals. But it's the same silliness that serves as its defense. Once you have mangled function names, there's no hope for the rest of the classic languages to feel like equals.

The trap has finally triggered. There's no going home anymore. C++ took a classic maneuver. Embrace, extend, extinguish. A Trojan horse. C++ used a time-tested technique for conquering a community and setting it off on a new mission.

Too often we developers think of great change as requiring discrete, atomic, massive events that stand out as a fork in the road. We envision corporate mandates, industry initiatives, an onslaught of PR releases, and carefully staged PowerPoint presentations as the only tools of change.

But like plate tectonics and evolution, great and enduring changes are also possible through purposefully directed actions in a small sequence of steps. It's even more powerful when your developers can use the legs they already have.

Eric Lippert

HOW MANY MICROSOFT EMPLOYEES DOES IT TAKE TO CHANGE A LIGHTBULB?[1]

Personally, I get quite cranky when 16-year-old programming prodigies who look really brave and strong on their blogs, hiding behind the fact that on the Internet nobody knows you have zits and braces, bitch and moan about how experienced developers are slow and incompetent. If I see one more child on Slashdot whining about how Windows XP, with its 37 googol lines of code, is "buggier than a lake in Minneapolis in the summertime" and acting like he (it is always a he, give it a rest) . . . acting like he could do better, if I see one more of these, I swear I'm going to puke.

The difference between programming as it is practiced in your high school class and programming as it is practiced in commercial software companies is huge. Once you've finished writing those five lines of code, there are a million other steps to making it into five lines of shippable code. Many students of computer science graduate without the foggiest idea of what it takes to make commercial software, beyond writing the code.

Eric Lippert was a key developer of Microsoft's scripting technologies, VBScript and JScript. Although this article comes across as making Microsoft sound bureaucratic, which is a little bit true, that bureaucracy arose for a reason, and anyone else writing software

---

1. Eric Lippert, "How Many Microsoft Employees Does It Take to Change a Lightbulb?" Eric Lippert's Blog: Fabulous Adventures in Coding (http://blogs.msdn.com/ericlippert), October 28, 2003. See http://blogs.msdn.com/ericlippert/archive/2003/10/28/53298.aspx.

*that needs to work perfectly for that proverbial blind Catalan user
without introducing security holes is going to need the same kind
of bureaucracy, and I thank Eric for maintaining his patience and
good humor while I would have sentenced these kids with their
"just five lines of code!" demands to 30 years of hard labor writing
a 3D word processor in COBOL for blind Catalonians. – Ed.*

~

Back when I was actually adding features to VBScript on a regular
basis, people would send me mail asking me to implement some new
feature. Usually the request was for a "one-off"—a feature that solved
their particular problem. Like, "I need to call `ChangeLightBulbWindow➡`
`HandleEx`, but there's no ActiveX control that does that and you can't call
Win32 APIs directly from a script; can you add a `ChangeLightBulb➡`
`WindowHandleEx` method to the VBScript built-in functions? It would only
be like five lines of code!"

I'd always tell these people the same thing—*if it is only five lines of
code then go write your own ActiveX object.* Because yes, you are
absolutely right—it would take me approximately five minutes to add
that feature to the VBScript runtime library. But how many Microsoft
employees does it actually take to change a lightbulb?

- One dev[2] to spend five minutes implementing
  `ChangeLightBulbWindowHandleEx`.

- One program manager (PM) to write the specification.

- One localization expert to review the specification for
  localizability issues.

- One usability expert to review the specification for accessibility
  and usability issues.

- At least one dev, one tester, and one PM to brainstorm security
  vulnerabilities.

- One PM to add the security model to the specification.

---

2. Dev = developer = an actual computer programmer – *Ed.*

- One tester to write the test plan.
- One test lead to update the test schedule.
- One tester to write the test cases and add them to the nightly automation.
- Three or four testers to participate in an ad hoc bug bash.
- One technical writer to write the documentation.
- One technical reviewer to proofread the documentation.
- One copy editor to proofread the documentation.
- One documentation manager to integrate the new documentation into the existing body of text, update tables of contents, indexes, etc.
- Twenty-five translators to translate the documentation and error messages into all the languages supported by Windows. The managers for the translators live in Ireland (European languages) and Japan (Asian languages), which are both severely time-shifted from Redmond,[3] so dealing with them can be a fairly complex logistical problem.
- A team of senior managers to coordinate all these people, write the checks, and justify the costs to their vice president.

None of these tasks takes very long individually, but they add up, and this is for a simple feature. You'll note that I've assumed that everything goes perfectly; what if there is a bug in those five lines of code? We'd have to add on the costs of finding the bug, writing regression tests, and so on.

That initial five minutes of dev time translates into many person-weeks of work and enormous costs, all to save one person a few minutes of whipping up a one-off VB6 control that does what they want. Sorry, but that makes no business sense whatsoever. At Microsoft we try very, very hard to not release half-baked software. Getting software right—by, among other things, ensuring that a legally blind Catalan-speaking Spaniard can easily use the feature without worrying about introducing a new security vulnerability—is rather expensive! But we have to get it

---

3. Where most development is done at Microsoft – *Ed.*

right because when we ship a new version of the script engines, hundreds of millions of people will exercise that code, and tens of millions will program against it.

Any new feature that does not serve a large percentage of those users is essentially *stealing* valuable resources that could be spent implementing features, fixing bugs, or looking for security vulnerabilities that do impact the lives of millions of people.

Michael "Rands" Lopp

WHAT TO DO WHEN YOU'RE SCREWED

5 Scenarios for High-Velocity Engineering Managers[1]

I first learned of "Rands" when I was too busy to update my own website. Some readers took to chatting among themselves about what to read while I was out of commission, and someone said something nice about "Rands in Repose," which looked like a typo or maybe two, but I checked it out, because even when I'm too busy to write, I'm never too busy to read

every

single

article

that a given blogger has ever posted.

Which I did, and which you will, after you finish this excellent article and head on down to http://www.randsinrepose.com *to make yourself blind reading*

every

single

article

there.

– Ed.

---

1. Michael "Rands" Lopp, "What To Do When You're Screwed," Rands in Repose (http://www.randsinrepose.com), July 10, 2004. See http://www.randsinrepose.com/archives/2004/07/10/what_to_do_when_youre_screwed.html.

~

Cabel Sasser of Panic[2] dropped a shirt off with me shortly before my first presentation at WWDC.[3]

The shirt reads, "Hi, I make macintosh software."

While Jimmy Eats World was ripping the tunes at the WWDC campus bash, I proudly wore the aforementioned shirt all over the campus. Coworkers quickly pointed out, "You don't make software anymore . . . you tell others to make software."

That's right.

I do.

Let's get started.

You're a manager now. Congratulations. Either you sucked at programming and wanted to try a different tack or maybe you're fed up with every other manager you've worked for and now you're going to REALLY SHOW US how it's done.

I'm here to help.

Your first five years as a manager are going to be full of lessons galore. Lesson #1 begins the moment someone asks you a question and you realize they're asking you not because you actually know the answer, but because the term *manager* is in your title and they'll believe any reasonable answer. Some folks call that power; I call it responsibility.

---

2. A Macintosh software developer – *Ed.* See http://www.panic.com/~cabel.

3. Apple's World Wide Developers Conference – *Ed.*

There are other lessons as well. There are the big three: hire, fire, and lay off. All of those are a nice kick in the teeth that'll be the source of significant insomnia. There's the little stuff, too. You'll find yourself saying "we" a lot. You'll notice you're repeating yourself . . . saying exactly the same thing to 12 different people. Some of it's entertaining, some of it's dull, but none of it compares to when you're screwed.

The state of being screwed is unique. You know when things are going smoothly because you can arrive in the morning and quietly sip your hot beverage until your first meeting at 11 a.m. Screwed is the opposite. Screwed is being accosted the moment you walk out of the elevator and being unable to even check your mail . . . until winter.

Screwed is mental paralysis.

Screwed is career panic.

Screwed is also an opportunity to hit it out of the park. Overcoming screwed will give you confidence, experience, and respect, but you need to figure out how screwed you actually are and then figure out how to fix it. If you aren't interested in unscrewing yourself, this article is not for you. I'm assuming you have passion regarding your professional career. You want to do more. You want to make more money, and if it all works out well, you want to change the world.

Maybe I haven't been kicked in the shins enough, but it baffles me when I run into folks who are coasting through life. Doing the bare minimum to get by and . . . enjoying it? What exactly are you enjoying? Hey, maybe your day job isn't your gig, but I like mine, so let's begin:

~

#1) I'm Missing a Document and People Are Yelling at Me

Screwedness: Low

Early in the product development process, everyone is talking about writing it down. Marketing specifications, engineering specifications . . . specs, specs, specs. Milestones are often constructed around these specifications, but, usually, these milestones come and go and no one really gets fussy about missing or incomplete specifications. That's the good news.

The absence of a particular document really isn't that relevant to your screwedness. The real question is "Who is asking for said specification and why?"

If the requestor is someone who has a legitimate need for the information, your potential screw-i-tude is high. Someone, somewhere is not able to do their job and that means someone could fail in their work and that's bad because they're going to be pissed off and pointing at you.

A tip: don't confuse the request for information as a request for a complete answer. You completionists out there do this a lot.[4] "I must answer the question thoroughly and completely; therefore, I must start by selecting a template for the information that best structures my response and BLAH BLAH BLAH" . . . Two weeks later and the requestor has moved on. You have officially missed your window to sound like you know what you're talking about and, guess what, you've also been pegged as hard to work with and unreliable. Way to go.

Larger organizations really believe they need to document more and they're right. Communication in big organizations is tricky because everyone's got an opinion and you never know who is going to have a bright idea. Big company policy on requiring documentation is furthered by layers of management struggling to ascertain and measure what is actually going on in large groups of people. (See "Status Reports Must Die."[5])

If you're feeling screwed by the absence of some important document, again, look at who is giving you that screwed feeling and ask yourself, "Is this an honest request for facts or a management boondoggle?" If the answer is facts, then face-to-face communication is always the way to go, especially if time is of the essence.

This section reads like I'm anti-documentation, which is silly because HELLO I WRITE A WEBLOG. Remember the context of this column, "When you're screwed . . ." I'm talking about situations when it appears

---

4. Michael Lopp defines the term "completionist" thus:

Completionists are dreamers. They have a very good idea of how to solve a given problem nd that answer is SOLVE IT RIGHT. Their mantra is "If you're going to spend the solve a problem, solve it in a manner that you aren't going to be solving it AGAIN months."

e in his article "Incrementalists & Completionists," online at http://www. pose.com/archives/2003/08/05/incrementalists_completionists.html. – *Ed.*

www.randsinrepose.com/archives/2003/11/20/status_reports_20.html.

the sky is falling and you need to move quickly. I could easily argue that diligent and frequent documentation is a handy way to avoid sky-falling situations because writing stuff down is a great way to make information scale . . . because you don't.

~

#2) A Significant Development Tool Does Not Exist on My Team

Screwedness: Varies by tool

There are an endless pile of tools engineers are fond of using in their development process, but there are only four that they really need:

- Editor
- Compiler
- Version control
- Bug tracking

I've never seen any engineering organization that hasn't had some form of an editor and compiler, but I've been shocked to find both version control and bug tracking missing when I've walked in the door.

If you ever find yourself in this situation, your first job . . . before you even sit down at your desk . . . is to get these tools in place and in use or you and your organization will be forever screwed. Any engineering organization with more than two people will fall flat on its face as soon as the product development process gains any sort of momentum unless version control and bug tracking are in use.

These tools empower engineers by allowing the entire team to

- Collaborate without stepping on each other's toes. *You do this, I'll do that.*
- Be accountable for their work. *Who's got that checked out? Whose bug is this anyway?*
- Measure their work. *How many bugs do I have? How about you?*
- Remember what they did. *Uh, who the hell checked in this crap?*

You'll find early on in your management stint that the main reason people make the trek to your office is because they need conflict resolution. Once the conflict participants stop yelling, you need to get them looking at facts because facts will ground them, and grounded means less yelling. All of the tools I describe above are excellent repositories of cold hard facts and that can help.

~

#3) I Can't Stand My Product/Program Manager or They Plain Don't Exist

Screwedness: Medium

As an engineering manager, you need to have two significant peers. First, you have a product manager . . . marketing. This person represents your conduit to your customer and their needs. Second, you have your program manager. This is your process and communication czar.

The program manager role is a bit harder to define because most engineering managers confuse a program manager's role with their own. A program manager owns the entire process of shipping a product. Think of it like this: you, the engineering manager, hand a DVD with your final product to the program manager and they make sure it shows up in the store in the right box. Don't think that isn't a huge amount of work because it is.

Again, both product and program managers are information brokers. For the product manager, they represent the customer's needs . . . they tell you what the customer wants and you build it. Once you're done, they tell you how it went. The program manager's information is organizational. For any given question, they know the answer or know who to ask. Good ones are also process wienies, which means things just don't fall through the cracks around them.

Program Manager Sidebar: My strong belief in the role of program manager comes from firsthand screwedness. My startup was 20 folks when I arrived as the first engineering manager. Over the next two years, we grew to 250 people and I was managing three product lines. The executive management team created the program office around that time and I was immediately suspect. "What do these boobs do? Take meeting notes? Jesus, what a waste." Wrong, wrong, wrong. Good program managers are detail drivers. They handle the piles of minutiae surrounding a release and you'll be shocked at the amount of time they'll save the average engineering manager.

If you're unable to work with these coworkers or if they just don't exist, you're pretty much at the same state of screwedness. You're going to have to do their jobs for them and that means less time to actually be an engineering manager. This isn't going to feel like screwed because you'll be busy, but you are, bit by bit, cheating your team and your product out of your time while you making sure the box art looks right.

Of the two, a missing or moronic product manager is probably more of an issue since their data affects the work of your entire team. You'll likely make things worse when, if pressed for time, you declare, "Well, I know what's best for the customer." Again, wrong. Unless your product is targeted at software engineering managers, it's unlikely your opinion is relevant. Sorry.

~

#4) My Product Is Nowhere Near Done

Screwedness: Less than you think (hopefully)

Let's first remember that the product development team loses their minds the last month of any significant product development cycle. Really. They're insane. They've been staring at this damned product for so long that they've developed a serious emotional attachment with the bits and that means irrational, goofy behavior that is not based on reality.

This is you. Mr. Insane Engineering Manager. It's two weeks until your product ships and you are sure there is no way you're going to make it. Your claim is "The product is crap."

Now, there are two situations, both of which are equally possible. First, you might be too close to the product to make a quality judgment.

Your intimacy with your product has clouded your judgment, and what you'd consider ready for prime time has nothing to do with whether a customer would be happy with it. If, in a moment of lucidity, you realize that this the situation you're in, it's best to find a person/party whose judgment you trust and get a sanity check. Your instinct will be to go to your QA organization, but they're equally in love with the product and probably more whacked about quality than you are.

Maybe your boss? Maybe another engineering manager? I don't know who, but it's got to be someone who has not spent the last three months living and breathing this product that's NEVER GOING TO SHIP. When you do find a designated sane person, they should ask questions like

1. Are the features done? How done? Are they testable?
2. How many bugs are left?
3. How many bugs are you fixing on a daily basis?
4. How many bugs are you willing to ship with?
5. What are your bug deferral criteria?
6. What's your update strategy?

This sane person's job is not to decide for you. Their job is to be neutral and to help you frame your decision by asking great questions. As a rookie manager, you're not going to seek external input because you'll think asking for help is a sign of weakness and, boy, are you wrong. Asking for help from team members allows these folks to apply their unique experience to whatever the problem might be and that's how you make better decisions while also building a stronger team. Asking for help is a big deal. Do it. Often.

That's situation #1 . . . getting a second opinion. This leads us to situation #2, which is, you're right . . . your product is nowhere near ready for customers and you're 14 working days from shipping. You and your team are charging forward to the ship date, but almost everyone is shaking their heads slowly and murmuring, "It's not ready."

And it's not. No need to get a second opinion. You're still finishing features. QA is sufficiently pissed off and your program manager is crying in his/her office.

Yes, it's really not ready.

As an individual contributor, your job is to bitch about the situation. I mean that in a good way. Bitching is one way of conveying data and if your manager is listening, they'll register it as such. Problem is, you're the manager and it's now YOUR JOB to initiate a course correction because late is better than crap.

If this is your first-ever course correction, you're going to believe you're more screwed than you are. Here's the truth: almost everyone believes that engineering is lying when they propose a schedule. It's what fancy word talkers call a truism. If engineering says it's going to take a month, it'll probably take three. OK, maybe lying is a bit strong. We're actually not lying, but we're doing the best we can, I swear. We honestly don't know how long it's going to take to finish that feature until we're halfway done.

Organizations insulate themselves in different ways against the lack of engineering certainty. Some product groups build in slip time. Others have mysteriously named milestones POST ship, which are the actual ship dates. The point is, if this the first proposed slip for any given product, you're going to be pleasantly surprised when the product team says, "How much time do you need?" Didn't know you were playing poker, did you? Well, you are.

DISCLAIMER: If you're interested in building any sort of credibility in your organization, I suggest that slipping your product late in the game is just bad PR. Any good engineering manager + program manager team is going to build in feature and schedule checkpoints where mid-game adjustments are made that give everyone higher confidence in a final schedule. Last-minute schedule changes violates Rule #3 of Rands Management No-No's: "No surprises."

~

#5) My Company/Job Sucks or Is About to Suck

Screwedness: High

True story. In the early '90s, Borland was taking it on the chin from Microsoft. Borland's big transition of their office applications to Windows was going abysmally. The Microsoft monopoly was in full force . . . they bundled their first version of the Office suite and were underpricing the competition. Good-bye Quattro Pro, Paradox, and dBASE.

After years of expansion and a move into a (still) amazing campus, Borland was about to implode and I was aware of this. That's the first step to get yourself unscrewed in this situation . . . detection . . . knowing the ship is sinking even though those execs continue to sound eternally optimistic in those all-hands meetings. Of course they sound positive; if the rank and file universally believe the sky is falling, those all-hands meetings will become utterly devoid of hands.

What'd I do? I jumped ship. I took my engineering title and moved up the peninsula to a now-defunct database company. Problem was, the new company was in much worse shape than Borland having imploded about a year earlier. I didn't know this until my hiring manager, who had presented a portrait of enthusiasm and vision, was gone one month after I started. I was suddenly debugging build systems and drinking really bad coffee with a bunch of chronically depressed database developers.

Ooops.

It's obvious, but there are two parts to getting descrewed when your company sucks. First, detection. There are people at Borland who, to this very day, are still bitching about that company the same way they were over a decade ago. Let's call them faux-Bitchers because for all their bitching, they're never going to do anything about it because bitching, apparently, is enough.

You are not a faux-Bitcher because you're still with me. You want to do something about your screwedness. You want to make an upwardly mobile move. You want to go somewhere where you're

A. Getting a raise

B. Getting a promotion

C. Getting to do something that interests you

D. Working for a company that doesn't suck

In my post-Borland move, I succeeded in A and B, but I blew D . . . and, it later turned out, C. It was my worst career transition ever and it took me a year to get back to a place that I felt I was moving forward. Good managers keep their teams, their products, and their careers full of velocity.

Velocity.

That's a better term than upward mobility. Constant forward momentum.

How you are going to achieve your own personal velocity is your own deal. My apparently endless stream of management advice is just that . . . advice. What you really want is my experience, but you can't have it because there is only one way to get it . . . you've got to put yourself a situation that allows you to get screwed. When you're deep in it and terrified, maybe some useful acquired advice will pop into your mind or maybe you'll construct more elegant solution. Either way, you'll come out the other side moving faster . . . or maybe slower.

Larry Osterman

LARRY'S RULES OF SOFTWARE ENGINEERING #2: MEASURING TESTERS BY TEST METRICS DOESN'T[1]

Larry Osterman introduces this piece with the words, "This one's likely to get a bit controversial." I disagree. I don't think it's controversial at all: it's absolutely and completely true that any attempt to measure the quality or productivity of testers by test metrics doesn't work. Most people just don't know it. Yet.

In fact, the same holds for developers, and managers, and just about anyone else doing knowledge work. The minute you try to measure how good a tester or developer is, using any metric you can think up, it will take only a few minutes for the tester or developer to optimize for that metric, i.e., game the system, in a way that gets them a great score, as measured, while reducing their true productivity.

There's always a tendency to think that you can tweak the metrics to make them work better. Experience has shown that you can't. Tweak the metrics and you'll just tweak the performance, but you won't accomplish anything. It's the fundamental idea of measuring that doesn't work.

1. Larry Osterman, "Larry's Rules of Software Engineering #2: Measuring Testers by Test Metrics Doesn't." Larry Osterman's WebLog, Confessions of an Old Fogey (http://blogs.msdn.com/larryosterman), April 20, 2004. See http://blogs.msdn.com/larryosterman/archive/2004/04/20/116998.aspx. Used with permission from Microsoft Corporation.

In my own products I'm very aware of this. The bug-tracking software I designed, FogBugz, does not include performance metrics and doesn't make it very easy to get them. We point out in our marketing material that if you try to penalize programmers for writing buggy code, the only thing you can be certain of is that sooner or later, the number of "bugs" in the bug-tracking database will approach zero, while the number of bugs in the software stays the same. We don't want FogBugz to be a crutch for the HR department. Just last week I spent some time on the phone with a potential customer who had a requirement that any bug-tracking software they used allow them to compile metrics on "how long it takes programmers to fix bugs." I explained why we didn't have that ability and why we probably never would, even if we have to lose them as a customer. I'd rather not have the customer in the first place than have my software blamed for your own mismanagement.

And you know what? It's not the end of the world. Managers still know who their good testers and developers are. They're the ones Paul Graham talked about in his piece "Great Hackers" on page 95. You really can tell who is not pulling their weight, using the normal critical facilities that came built into your brain when you were born. You don't need an artificial, easily gamed metric. – Ed.

~

This one's likely to get a bit controversial ☺.

There is an unfortunate tendency among test leads to measure the performance of their testers by the number of bugs they report.

As best as I've been able to figure out, the logic works like this:

Test Manager 1: "Hey, we want to have concrete metrics to help in the performance reviews of our testers. How can we go about doing that?"

Test Manager 2: "Well, the best testers are the ones who file the most bugs, right?"

Test Manager 1: "Hey that makes sense. We'll measure the testers by the number of bugs they submit!"

Test Manager 2: "Hmm. But the testers could game the system if we do that—they could file dozens of bogus bugs to increase their bug count. . . "

Test Manager 1: "You're right. How do we prevent that then? . . . I know, let's just measure them by the bugs that are resolved 'fixed'—the bugs marked 'won't fix,' 'by design,' or 'not reproducible' won't count against the metric."

Test Manager 2: "That sounds like it'll work; I'll send the email out to the test team right away."

Sounds good, right? After all, the testers are going to be rated by an absolute value based on the number of real bugs they find—not the bogus ones, but real bugs that require fixes to the product.

The problem is that this idea falls apart in reality.

Testers are given a huge incentive to find nit-picking bugs—instead of finding significant bugs in the product, they try to find the bugs that increase their number of outstanding bugs. And they get very combative with the developers if the developers dare to resolve their bugs as anything other than "fixed."

So let's see how one scenario plays out using a straightforward example:

My app pops up a dialog box with the following:

Without a review metric, most testers would file a bug with a title of "Multiple errors in password dialog box," which then would call out the spelling error and the alignment error on the edit control.

They might also file a separate localization bug because there's not enough room between the prompt and the edit control (separate because it falls under a different bug category).

But if the tester has their performance review based on the number of bugs they file, they now have an incentive to file as many bugs as possible.

So the one bug morphs into two bugs—one for the spelling error, the other for the misaligned edit control.

This version of the problem is a total and complete nit; it's not significantly more work for me to resolve one bug than it is to resolve two, so it's not a big deal.

But what happens when the problem *isn't* a real bug—remember, bugs that are resolved "won't fix" or "by design" don't count against the metric so that the tester doesn't flood the bug database with bogus bugs artificially inflating their bug counts.

> Tester: "When you create a file when logged on as an administrator, the owner field of the security descriptor on the file's set to BUILTIN\Administrators, not the current user."
>
> Me: "Yup, that's the way it's supposed to work, so I'm resolving the bug as by design. This is because Microsoft® Windows NT® considers all administrators as interchangable, so when a member of BUILTIN\Administrators creates a file, the owner is set to the group to allow any administrator to change the DACL on the file."

Normally the discussion ends here. But when the tester's going to have their performance review score based on the number of bugs they submit, they have an incentive to challenge every bug resolution that isn't "Fixed." So the interchange continues:

> Tester: "It's not by design. Show me where the specification for your feature says that the owner of a file is set to the BUILTIN\Administrators account."
>
> Me: "My spec doesn't. This is the way that NT works; it's a feature of the underlying system."
>
> Tester: "Well then, I'll file a bug against your spec since it doesn't document this."
>
> Me: "Hold on—my spec shouldn't be required to explain all of the intricacies of the security infrastructure of the operating system. If you have a problem, take it up with the NT documentation people."
>
> Tester: "No, it's YOUR problem—your spec is inadequate, so fix your specification. I'll only accept the 'by design' resolution if you can show me the NT specification that describes this behavior."
>
> Me: "Sigh. OK, file the spec bug and I'll see what I can do."

So I have two choices—either I document all these subtle internal behaviors (and security has a bunch of really subtle internal behaviors, especially relating to ACL inheritance) or I chase down the NT program manager responsible and file bugs against that program manager—neither of which gets us closer to shipping the product. It may make the NT documentation better, but that's not one of MY review goals.

In addition, it turns out that the "most bugs filed" metric is often flawed in the first place. The tester who files the most bugs *isn't* necessarily the best tester on the project. Often the tester who is the most valuable to the team is the one who goes the extra mile and spends time investigating the underlying causes of bugs and files bugs with detailed information about possible causes of bugs. But they're not the most prolific testers because they spend the time to verify that they have a clean reproduction and have good information about what is going wrong. They took the time that they would have spent finding nit bugs and instead spent it making sure that the bugs they found were high quality— they found the bugs that would have stopped us from shipping, and not the "the florblybloop isn't set when I twiddle the frobjet" bugs.

I'm not saying that metrics are bad. They're not. But basing people's annual performance reviews on those metrics is a recipe for disaster.

There was a tester for Windows NT 3.1 who was an absolute nut about data corruption problems. He worked on solving data corruptions problems tirelessly. And he didn't find very many of them. But every single one of the data corruption problems he found was absolutely critical to the success of the product. If he'd been measured by a "number of bugs found" metric, then he'd have been dinged horribly on his evaluations, because his bug production was relatively low compared to other testers in the organization. But his value to the organization was as high or higher than the value of any of the other testers. An absolute metric, however, would not have recognized his contributions to the product.

~

Somewhat later: After I wrote the original version of this, a couple of other developers and I discussed it a bit at lunch. One of them pointed out that one of the things I missed in my discussion earlier is that there should be two halves of a performance review:

- Measurement: Give me a number that represents the quality of the work that the user is doing.
- Evaluation: Given the measurement, is the employee doing a good job or a bad job? In other words, you need to assign a value to the metric—how relevant is the metric to your performance?

He went on to discuss the fact that any metric is worthless unless it is reevaluated each time to determine how relevant the metric is—a metric is only as good as its validity.

One other comment was that absolute bug count metrics cannot be a measure of the worth of a tester. The tester who spends two weeks and comes up with four buffer overflow errors in my code is likely to be more valuable to my team than the tester who spends the same two weeks and comes up with 20 trivial bugs. Using the severity field of the bug report was suggested as a metric, but my colleague pointed out that this only worked if the severity field actually had significant meaning, and it often doesn't (it can be very difficult to determine the relative severity of a bug, and often the setting of the severity field is left to the tester, a strategy that has the potential for abuse unless all bugs are externally triaged, which doesn't always happen).

By the end of the discussion, we had all agreed that bug counts were an *interesting* metric, but they couldn't be the *only* metric.

Mary Poppendieck

———

TEAM COMPENSATION[1]

The biggest myth in human resource departments is that you can set up kindergarten-like gold star–based economies in which you reward employees for doing the things you want them to do, and punish the ones who don't live up to expectations, by gluing little gold stars to their charts and giving them enough money for a hot dog and a pop, and thus achieve better results.

Hogwash.

This is so completely wrong that the very idea makes me sputter and spit angrily, which prevents me from clearly explaining just how completely wrong it is. And yet every big software company I know of and most of the small ones persevere in nineteenth-century-style performance measurement even when it's been thoroughly and exhaustively explained to be wrong, wrong, wrong!

Phbtft.

Luckily, Mary Poppendieck kept her wits about her long enough to calmly and patiently instruct us, by which I mean you, on precisely why performance measurement for knowledge workers is always counterproductive, and she does so with a lot less—how can I put this nicely—contempt and vitriol than I would have used, if I had been able to calm down long enough to write about it. – Ed.

---

1. Article originally published in *Better Software Magazine*, August 2004, under "Unjust Deserts."

~

The team had done an incredible job, and they knew it. Iteration by iteration they had built a new software product, and when the deadline came, everything that had to be operational was working flawlessly. At an afternoon celebration, the division vice president thanked everyone who had contributed to the effort, and the team members congratulated one another as they relived some of the more harrowing moments of the last six months.

~

The Morning After

The next day, the team's Scrum Master[2] was catching up on long-ignored email when Dave, the development manager, called. "Say, Sue," he said, "great job your team did! I've been waiting for the product launch before I bothered you with this, but the appraisal deadline is next week. I need your evaluation of each team member. And if you could, I'd like you to rank the team from who contributed the most down to who contributed the least."

Sue could almost hear the air escaping as her world deflated. "I can't do that," she said. "Everyone pitched in 100 percent. We could not have done it otherwise. In fact, collaboration is at the core of our Agile process."

"But Sue," Dave said, "there must have been a most valuable player, a runner-up, and so on."

"No, not really," Sue replied. "But what I can do is evaluate everyone's contribution to the effort."

Sue filled out an appraisal input form for each team member. She rated everyone's performance but found that she had to check the "far exceeded expectations" box for each team member. After all, getting out the product on time was a spectacular feat, one that far exceeded everyone's expectations.

Scrum is one of those trendy Agile methodologies. – *Ed.*

~

The Aftershocks

Two days later, Sue got a call from Janice in human resources. "Sue," she said, "great job your team did! And thanks for filling out those appraisal input forms. But really, you can't give everyone a top rating. Your average rating should be 'meets expectations.' You can only have one or two people who 'far exceeded expectations.' Oh, and by the way, since you didn't rank the team members, would you please plan on coming to our ranking meeting next week? We are going to need your input on that. After all, at this company we pay for performance, and we need to evaluate everyone carefully so that our fairness cannot be questioned."

Sue felt like a flat tire. In the past, when she had a particularly difficult problem, she had always consulted the team, and they had always come up with creative solutions; so she decided to consult them once again. She thought she might convince them to elect an MVP or two, to help her put some variation into the evaluations.

The next morning, the entire team listened as Sue explained her problem. Sue was disappointed and surprised when after hearing her dilemma, instead of jumping in to help solve the problem, the team members deflated just as quickly as she had. The best they could do was insist that everyone had given 200 percent effort, that they had all helped each other, and that they had thought that every single person had done a truly outstanding job. They were not interested in electing a *most* valuable player, but they were willing to choose a *least* valuable player: the unnamed manager who was asking Sue to choose among them.

Now Sue really had a problem. She had no idea how to respond to Dave and Janice, and her plan to involve the team had only succeeded in making them angry and suspicious. Tomorrow, they would have to start working together on the next release. How could something that was supposed to boost performance do such a thorough job of crushing the team's spirit?

Sue is not the only one who has had trouble with merit pay evaluation and ranking systems. One of the greatest thought leaders of the twentieth century, W. Edwards Deming, wrote that immeasurable damage is created by ranking systems, merit raises, and incentive pay.

Deming believed that every business is a system, and the performance of individuals is largely the result of the way the system operates. In his view, the system causes 80 percent of the problems in a business, and the system is management's responsibility. He wrote that using exhortations and incentives to get individuals to solve management problems simply doesn't work. Deming opposed ranking because it destroys pride in workmanship, and he opposed merit raises because they address the symptoms, rather than the causes, of problems.

It's a bit difficult to take Deming at face value on this; after all, companies have been using merit pay systems for decades, and their use is increasing. Moreover, Deming was mainly involved in manufacturing, so possibly his thinking does not apply directly to knowledge work like software development. Still, someone as wise as Deming is not to be ignored; so let's take a deeper look into employee evaluation and reward systems and explore what causes them to become dysfunctional.

~

Dysfunction #1: Competition

As Sue's team instinctively realized, ranking people for merit raises pits individual employees against each other and strongly discourages collaboration, a cornerstone of Agile practices. Even when the rankings are not made public, the fact that they happen does not remain a secret. Sometimes ranking systems are used as a basis for dismissing the lowest performers, making the practice even more threatening. When team members are in competition with one another for their livelihood, teamwork quickly evaporates.

Competition between teams, rather than individuals, may seem like a good idea, but it can be equally damaging. Once, I worked in a division in which there were two separate teams developing software products that were targeting similar markets. The members of the team who attracted the larger market share were likely to have more secure jobs and enhanced career opportunities. So, each team expanded the capability of its product to attract a broader market. The teams ended up competing fiercely with each other for the same customer base as well as for division resources. In the end, both products failed. A single product would have had a much better chance at success.

~

Dysfunction #2: The Perception of Unfairness

There is no greater demotivator than a reward system that is perceived to be unfair. It doesn't matter whether the system is fair or not. If there is a perception of unfairness, then those who think that they have been treated unfairly will rapidly lose their motivation.

People perceive unfairness when they miss out on rewards they think they should have shared. What if the vice president had given Sue a big reward but not rewarded the team? Even if Sue had acknowledged the hard work of her team members, they would probably have felt that she was profiting at their expense. You can be sure that Sue would have had a difficult time generating enthusiasm for work on the next release, even if the evaluation issues had not surfaced.

Here's another scenario: what would have happened if Sue's team had been asked out to dinner with the VP and each member had been given a good-sized bonus? The next day the operations people who worked late nights and weekends to help get the product out on time would have found out and felt cheated. The developers who took over maintenance tasks so their colleagues could work full time on the product also would have felt slighted. Other teams might have felt that they could have been equally successful, except that they got assigned to the wrong product.

~

Dysfunction #3: The Perception of Impossibility

Sue's team met its deadline by following the Scrum practice of releasing a high-quality product containing only the highest-priority functionality. But let's try a different scenario: let's assume that the team was given a non-negotiable list of features that had to be done by a non-negotiable deadline, and let's further speculate that the team was 100 percent positive that the deadline was impossible. (Remember this is hypothetical; surely this would never happen in real life.) Finally, let's pretend that the team members were promised a big bonus if they met the deadline.

There are two things that could happen in this scenario. Financial incentives are powerful motivators, so there is a chance that the team might have found a way to do the impossible. However, the more likely case is that the promise of a bonus that was impossible to achieve would make the team cynical, and the team would be even less motivated to meet the deadline than before the incentive was offered. When people find management exhorting them to do what is clearly impossible rather than helping to make the task possible, they are likely to be insulted by the offer of a reward and give up without even trying.

~

Dysfunction #4: Suboptimization

I recently heard of a business owner who offered testers five dollars for every defect they could find in a product about to go into beta release. She thought this would encourage the testers to work harder, but the result was quite different. The good working relationship between developers and testers deteriorated as testers lost their incentive to help developers quickly find and fix defects before they propagated into multiple problems. After all, the more problems the testers found, the more money they made.

When we optimize a part of a chain, we invariably suboptimize overall performance. One of the most obvious examples of suboptimization is the separation of software development from support and maintenance. If developers are rewarded for meeting a schedule even if they deliver brittle code without automated test suites or an installation process, then support and maintenance of the system will cost far more than was saved during development.

~

Dysfunction #5: Destroying Intrinsic Motivation

There are two approaches to giving children allowances. Theory A says that children should earn their allowances; money is exchanged for work. Theory B says that children should contribute to the household without being paid, so allowances are not considered exchange for work. I know one father who was raised with Theory B but switched to Theory A for his children. He put a price on each job and paid the children weekly for the jobs they had done. This worked for a while, but then the kids discovered that they could choose among the jobs and avoid doing the ones they disliked. When the children were old enough to earn their own paychecks, they stopped doing household chores altogether, and the father found himself mowing the lawn alongside his neighbors' teenage children. Were he to do it again, this father says he would not tie allowance to work.

In the same way, once employees get used to receiving financial rewards for meeting goals, they begin to work for the rewards, not the intrinsic motivation that comes from doing a good job and helping their company be successful. Many studies have shown that extrinsic rewards like grades and pay will, over time, destroy the intrinsic reward that comes from the work itself.

~

One Week Later

Sue was nervous as she entered the room for the ranking meeting. She had talked over her problem with her boss, Wayne, and, although he didn't have any easy solutions, he suggested that she present her problem to the management team. Shortly after the meeting started, Janice asked Sue how she would rank her team members. Sue took a deep breath, got a smile of encouragement from Wayne, and explained how the whole idea of ranking made no sense for a team effort, especially in an Agile environment. She explained how she had asked for advice from the team and ended up with an angry and suspicious team.

"You should never have talked to the team about this," said Janice.

"Hold on a minute," Wayne jumped in. "I thought our goal in this company is to be fair. How can we keep our evaluation policies secret and expect people to consider them fair? It doesn't matter if *we* think they are fair; it matters if employees think they are fair. If we think we can keep what we are doing a secret, we're kidding ourselves. We need to be transparent about how we operate; we can't make decisions behind closed doors and then try to tell people, 'Don't worry, we're being fair.'"

Sue was amazed at how fast the nature of the discussion changed after Wayne jumped to her defense. Apparently, she wasn't the only one who thought this ranking business was a bad idea. Everyone agreed that Sue's team had done an excellent job, and the new product was key to their business. No one had thought that it could be done, and indeed the team as a whole had far exceeded everyone's expectations. It became apparent that there wasn't a person in the room who was willing to sort out who had contributed more or less to the effort, so Sue's top evaluation for every team member was accepted. More important, the group was concerned that a de-motivated team was a serious problem. Eventually, the vice president agreed to go to the next meeting of the team and discuss the company's evaluation policies. Sue was sure that this would go a long way to revitalize the team spirit.

Now the management team members had a problem of their own. They knew that they had to live within a merit pay system, but they suspected they needed to rethink the way it was implemented. Since changes like that don't happen overnight, they formed a committee to look into various evaluation and pay systems.

The committee started by agreeing that evaluation systems should not be used to surprise employees with unexpected feedback about their performance. Performance feedback loops must be far shorter than annual, or even quarterly, evaluation cycles. Appraisals are good times to review and update development plans for an employee, but if this is the only time the employees find out how they are doing, a lot more needs fixing than the appraisal system.

With this disclaimer in mind, the committee developed some guidelines for dealing with various forms of differential pay systems.

~

Guideline #1: Make Sure the Promotion System Is Unassailable

In most organizations, significant salary gains come from promotions that move people to a higher salary grade, not from merit increases. Where promotions are not available, as is the case for many teachers, merit pay systems have a tendency to become contentious, because merit increases are the only way to make more money. When promotions are available, employees tend to ignore the merit pay system and focus on the promotion system. Of course, this system of promotions tends to encourage people to move into management as they run out of promotional opportunities in technical areas. Companies address this problem with "dual ladders" that offer management-level pay scales to technical gurus.

The foundation of any promotion system is a series of job grades, each with a salary range in line with industry standards and regional averages. People must be placed correctly in a grade so that their skills and responsibilities match the job requirements of their level. Initial placements and promotion decisions should be made carefully and reviewed by a management team.

Usually, job grades are embedded in titles, and promotions make the new job grade public through a new title. A person's job grade is generally considered public information. If employees are fairly placed in their job grades and promoted only when they are clearly performing at a new job grade, then salary differences based on job grade are generally perceived to be fair. Thus, a team can have both senior and junior people, generalists and highly skilled specialists, all making different amounts of money. As long as the system of determining job grades and promotions is transparent and perceived to be fair, this kind of differential pay is rarely a problem.

The management team at Sue's company decided to focus on a promotion process that did not use either a ranking or a quota system. Instead, clear promotion criteria will be established for each level; when someone has met the criteria, that person will be eligible for promotion. A management committee will review each promotion proposal and gain a consensus that the promotion criteria have been met. This will be similar to existing committees that review promotions to fill open supervisor or management positions.

~

Guideline #2: De-emphasize the Merit Pay System

When the primary tool for significant salary increases is promotion, then it's important to focus as much attention as possible on making sure the promotion system is fair. When it comes to the evaluation system that drives merit pay, it's best not to try too hard to sort people out. Studies show that, when information sharing and coordination are necessary, organizations that reduce pay differences between the highest- and the lowest-paid employees tend to perform better over time.

Use evaluations mainly to keep employees at an appropriate level in their salary grade. Evaluations might flag those who are ready for promotion and those who need attention, but that should trigger a separate promotion or corrective action process. About four evaluation grades are sufficient, and a competent supervisor with good evaluation criteria and input from appropriate sources can make fair evaluations that accomplish these purposes.

Even when annual raises are loosely coupled to merit, evaluations will always be a big deal for employees, so attention should be paid to making them fair and balanced. Over the last decade, balanced scorecards have become popular for management evaluations—at least in theory. Balanced scorecards ensure that the multiple aspects of a manager's job all receive attention. A simple version of a balanced scorecard also might be used for merit pay evaluations, to emphasize the fact that people must perform well in many dimensions to be effective. A supervisor might develop a scorecard with each employee that takes into account team results, new competencies, leadership, and so on. It is important that employees perceive that the input to the scorecard is valid and fairly covers the multiple aspects of their job. It is important to keep things simple because too much complexity will unduly inflate the attention paid to a pay system that works better when it is understated. Finally, scorecards should not be used to feed a ranking system.

~

Guideline #3: Tie Profit Sharing to Economic Drivers

Nucor Steel decided to get into the steelmaking business in 1968, and 30 years later it was the biggest steel company in the United States. When Nucor started up, Bethlehem Steel considered it a mere gnat, but 35 years later, Bethlehem Steel was not only bankrupt but sold off for assets. So, Nucor Steel is one very successful company that has done a lot of things right in a tough industry. Quite surprisingly, Nucor has a decades-old tradition of paying for performance. How does the company avoid the dysfunctions of rewards?

Nucor Steel started with the realization that profit per ton of finished steel was its key economic driver, and based its profit-sharing plan on the contribution a team makes to improve this number. So, for example, a team that successfully develops a new steel-making process or starts up a new plant on schedule will not see an increase in pay until the process or plant has improved the company's profit per ton of steel. Thus, Nucor avoids suboptimization by tying its differential pay system as closely to the economic driver of its business as possible.

~

Guideline # 4: Reward Based on Span of Influence, Not Span of Control

Conventional wisdom says that people should be evaluated based on results that are under their control. However, evaluating individual results, rather than group results, creates competition rather than collaboration among the team members. To encourage collaboration, Nucor makes sure that its profit-sharing formula rewards relatively large teams, not just the individuals or small groups who have direct responsibility for an area. According to their policies and principles, if a software program creates a significant profit increase, everyone, including those who brought the idea into the company, the developers and testers, the operations and support people, and the end users, should share in any reward. This reward system fits particularly well within an Agile environment, which naturally takes the same broad approach of involving everyone (end users, testers, support people, etc.) in the development process.

Nucor Steel works hard to create a learning environment where experts move from one plant to another, machine operators play a significant role in selecting and deploying new technology, and tacit knowledge spreads rapidly throughout the company. Its reward system encourages knowledge sharing by rewarding people for influencing the success of areas they do not control.

How, exactly, can rewards be based on span of influence rather than span of control? I recommend a technique called "Measure UP." No matter how hard you try to evaluate knowledge work or how good a scorecard you create, something will go unmeasured. Over time, the unmeasured area will be de-emphasized, and problems will arise. We have a tendency to add more measurements to the scorecard to draw attention to the neglected areas.

However, it is a lot easier to catch everything that falls between the cracks by reducing the number of measurements and raising them to a higher level. For instance, instead of measuring software development with cost, schedule, and earned value, try creating a P&L or ROI for the project and helping the team use these tools to drive trade-off decisions.

Guideline #5: Find Better M than Money

While monetary rewards can be a powerful driver of behavior, the motivation they provide is not sustainable. Once people have an adequate income, motivation comes from things such as achievement, growth, control over one's work, recognition, advancement, and a friendly working environment. No matter how good your evaluation and reward system may be, don't expect it to do much to drive stellar performance over the long term.

In the book *Hidden Value,* Charles O'Reilly and Jeffrey Pfeffer present several case studies of companies that obtain superb performance from ordinary people. These companies have people-centered values that are aligned with actions at all levels. They invest in people, share information broadly, rely on teams, and emphasize leadership rather than management. Finally, they do not use money as a primary motivator; they emphasize the intrinsic rewards of fun, growth, teamwork, challenge, and accomplishment.

Treat monetary rewards like explosives because they will have a powerful impact whether you intend it or not. So use them lightly and with caution. They can get you into trouble much faster than they can solve your problems. Once you go down the path of monetary rewards, you may never be able to go back, even when they cease to be effective, as they inevitably will. Make sure that people are fairly and adequately compensated, and then move on to more effective ways to improve performance.

Six Months Later

Sue's team is having another celebration. The team members had been surprised when the VP came to their team meeting six months earlier. But they quickly recovered and told her that they each wanted to be the st, they wanted to work with the best, and they did not appreciate the implication that some of them were better than others. When the VP left, the team cheered Sue for sticking up for them and then got down to work with renewed enthusiasm. Now, two releases later, the customers were showing their appreciation with their pocketbooks.

There haven't been any dramatic pay increases and only the occasional, well-deserved promotion; however, the company has expanded its training budget, and team members have found themselves mentoring other teams. Sue is rather proud of them all as she fills out the newly revised appraisal input forms, which have more team-friendly evaluation criteria. This time, Sue is confident that her judgment will not be questioned.

Rick Schaut

MAC WORD 6.0[1]

When Word 6.0 for the Macintosh first came out, it was loathed. It received absolutely horrid reviews.

In my opinion, Mac Word 6.0 had two problems, one real, one political.

The real reason was that it was slow and buggy, and that it had arbitrary UI differences from Mac Word 5.0 that required relearning.

But there was a political reason too. To understand the political reason, you have to understand that when the Macintosh first came out, it was completely revolutionary, with its WIMP user interface (Windows, Icons, Menus, and . . . um. . . Pterodactyls? One forgets. . .) and fonts and bitmapped screen and the ability to make a "beep!" sound unlike any computer beep that had ever been heard before.

Many software publishers did not quite grok the newness and superiority of the Mac. They just thought it was yet another computer. So they took their old DOS programs and sort of ported them to the Mac, keeping the ridiculous DOS text mode interface and ignoring all the icons and menus and that stuff.

These DOS ports were horrible, and Apple was terrified that if this trend continued, the Mac's distinctive GUI advantage would be lost.

So Apple evangelists like Guy Kawasaki spread the mantra to the Mac faithful: Ports Are Bad. The only true way of the Mac religion

---

1. Rick Schaut, "Mac Word 6.0," Buggin' My Life Away: Musings of a Mad Mac Maven (http://blogs.msdn.com), February 26, 2004. See http://blogs.msdn.com/rick_schaut/archive/2004/02/26/80193.aspx.

was a completely new, ground-up rewrite to take advantage of the GUI. Mac users were successfully trained by Apple to reject any applications that were just ports from character-mode DOS.

The trouble was that they were trained a little bit too well. So when Word for Windows was ported to the Macintosh creating Word 6.0, even though it still had menus and icons and whatnot and was a reasonably Mac-like product, the Mac faithful got wind of what had happened and started chanting their mantra: Ports Are Bad, Ports Are Bad—even though the port was from Windows, not DOS, and Windows was a clone of the Mac in the first place.

So that was the political problem. And even though I'm poking fun at it, it's a real problem. You can't make a product successful if it doesn't assuage the real and imagined prejudices of its target audience. That's why nowadays Microsoft has a whole business unit in Silicon Valley that makes Macintosh software and they always try to include at least one feature in the Mac version that the Windows version doesn't have, to keep on the Mac acolytes' good side even if there's something irrational about it.

The vocal Mac community still chants regularly about how they want native, ground-up applications for the Mac, not plain ports, which, by the way, hurts them a lot more than it helps them, because it scares away software publishers who might have been able to afford a port but do not have the resources to do a whole new product... but that's a different story.

One of the reasons I loved reading Rick's account of Mac Word 6.0 is that it reminded me of the early 1990s, when I worked at Microsoft, when every decision was carefully taken after much debate and deliberation by very, very smart people, and yet, to the outside peanut gallery throwing stones, to mix a metaphor, those decisions looked stupid and incompetent. That's the way it always is. Design decisions involve extremely hard trade-offs, especially when you have limited memory and CPU power, and it's easy to criticize the result without understanding all the factors that the programming team had to consider. So journalists writing reviews of our products have fairly legitimate complaints about how the software behaves, and any attempt to

explain that behavior can only be understood by another pro-
grammer.

Everyone involved, fortunately, had stock options and now
owns a very nice house on Mercer Island, another loft in down-
town Seattle, a Bentley convertible, and a big boat. So don't feel
too sorry for them. – Ed.

~

Mom always said, "The only good thing about beating your head against the wall is that it feels good when you stop." Well, sorry Mom, but that's not fully true. While you're sitting on the couch buried beneath an ice pack, you tend to come up with a few ways to mind your head.

Shipping a crappy product is a lot like beating your head against the wall. It really does feel good when you ship a great product as a follow-up, and it really does motivate you to spend some time trying to figure out how not to ship a crappy product again.

Mac Word 6.0 was a crappy product. And we spent some time trying to figure out how not to do that again. In the process, we learned a few things, not the least of which was the meaning of the term "Mac-like."

In order to understand why Mac Word 6.0 was a crappy product, we need to understand both the historical background that led to some key decisions, and we need to understand some of the technical problems that resulted from those decisions.

~

Mac Word 5 and Pyramid

On October 5, 1991, we shipped Mac Word 5.0. The reviews were glowing. For the effort, we received the Mac software equivalent of a Tony award: the Mac World Eddy. Even today, there are people who say that Mac Word 5.0/5.1 comprise the best version of Mac Word we've ever shipped.

While Mac Word 5 was a great product, there was one problem with it: Win Word 2. They both shipped at about the same time, but Win Word 2 had more features (most notably a macro language,[2] but there were a few others). This was a major sore point for Mac Word users. They wanted feature parity, and they wanted it now! The longer they had to wait for feature parity between Win Word and Mac Word, the more we got raked over the coals.

But we had a problem. Actually, we had a couple problems, the first being that Win Word and Mac Word were built from separate code bases. The other problem was WordPerfect. At that time, it still represented a major competitor to Windows, and we still had some catch-up work to do in order to get better than WordPerfect. If we had continued to develop Mac Word and Win Word from separate code bases, Mac Word would never have caught up to Win Word in terms of feature parity.

As of October 1991, we already had a plan to address the first problem: the Pyramid project. It was a complete rewrite of Word intended both to address some nagging issues with what had, by that time, become somewhat of a crusty code base and to address the separate code base problem. Both Win Word and Mac Word would be built from that same code base.

~

Exit Jeff Raikes, Enter Chris Peters

Feature parity problem solved. Well, not quite. At the same time, Jeff Raikes was promoted from Word business unit manager to some other position in Microsoft (I forget exactly which), and Chris Peters was promoted to fill Jeff Raikes' position. Almost everyone knows about Jeff Raikes these days. Chris Peters, however, had been the development manager for Excel before moving to Word. His favorite pastime is bowling, and he was known for having huge stacks of empty Coke cans in his office.

---

2. WordBasic was a surprisingly complete programming environment that allowed you to build pretty incredible applications with a fully functional word processor at their heart. – *Ed.*

While Jeff Raikes thought the Pyramid project was a good idea, Chris Peters looked at the WordPerfect problem and decided that Pyramid was a bad way to solve the feature parity problem. A complete code rewrite is risky. The whole point of a complete rewrite is to take a few steps backward in the short run in order to be able to make some greater strides in the long run. Chris Peters decided that we couldn't afford to take the short-run hit that Pyramid required.

So, Chris Peters killed Pyramid. At that point, the only way to solve the feature parity issue was to start both Mac Word and Win Word from the Win Word 2.0 code base, which is exactly what we did.

But that's not the full effect of Chris Peters' decision. At the time Chris Mason was the development manager for Word, and he strongly disagreed with Chris Peters' decision. As a result, Chris Mason left the Word group to work on other things at Microsoft. Chris Mason understood the Mac, and had been a Word developer going back to Mac Word 3.0. Chris Mason was replaced by Ed Fries, who was far less of a Mac person than Chris Mason was, so we lost a good bit of Mac understanding in the higher-level management of the Word group.[3] While it's impossible to say exactly what effect this had, there's a high probability that some of the trade-offs we made with Mac Word 6.0 would have gone in a different direction.

~

Technical Hurdles

Starting from the Win Word 2.0 code base presented a couple of technical problems for those of us on the Mac side. The first was that it was written to the Windows APIs. Solving this problem isn't simply a matter of writing a layer that emulates the Windows APIs on the Mac. The way the two systems handle windows are fundamentally different, though it's interesting to note that the new Carbon APIs are far more similar to the way Windows does things. The biggest problem is that Windows has the

---

3. Ed Fries is an accomplished programmer who will probably be best remembered for inventing the concept of a screensaver where little fish swim around on your screen, although he did incredible stuff on Excel, Word, and the Xbox. – *Ed.*

concept of child windows,[4] while the Mac does not. The other is that, on Windows, everything is a subclass of the window object. Even controls are windows.[5]

The other problem was a limitation in the Mac OS. While 68K Classic Mac OS was a nice operating system, it had one very glaring flaw. It didn't do memory management very well. In fact, it barely did any memory management at all. Users had to tell the OS how much memory a program needed in order to run, and that's how much memory the program got regardless of what the program might need at any given time during execution.

The memory problem was worse on 68K machines, because the memory given to a program, regardless of the virtual memory settings, was what the program got to use for both code and data. Under 68K, code was contained in something called a "code resource." Now, you could swap these code resources in and out of memory as needed, which meant that the actual memory needs of your program could change drastically depending on what the user wanted to do.

For example, consider a grammar checker. The user isn't going to want to check grammar all the time, so the grammar checker doesn't need to be loaded into memory all the time. But a grammar checker isn't a simple piece of code. It's a memory pig. The way 68K Classic Mac OS handled memory meant that you had to set a minimum amount of memory for your application such that you could load that memory pig of a grammar checker.

I'm making a distinction between 68K Classic Mac OS and PowerPC Classic Mac OS, because Apple changed how code was stored, loaded, and executed on the PowerPC. For those of you who remember, when you did Get Info on an application, it would show you two different memory requirements: one with virtual memory turned on and one with virtual memory turned off. With virtual memory turned on, the application's code could be handled through something called "demand paged" virtual memory, so the code no longer had to fit in the application's memory partition. That notorious grammar checker didn't have to be taken into account when trying to figure out the application's minimum memory requirements.

---

4. A child window is a window inside another window. For example, on a Yes/No dialog box, the Yes and No buttons are both child windows of the dialog box. – *Ed.*

5. *Controls* are things like buttons, edit boxes, scrollbars, etc. – *Ed.*

I want to be careful, here, not to lay blame for this at Apple's feet. Doing true virtual memory requires hardware support. Microprocessors in 1984 didn't have the full functionality required to support full demand paged virtual memory, so designing it into the original Mac OS would have been a waste of time. We often make design decisions that make perfect sense in light of current system limitations, only to have those design decisions come back to haunt us when Moore's Law makes those systems orders of magnitude more powerful. There's a reason Apple scrapped the Motorola 68K line of processors in favor of the PowerPC, not the least of which is the fact that it afforded them an opportunity to revisit some of those early design decisions.

~

Technical Achievement

Having reaped the benefits of a decade's worth of Moore's Law, we who now think very little of putting 128MB or even a half a GB of memory into a laptop computer might find it difficult to grasp just how much of a problem the 68K memory wall presented for Mac Word 6.0. But we were trying to get the whole thing to run in 4MB of memory—that's total system memory, not just the application partition.

This was no small matter. Word 6 was getting a bevy of new features over and above Win Word 2.0. Relative to Mac Word 5.0, this was two major releases' worth of feature changes. OLE;[6] the built-in lexical analyzer and rule-based inference engine required for AutoCorrect/ AutoFormat; and a grammar checker that included state-of-the-art natural language processing technology (which made the grammar checker even more of a memory pig) combined with things like a full-blown macro language (WordBasic) to make Mac Word 6.0 huge relative to common Mac systems of that time.

Please note the "relative" qualifier to the word "huge" back there. To see this in perspective, fire up BBEdit on your Mac OS X machine, open the Terminal window, and type "top" at the command line. Now

---

6. OLE = Object Linking and Embedding, a feature that lets you embed one kind of document in another, like a picture or a piece of a spreadsheet in a word processing document. – *Ed.*

read the values in the RSIZE and VSIZE columns. When I open my .tcshrc file in BBEdit, those values are 12.1MB and 164MB, respectively. As I type this document into my most recent build of Word 2004, those values are 36.6MB and 222MB, respectively—and Word is a full-blown word processor.

The amazing thing is that we actually managed to get Word 6.0 to run on systems that had only 4MB of memory (well, "walk" might be a better word than "run," but you get the point). To fully grasp the extent of this achievement, we need to understand a little bit about how programs are written and how they execute. What follows is my attempt to explain a fairly technical issue in lay terms. If your eyes start rolling into the back of your head, feel free to jump ahead to the next section.

Programs are written in relatively small chunks of code called "functions." Each function represents a single, functional aspect of the program. Functions can represent high-level concepts (e.g., lay out a page of text) or low-level concepts (format a single line of text within a page). Higher-level functions perform their work by calling lower-level functions, and there's a protocol that helps the computer to know how to return from a low-level function back to the high-level function that called it. This protocol is known as "procedure prologue and epilogue," and it involves something known as a "call stack." While the lower-level code is running, the higher-level code that called it is said to be "on the call stack."

Trying to get a body of code to run in a memory space that's smaller than the code itself involves something called *code swapping*. This is generally very easy to do if the code that you're swapping out doesn't cross these high-level to low-level boundaries. Our grammar checker is a good example. It represents a distinct functional unit, so we can swap the grammar checker's code out of memory if we no longer need that code around without having to worry about swapping it back in when we're done executing the current chunk of code.

But we can group code at a level of granularity that crosses high-level to low-level functional boundaries. For example, the code that lays out a page of text can be in one module (or code segment), while the code that formats a single line of text can be in another module. When you're laying out a single line of text, you really don't need the code that lays out the whole page in memory. Conceptually, at least, you can swap out the page layout code while running the format line code.

There's a problem with this idea: the page layout code calls the format line code, which means that the page layout code is still on the call stack. When the format line code is finished, the protocol that allows the computer to know how to return execution back to the page layout code needs to know that the page layout code is no longer in memory. This is such a difficult problem that Apple's documentation claimed that it was simply not possible to swap out code that was still on the call stack. Yet this is exactly what we were able to do with Word 6.0.

There is an unfortunate downside to being able to swap out code that's on the call stack. It leads to something called thrashing. Consider our page layout/format line example. Page layout works by calling a format line for each line of text on the page. Every time we cross the boundary between the page layout code and the format line code, we need to stop and load a chunk of code into memory, which will, in turn, require removing another chunk of code from memory.

Now, I've grossly oversimplified the whole process to explain what was going on. The swapping algorithm is a bit smarter about deciding what parts of the program to swap out of memory in order to be able to swap in a piece of code that's needed immediately. In practice, then, it's highly unlikely that page layout and format line code would ever thrash by themselves. Nonetheless, thrashing does occur when the available memory is small enough. When the system thrashes like this, performance goes down the toilet.

~

Learning the Meaning of "Mac-Like"

OK, so Mac Word 6.0 was big and slow relative to the memory that most computers had available at the time we shipped it, but that's not the reason why Mac Word 6.0 was such a crappy product, or at least not directly. Not long after Word 6.0 shipped, people could afford to add more memory to accommodate the added features of Mac Word 6.0. Those people who found those features to be very useful—and you'll run into a few of them even today—felt that the cost of the added memory was worth the work-savings that those features afforded them. Moore's Law, and the PowerPC, would have solved the memory problem in due time.

Moreover, while people complained about the performance, the biggest complaint we kept hearing about Mac Word 6.0 was that it wasn't "Mac-like." So we spent a lot of time drilling down into what people meant when they said it wasn't "Mac-like." We did focus groups. Some of us hung out in various Usenet newsgroups. We talked to product reviewers. We talked to friends who used the product. It turns out that "Mac-like" meant Mac Word 5.0.

We spent so much time, and put so much effort into, solving all the technical problems of Mac Word 6.0 that we failed to make the UI of Mac Word 6.0 behave like Mac Word 5.0. As a result, there were many differences, some little, some huge, and even some that were simply gratuitous, between the way Mac Word 6.0 did things and the way Mac Word 5.0 did things. The end result was a UI that could only be described as clunky relative to Mac Word 5.0's elegance. More importantly, Mac Word users had to unlearn all the ways they had come to do certain things, and relearn the Word 6.0 way of doing them.

My favorite example of this is the way you defined styles. In Mac Word 5.0, style definition was a semi-modal task. You defined or modified a style the same way you changed the font or paragraph properties in the document itself. In Mac Word 6.0, the task was completely modal. The entire array of menus and toolbar buttons that you could use in Mac Word 5.0 (and with which you were quite familiar as a user) was replaced by a single drop-down menu in the New/Modify Style dialog box. Even today, you can't use the Formatting palette to change the font or paragraph information in a style in Word 2001 or Word X, and this remains one of the things I want to fix in Word before I leave MacBU.[7]

The other thing we figured out as a result of coming to understand what "Mac-like" meant was that we weren't going to be able to deliver "Mac-like" products if Office remained a singular product from which both the Win and Mac versions were built. The mere fact that "Mac-like" was an issue at all meant that there were some fundamental differences between the Win Word market and the Mac Word market. If we were to understand both those markets, then our Mac products and Win products needed separate marketing and PGM organizations. The lessons we learned from Mac Word 6.0 are some of the reasons why MacBU exists today.

---

7. The Macintosh Business Unit at Microsoft – *Ed.*

We still bang our heads against the wall from time to time. Understanding users isn't an exact science. But we do it far less often than we used to. And it really does feel much better.

Clay Shirky

A GROUP IS ITS OWN WORST ENEMY[1]

In the late 1980s, software went through a major transition.

Before about 1985, the primary goal of software was making it possible to solve a problem, by any means necessary. Do you need to punch cards with your input data? No big deal. A typo on one card means you have to throw it away and start over? No problem. Humans will bend to the machines, like Charlie Chaplin in Modern Times.

Suddenly with personal computers the bar was raised. It wasn't enough just to solve the problem: you had to solve it easily, in a way that takes into account typical human frailties. The backspace key, for example, to compensate for human frailty, not to mention menus, icons, windows, and unlimited Undo. And we called this usability, and it was good.

Lo and behold, when the software industry tried to hire experts in usability, they found that it was a new field, so nobody was doing this. There was this niche field in psychiatry called ergonomics, but it was mostly focused on things from the physical world, like finding the optimal height for a desk chair.

Eventually usability came into its own as a first-class field of study, with self-trained practitioners and university courses, and no software project could be considered complete without at least a cursory glance at usability.

---

1. This is a lightly edited version of the keynote Clay Shirky gave on social software at the O'Reilly Emerging Technology conference in Santa Clara on April 24, 2003. See http://www.shirky.com/writings/group_enemy.html.

We're about to undergo a similar transition.

As soon as the Internet happened, software stopped being solely about computer-to-human interaction and started being about human-to-human interaction. We had new applications like the Web, email, instant messaging, and bulletin boards, all of which were about humans communicating with one another through software.

Now, suddenly, when you create software, it isn't sufficient to think about making it possible to communicate; you have to think about making communication socially successful. In the age of usability, technical design decisions had to be taken to make software easier for a mass audience to use; in the age of social software, design decisions must be taken to make social groups survive and thrive and meet the goals of the group even when they contradict the goals of the individual. A discussion group designed by a usability expert might be optimized to make it easy to post spam about Viagra. But in social software design it's pretty obvious that the goal is to make certain things harder, not easier, and if you can make it downright impossible to post spam, you've done your job. Features need to be designed to make the group successful, not the individual.

Today, hardly anybody really studies how to design software for human-to-human interaction. The field of social software design is in its infancy. In fact, we're not even at the point yet where the software developers developing social software realize that they need to think about the sociology and the anthropology of the group that will be using their software, so many of them just throw things together and allow themselves to be surprised by the social interactions that develop around their software.

Clay Shirky has been a pioneer in this field, and his talk A Group Is Its Own Worst Enemy *will be remembered as a watershed in the widespread realization that in this new era, sociology and anthropology are just as crucial to software design as usability was in the last. – Ed.*

~

Good morning, everybody. I want to talk this morning about social software, and about a pattern I've seen over and over again in social software that supports large and long-lived groups. In particular, I want to talk about what I now think is one of the core challenges for designing large-scale social software, the pattern described in the title of this talk: "A Group Is Its Own Worst Enemy."

Let me offer a definition of social software, because it's a term that's still fairly amorphous. My definition is quite simple: it's software that supports group interaction. I also want to emphasize, though that's a fairly simple definition, how radical social software is. The Internet supports lots of communications patterns, principally point-to-point and two-way, one-to-many outbound, and many-to-many two-way.

Prior to the Internet, we had lots of patterns that supported point-to-point two-way. We had telephones; we had the telegraph. We were familiar with technological mediation of those kinds of conversations. Prior to the Internet, we had lots of patterns that supported one-way broadcast of information. I could put something on television or the radio; I could publish a newspaper. We had the printing press. So although the Internet does good things for those ways of communicating, technological support for point-to-point and broadcast well predate the Internet.

Software for groups is different. Prior to the Internet, the last technology that had any real effect on the way people sat down and talked together was the table. There was no technological mediation for group conversations. The closest we got was the conference call, which never really worked right—"Hello? Do I push this button now? Oh, shoot, I just hung up." It's not easy to set up a conference call, but it's very easy to email five of your friends and say, "Hey, where are we going for pizza?"—so ridiculously easy group forming is quite a new pattern, something technology has never made easy before.

We've had social software for 40 years at most, dated from the Plato BBS system, and we've only had a decade or so of widespread availability, so we're just finding out what works. We're still learning how to make these kinds of things.

Now, software that supports group interaction is a fundamentally unsatisfying definition in many ways, because it doesn't point to a specific class of technology. If you look at email, it obviously supports social patterns, but it can also support a broadcast pattern. If I'm a spammer, I'm going to mail things out to a million people, but they're not going to be talking to one another, and I'm not going to be talking to them—spam is email, but it isn't social. If I'm mailing you, and you're mailing me back, we're having a point-to-point conversation, but not one that creates group dynamics.

So sometimes email supports social patterns, and sometimes it doesn't. Ditto weblogs. If I'm Glenn Reynolds of Instapundit.com,[2] and I'm publishing something to a million users a month, with comments turned off on my blog, that's really broadcast—Glenn's users aren't talking back to him, and they aren't talking to each other. It's obviously interesting that Glenn can reach that many people as a single individual, but the pattern is closer to MSNBC than it is to a conversation. If it's a cluster of half a dozen LiveJournal[3] users, on the other hand, talking about their lives with one another, that's social. So weblogs are not necessarily social, although they can support social patterns.

While that definition—software for group interaction—cuts across existing categories, I think it is the right one, because it recognizes the fundamentally social nature of the problem. Groups are a runtime effect. You cannot specify in advance what any given group will do, and so you can't instantiate in software everything you expect to have happen.

Now, there's a large body of literature saying, "We built this software, a group came and used it, and they began to exhibit behaviors that surprised us enormously, so we've gone and documented these behaviors." Over and over and over again this pattern comes up. (I hear Stewart[4] laughing. The WELL is one of those places where this pattern came up over and over again.)

With that background out of the way, the rest of this talk is in three parts. The best explanation I have found for the kinds of things that happen when groups of humans interact is psychological research that

---

2. A popular political weblog – *Ed.*

3. An online journal service, similar to blog software with more of an emphasis on community – *Ed.*

4. Stewart Brand, of the WELL, a very early online community that predates the Internet, now a part of Salon.com. – *Ed.*

predates the Internet, so the first part is going to be about W. R. Bion's research, which I will talk about in a moment, research that I believe helps explain how and why a group is its own worst enemy.

The second part is: why now? What's going on now that makes this worth thinking about? I think we're seeing a revolution in social software in the current environment that's really interesting.

And third, I want to identify some things, about half a dozen things, in fact, that I think are core to any software that supports large, long-lived groups.

~

Part One: How Is a Group Its Own Worst Enemy?

So, Part One. The best explanation I have found for the ways in which this pattern establishes itself, the group is its own worst enemy, comes from a book by W. R. Bion called *Experiences in Groups*, written in the middle of the last century.

Bion was a psychologist who was doing group therapy with groups of neurotics. (Drawing parallels between that and the Internet is left as an exercise for the reader.) And while he was trying to treat these patients, he realized that they were, as a group, conspiring to defeat therapy.

There was no overt communication or coordination. But he could see that whenever he would try to do anything that was meant to have an effect, the group would somehow quash it. And he was driving himself crazy, in the colloquial sense of the term, trying to figure out whether or not he should be looking at the situation as "Are these individuals taking action on their own, or is this a coordinated group?"

He could never resolve the question, and so he decided that the unresolvability of the question was the answer. To the question "Do groups of people behave as aggregations of individuals or as a cohesive group?" Bion's answer was that human groups are "hopelessly committed to both," which is to say hopelessly committed to individual identity *and* to group membership.

He said that humans are fundamentally individual, and also fundamentally social. Every one of us has a kind of rational decision-making mind that allows us to assess what's going on and make decisions and act on them. And we are all also able to enter viscerally into emotional bonds with other groups of people who transcend the intellectual aspects of the individual.

In fact, Bion was so convinced that this was the right answer that the image he put on the front cover of his book was a Necker cube, one of those cubes that you can look at and resolve in one of two ways, but you can never see both views of the cube at the same time. So groups can be analyzed both as collections of individuals and as having this kind of emotive group experience.

Now, it's pretty easy to see how with groups of people who have formal memberships—groups that have been labeled and named like "I am a member of such-and-such a guild in a massively multiplayer online role-playing game"—you would have some kind of group cohesion there. But Bion's thesis is that this effect is much, much deeper, and kicks in much, much sooner than many of us expect. So I want to illustrate this with a story, and to illustrate the illustration, I'll use a story from your life. Because even if I don't know you, I know that what I'm about to describe has happened to you.

You are at a party, and you get bored. You say "This isn't doing it for me anymore. I'd rather be someplace else. I'd rather be home asleep. The people I wanted to talk to aren't here." For whatever reason, the party fails to meet some threshold of interest. And then a really remarkable thing happens: you don't leave. You make a decision: "I don't like this." If you were in a bookstore and you said, "I'm done," you'd walk out. If you were in a coffee shop and said, "This is boring," you'd walk out.

You're sitting at a party, and you decide, "I don't like this; I don't want to be here." And then you don't leave. That kind of social stickiness is what Bion is talking about.

And then, another really remarkable thing happens. Twenty minutes later, one person stands up and gets their coat, and what happens? Suddenly everyone is getting their coats on, all at the same time. Which means that everyone had decided that the party was not for them, and no one had done anything about it, until finally this triggering event let the air out of the group, and everyone kind of felt okay about leaving.

This effect is so common that it's sometimes called the "paradox of groups." It's obvious that there are no groups without members. But what's less obvious is that there are no members without a group—because what would you be a member of?

So there's this very complicated moment of a group coming together, where enough individuals, for whatever reason, sort of agree that something worthwhile is happening, and the decision they make at that moment is "This is good and must be protected." And at that moment, even if it's subconscious, you start getting group effects. And the effects that we've seen come up over and over and over again in online communities.

Now, Bion decided that what he was watching with the neurotics was the group defending itself against his attempts to make the group do what they said they were supposed to do. This group of people was in therapy to get better, but they were during therapy defeating the very things that might help them get better. And after years of these observations, Bion said there are some very specific patterns that they're entering into in order to defeat the ostensible purpose of the group meeting together. And he detailed three patterns.

The first is sex talk, what he called, in his mid-century prose, "A group met for pairing off." And what that means is, the group conceives of its purpose as the hosting of flirtatious or salacious talk or emotions passing between pairs of members.

Imagine going on IRC (internet relay chat, a global set of chat rooms)—you scan the list of channel names, and you say, "I know what they are talking about on the #hamradio channel, because I can see the channel name." But when you go into the group, you will also almost invariably find that it's about sex talk as well, usually expressed as double entendres. The topic of sex is always in scope in live human conversations, according to Bion. (Interestingly, it is a much less frequent pattern in asynchronous communication, like mailing lists, than in synchronous ones, like IRC.) That is one basic pattern that groups can always devolve into, away from the sophisticated purpose and toward one of these basic purposes.

The second basic pattern that Bion detailed is the identification and vilification of external enemies. This is a very common pattern. Anyone who was around the open source movement in the mid-1990s could see this all the time. If you cared about Linux on the desktop, there was a big list of jobs to do. But you could always instead get a conversation going about Microsoft and Bill Gates. And people would start bleeding from their ears, they would get so mad.

The open source movement at the time seemed pretty enemy-free, because of their mode of working: if you want to make it better, there's a list of things to do. Just fix it. But you could always get people wound up on the subject of Microsoft and Bill Gates, and the foam would start coming out of their mouths.

Nothing causes a group to galvanize like an external enemy. So even if someone isn't really your enemy, identifying them as an enemy can cause a pleasant sense of group cohesion. And groups often gravitate toward members who are the most paranoid and make them leaders, because those are the people who are best at identifying external enemies.

The third pattern Bion identified is religious veneration—the nomination and worship of a religious icon or a set of religious tenets. The religious pattern is, essentially, we have nominated something that's beyond critique. You can see this pattern on the Internet any day you like. Go onto a Tolkien newsgroup or discussion forum, and try saying, "You know, *The Two Towers* is a little dull. I mean loooong. We didn't need that much description about crossing the forest, because it's pretty much the same forest all the way."

Try having that discussion. On the door of the group it will say, "This is for discussing the works of Tolkien." Go in and try and have that discussion.

Now, in some places people say, "Yes, but it needed to, because it had to convey the sense of lassitude," or whatever. But in most places you'll simply be flamed to high heaven, because you're interfering with the religious text. Groups often have some small set of core tenets, beliefs, or interests that are beyond criticism, because they are the things that hold the group together. Even in groups founded for fairly intellectual discussion, the emotional piece comes out whenever you threaten one of these core beliefs, because when you take on those beliefs, you are not just offering an opinion, you are threatening group cohesion.

Bion's patterns have shown up on the Internet, not because of the software, but because it's being used by humans. Bion has identified this possibility of groups sandbagging their sophisticated goals with these basic urges. And what he finally came to, in analyzing this tension, is that group structure is necessary. Robert's Rules of Order are necessary.

Constitutions are necessary. Norms, rituals, laws, the whole list of ways that we say, out of the universe of possible behaviors, we're going to draw a relatively small circle around the acceptable ones, all of those are ways to keep groups from just wallowing in these patterns and never actually getting anything done. Anyone who has been in a competitive industry knows you can kill a two-hour meeting by mentioning what the competition is up to, at which point everyone will stop thinking about the hard work of actually getting anything done, and will switch to alternately vilifying the competition and assuring themselves that there is no threat.

Most importantly, Bion said the various forms of group structure we have created over the centuries are necessary to defend the group from itself. Group structure exists to keep a group on target, on track, on message, on charter, to keep a group focused on its own sophisticated goals and away from sliding into these basic patterns. Group structure defends the group from the action of its own members.

This is a pattern that's shown up on the network over and over again. In the 1970s, a BBS called Communitree launched, one of the very early dial-up BBSs. This was launched when people didn't own computers— institutions owned computers.

Communitree was founded on the principles of open access and free dialogue. ("Communitree"—doesn't that say "California in the '70s"?) And the notion was, effectively, throw off structure and new and beautiful new social patterns will arise.

And, indeed, as anyone who has put discussion software into groups that were previously disconnected has seen, that does happen. Incredible things happen. The early days of Echo,[5] the early days of Usenet, the early days of Lucasfilms' Habitat (one of the original multiplayer games), over and over again, you see all this incredible upwelling of people who suddenly are connected in ways they weren't before.

But it's not all beautiful; as time sets in, difficulties emerge. In this case, one of the difficulties was occasioned by the fact that one of the institutions that joined Communitree was a high school. And who, in 1978, was hanging out in the room with the computer and the modems in it but the boys of that high school. And the boys weren't terribly

---

5. A small but prestigious online community in New York City, which also predates the Internet, created by Stacy Horn at NYU. – *Ed.*

interested in sophisticated adult conversation. They were interested in fart jokes. They were interested in salacious talk. They were interested in running amok and posting four-letter words and nyah-nyah-nyah all over the bulletin board.

And the adults who had set up Communitree were horrified, because they were being overrun by these students. The place that was founded on open access had too much open access, too much openness. They couldn't defend themselves against their own users. The place that was founded on free speech had too much freedom. They had no way of saying, "No, that's not the kind of free speech we meant."

But that was a requirement. In order to defend themselves against being overrun, that was something that they needed to have that they didn't have, and in the end, they simply shut the site down.

Now you could ask whether or not the founders' inability to defend themselves from this onslaught, from being overrun, was a technical or a social problem. Did the software not allow the problem to be solved? Or was it the social configuration of the group that founded it, where they simply couldn't stomach the idea of adding censorship to protect their system. But in a way, it doesn't matter, because technical and social issues are deeply intertwined. There's no way to completely separate them.

What matters is, a group designed this and then was unable, in the context they'd set up, to save it from this attack from within, and that context was partly technical and partly social. The lesson of Communitree is that attack from within is what matters. Communitree wasn't shut down by people trying to crash the server or flood it from the outside. It was shut down by people logging in and posting, which is what the system was designed to allow. The technological patterns of normal use and attack were so similar at the machine level, there was no way to specify technologically what should and shouldn't happen. Some of the users wanted the system to continue to exist and to provide a forum for discussion. And other of the users, the high school boys, either didn't care or were actively inimical. And the system provided no way for the former group to defend itself from the latter.

This pattern has happened over and over and over again. Someone built the system; they assumed certain user behaviors. The users came on and exhibited different behaviors. And the people running the system discovered to their horror that the technological and social issues could not in fact be decoupled. This story has been written many times. It's actually frustrating to see how many times it's been written, because although there's a wealth of documentation from the field, people starting similar projects often haven't read these accounts.

The most charitable description of this repeated pattern is "learning from experience," but learning from experience is the worst possible way to learn something. Learning from experience is one up from remembering—that's not great. The best way to learn something is when someone else figures it out and tells you: "Don't go in that swamp. There are alligators in there."

Learning from experience about the alligators is lousy, compared to learning from reading, say. There hasn't been, unfortunately, in this arena, a lot of learning from reading. And so, the essay "Lessons from Lucasfilms' Habitat,"[6] written in 1990, reads a lot like Rose Stone's description of Communitree from 1978.

There's a great document called "LambdaMOO Takes a New Direction," which is about the wizards of LambdaMOO, Pavel Curtis's Xerox PARC experiment in building a MUD[7] world. And one day the wizards of LambdaMOO announced, "We've gotten this system up and running, and all these interesting social effects are happening. Henceforth we wizards will only be involved in technological issues. We're not going to get involved in any of that social stuff."

And then, I think about 18 months later, the wizards come back, extremely cranky. And they say, "What we have learned from you whining users is that we can't do what we said we would do. We cannot separate the technological aspects from the social aspects of running a virtual world.

"So we're back, and we're taking wizardly fiat back, and we're going to do things to run the system. We are effectively setting ourselves up as a government, because this place needs a government, because without us, everything was falling apart."

People who work on social software are closer in spirit to economists and political scientists than they are to people making compilers. They both look like programming, but when you're dealing with groups of people as one of your runtime phenomena, you have an incredibly

---

6. See http://www.fudco.com/chip/lessons.html.

7. Multiuser Dungeon, a textual online multiplayer adventure game – *Ed.*

different practice. In the political realm, we would call these kinds of crises a constitutional crisis. It's what happens when the tension between the individual and the group, and the rights and responsibilities of individuals and groups, gets so serious that something has to be done.

And the worst crisis is the first crisis, because it's not just "We need to have some rules." It's also "We need to have some rules for making some rules." And this is what we see over and over again in large and long-lived social software systems. Constitutions are a necessary component of large, long-lived, heterogeneous groups.

Geoff Cohen has a great observation about this. He said, "The likelihood that any unmoderated group will eventually get into a flame-war about whether or not to have a moderator approaches one as time increases." As a group commits to its existence as a group, and begins to think that the group is good or important, the chance that they will begin to call for additional structure, in order to defend themselves from themselves, gets very, very high.

~

Part Two: Why Now?

If these things I'm saying have happened so often before, have been happening and been documented and we've got psychological literature that predates the Internet, what's going on now that makes this important?

I can't tell you precisely why, but observationally there is a revolution in social software going on. The number of people writing tools to support or enhance group collaboration or communication is astonishing.

The Web turned us all into size queens for six or eight years there. It was loosely coupled, it was stateless, it scaled like crazy, and everything became about how big you could get. "How many users does Yahoo have? How many customers does Amazon have? How many readers does MSNBC have?" And the answer could be "A lot!" But MSNBC, say, could only get a lot if they didn't have to be talking with their users, just talking to them, and they didn't have to figure out a way to let those readers talk to each other.

The downside of going for size and scale above all else is that the dense, interconnected pattern that drives group conversation and collaboration isn't supportable at any large scale. Less is different—small groups of people can engage in kinds of interaction that large groups can't, and during the Web years, we blew past that interesting scale of small groups. In groups of larger than a dozen but smaller than a few hundred, there are conversational forms that can't be supported when you're talking about thousands or millions of users a single group.

We've had things like mailing lists and BBSs for a long time. More recently we've had IM, and we've had these various tools for a while. But now, all of a sudden, a bunch of new forms are spreading. We've gotten weblogs and wikis, and I think, even more importantly, we're getting platform stuff. We're getting RSS. We're getting shared Flash objects. We're getting ways to quickly build on top of some infrastructure we can take for granted, that lets us try new things very rapidly.

I was talking to Stewart Butterfield about Flickr, the application they're launching here. I said, "Hey, how's that going?" He said, "Well, we only had the idea for it two weeks ago. So this is the launch." When you can go from "Hey, I've got an idea" to "Let's launch this in front of a few hundred serious geeks and see how it works," that suggests that there's a platform there that is letting people do some really interesting things really quickly. It's not that you couldn't have built a similar application a couple of years ago, but the cost would have been much higher. And when you lower costs, interesting new kinds of things happen.

So the first answer to Why Now? is simply, "Because it's time." I can't tell you why it took as long for weblogs to happen as it did, except to say it had absolutely nothing to do with technology. We had every bit of technology we needed to do weblogs in 1994, the day Mosaic launched the first forms-capable browser. Every single piece of it was right there. Instead, we got Geocities. Why did we get Geocities and not weblogs? We didn't know what we were doing.

One was a bad idea; the other turns out to be a really good idea. It took a long time to figure out that people talking to one another, instead of simply uploading badly scanned photos of their cats, would be the real source of value.

We got the weblog pattern in around '96 with Drudge. We got weblog platforms starting in '98. The thing really was taking off in

2000. By last year, it was "Omigod, this thing is going mainstream, and it's going to change everything."

The vertigo moment for me was when Phil Gyford launched the Pepys weblog, Samuel Pepys' diaries of the 1660s turned into a weblog form, with a new post every day from Pepys' diary. What that said to me was that Phil was asserting, and I now believe, that weblogs will be around for at least 10 years, because that's how long Pepys kept a diary. And that was this moment of projecting into the future: this is now infrastructure we can take for granted.

Why was there an eight-year gap between a forms-capable browser and the Pepys diaries? It just takes a while for people to get used to these ideas, to understand the technical form well enough to put it to socially novel uses.

The other big change is that the social software people are building now is web-native, built on the Web from the ground up. When you got social software on the Web in the mid-1990s, a lot of it was enterprise software with a web front-end slapped on: "This is the Giant Lotus Dreadnought, now with New Lightweight Web Interface!" It never felt like the Web. It felt like this hulking thing tarted up with some clickable icons.

A weblog is web-native. It's the Web all the way in. A wiki is a web-native way of hosting collaboration. It's lightweight, it's loosely coupled, it's easy to extend, it's easy to break down. And it's not just the surface, like "Oh, you can just do things in a form." It assumes HTTP is transport. It assumes markup in the coding. RSS is a web-native way of doing syndication. So we're taking all of these tools and we're extending them in a way that lets us build new things really quickly.

The third thing that's happening now to accelerate social software is that, in David Weinberger's felicitous phrase, we have a "Small Pieces Loosely Joined" way of making software. It's really worth looking into what Joi Ito is doing with the Emergent Democracy movement, even if you're not interested in the themes of emerging democracy. This started because a conversation was going on, and Ito said, "I am frustrated. I'm sitting here in Japan, and I know all of these people are having these conversations in real time with one another. I want to have a group conversation, too. I'll start a conference call.

"But since conference calls are so lousy on their own, I'm going to bring up a chat window at the same time." And then, in the first meeting, I think it was Pete Kaminski who said, "Well, I've also opened up a wiki, and here's the URL." And he posts the URL of the wiki in the chat window. And people on the call also start annotating things in the wiki, adding bookmarks in the chat channel, and so on. The meeting is going on in three separate modes at the same time, two in real time (the phone and the chat) and one annotated (the wiki).

You know how conference calls usually are: either one or two people dominate it, or everyone's walking over each other, interrupting and cutting each other off. It's very difficult to coordinate speakers in a conference call because people can't see one another, which makes it hard to manage the interrupt logic. In Joi's conference call, the interrupt logic got moved to the chat room. People would type "Hand," and the moderator of the conference call will then type, "You're speaking next," in the chat. So the conference call flowed incredibly smoothly, because the chat provided a kind of control channel for the speaking.

Meanwhile, in the chat, people are annotating what people are saying. "Oh, that reminds me of So-and-so's work." Or "You should look at this URL. . . you should look at that ISBN number." In a conference call, to read out a URL, you have to spell it out—"No, no, no, it's w w w dot net dash. . ." In a chat window, you get it and you can click on it right there. You can say, in the conference call or the chat: "Go over to the wiki and look at this."

This is a broadband, multimedia conference call, but it isn't implemented as a single giant thing. It's just three little pieces of software, laid next to each other and held together with a little bit of social glue. This is an incredibly powerful pattern. It's different from "Let's take the Lotus juggernaut and add a web front-end."

And the fourth and final driving the current revolution in social software is ubiquity. The Web has been growing for a long, long time. In the beginning, just a few people had web access, and then lots of people had web access, and then most people had web access. But something different is happening now. In many situations, *all* people have access to the network. And "all" is a different kind of amount than "most." "All" lets you start taking things for granted.

Now, the Internet isn't everywhere in the world. It isn't even everywhere in the developed world. But for some groups of people—students, people in high-tech offices, knowledge workers—everyone they work with is online. Everyone they're friends with is online. Everyone in their family is online.

This pattern of ubiquity lets you start taking this for granted. Bill Joy once said, "My method is to look at something that seems like a good idea and assume it's true." We're starting to see software that simply assumes that all offline groups will have an online component, no matter what. It is now possible for every grouping, from a Girl Scout troop on up, to have an online component, and for it to be lightweight and easy to manage. And that's a different kind of thing than the old pattern of "online community." I have this Venn diagram image of two hula hoops, where my real life is off to the left, and my online life is off to the right, and I'm the only thing in common between the two; people in my offline world are different than people in my online world. And for most of the last 30 years, the Net has been like that—you had different friends online than offline. If the hula hoops are swung together, though, so that everyone who's offline is also online, that's a different kind of pattern. In a world of ubiquitous Net access, the split between offline and online is not between different groups, but between different modes of interacting in one group.

There's a second kind of ubiquity, which is the kind we're enjoying here at the conference, thanks to the Wifi network at the conference. If you assume whenever a group of people are gathered together that they can be both face to face and online at the same time, you can start to do different kinds of things than if real versus virtual communications are treated as separate cases. I don't run a real-world meeting now without either having a chat room or a wiki up and running. Three weeks ago I ran a meeting for the Library of Congress. We had a wiki, set up by Socialtext, and used it during the meeting to capture a large and very dense amount of technical information on long-term digital preservation.

It really quickly becomes an assumption that a group can do things like "Oh, I took my PowerPoint slides, I showed them, and then I dumped them into the wiki. So now you can get at them." It becomes a sort of shared repository for group memory. This is new. These kinds of ubiquity, both "everyone is online," and "everyone who's in a room can be online together at the same time," are leading to new patterns.

~

Part Three: What Can We Take for Granted?

If these assumptions are right—first that a group is its own worst enemy, and second, we're seeing this explosion of social software—what should we do? Can we say anything with any certainty about building social software, at least for large and long-lived groups?

I think we can. A little over 10 years ago, I quit my day job, because Usenet was so interesting. I thought at the time, "This is really going to be big." And I actually wrote a book called *Voices from the Net*, about Net culture at the time, Usenet, the Well, Echo, IRC, and so forth. It was published in April of '95, just as that world was being washed away by the Web. But it was my original interest, so I've been looking at this problem in one way or another for 10 years, and I've been looking at it pretty hard for a year and a half or so.

So there's this question: "What is required to make a large, long-lived online group successful?" I think I can now answer with some confidence: "It depends." (I'm hoping to flesh that answer out a little bit in the next 10 years.)

But I can at least say some of the things it depends on. The Calvinists had a doctrine of natural grace and supernatural grace. Natural grace was, "You have to do all the right things in the world to get to heaven. . ." and supernatural grace was, ". . .and God has to anoint you." And you never knew if you had supernatural grace or not. This was their way of getting around the fact that the book of Revelation put an upper limit on the number of people who were going to heaven.

Social software is like that. You can find the same piece of code running in many, many environments. And sometimes it works and sometimes it doesn't. So there is something supernatural about groups, where having good software alone isn't enough, because the social behavior of groups is a runtime experience.

The normal experience of social software is failure. If you go into Yahoo groups and you map out the subscriptions, it is, unsurprisingly, a power law. There's a small number of highly populated groups, a moderate number of moderately populated groups, and this long, flat tail of failure. And the failure is inevitably more than 50% of the total mailing lists in any category. So it's not like a cake recipe. There's nothing you can do to make it come out right every time.

There are, however, I think, about half a dozen things that are broadly true of all the groups I've looked at and all the online constitutions I've read for software that supports large and long-lived groups. And I'd break that list in half. I'd say, if you are going to create a piece of social software designed to support large groups, you have to accept three things, and design for four things.

Three Things to Accept

1.) Of the things you have to accept, the first is that you cannot completely separate technical and social issues. There are two attractive patterns for thinking about the intersection of social and technological issues. One says, "We'll handle technology over here, we'll do social issues there. We'll have separate mailing lists with separate discussion groups, or we'll have one track here and one track there." This doesn't work; you can't separate the two. It's never been stated more clearly than in the pair of documents called "LambdaMOO Takes a New Direction" that I referred to earlier. I can do no better than to point you to those documents.

This may seem obvious, but it's one of those patterns that gets endlessly repeated. I recently was on a social software discussion list, and someone said, "Hey everybody, I know! Let's set up a second mailing list for just discussing the technical issues." The LambdaMOO docs were written in the early '90s, here it is 2003, and people still want to believe that the technology has some kind of clean edge that separates from the behavior of the mere users. And of course what happened when the second technical mailing list was created? Nothing. Nothing happened. No one moved the conversations away from the first list; no one could fork the conversation between social and technical issues, because the conversation can't be forked.

There's another way of thinking about tech and social dynamics that's very, very attractive—anybody who looks at this stuff has the same epiphany: "Omigod, the software is determining what people do!" And that is true, up to a point. But you cannot completely program social issues either—different mailing lists run on the same software but have different cultures; both Slashdot and Plastic.com run on the same software platform, but they have very different cultures too.

You can't separate technological effects from social ones, and you can't specify all social issues in technology. The group is going to assert its existence independently of the software somehow, and you're going to get a mix of social and technological effects.

The group is real. It will exhibit emergent effects. It can't be ignored, and it can't be programmed, which means you have an ongoing issue. And the best pattern, or at least the pattern that's worked the most often, is to put into the hands of the group itself the responsibility for defining what value is, and defending that value, rather than trying to describe everything in the software up front.

2.) The second thing you have to accept: members are different from users. A pattern will arise in which there is some group of users that cares more than average about the integrity and success of the group as a whole. And that becomes your core group, Art Kleiner's phrase for "the group within the group that matters most."

The core group on Communitree was undifferentiated from the group of random users that came in. They were separate in their own minds, because they knew what they wanted to do, but they couldn't defend themselves against the other users. But in all successful online communities that I've looked at, a core group arises that cares about the community as a whole—not just their part of it—and that gardens effectively and takes care of the social environment by encouraging good behavior and discouraging bad behavior.

Now, if the software does not always allow the core group to express itself, it will invent new ways of doing so. On alt.folklore.urban, the Usenet discussion group about urban folklore, a group of people hung out together and, over time, got to be friends. Enough of these AFU regulars were also Silicon Valley dwellers that they decided to get together for a real-world barbecue, and to coordinate that, they set up a separate mailing list, which they called the Old Hats list.

After the barbecue, though, the mailing list stayed up, and membership was extended to other AFU readers, but only selectively, only to those members who'd been around AFU long enough to get to know everyone—the average reader of AFU didn't even know the mailing list existed. Old Hats became a place for meta-discussion, discussion about AFU, and the members of Old Hats began to coordinate efforts formally if they were going to troll someone or flame someone or ignore someone in alt.folklore.urban itself.

Then, as Usenet kept growing, many newcomers arrived and seemed to like the environment, because it was well run. In order to defend themselves from the scaling issues that come from of adding a lot of new members to the Old Hats list, they said, "We're starting a second list, called the Young Hats."

So AFU ended up with this three-tier system, not dissimilar to the tiers of anonymous cowards, logged-in users, and people with high karma on Slashdot. But because Usenet didn't let the AFU core group do it in the software, they brought in other pieces of software, these mailing lists, that they needed to build the structure. So you don't get the program users—in any healthy group, the members in good standing will find one another and be recognized by one another.

3.) The third thing you need to accept: the core group has rights that trump individual rights in some situations. This pulls against the libertarian view that's quite common on the network, and it absolutely pulls against the one-person/one-vote notion. But you can see examples of how bad an idea voting is when citizenship is the same as ability to log in.

In the early '90s, a proposal went out to create a Usenet newsgroup for discussing Tibetan culture, to be called soc.culture.tibet. And it was voted down, in large part because a number of Chinese students who had Internet access voted it down, on the logic that Tibet wasn't a country; it was a region of China. And in their view, since Tibet wasn't a country, there oughtn't be any place to discuss its culture, because that was oxymoronic.

Now, everyone could see that this was the wrong answer. The people who wanted a place to discuss Tibetan culture should have it. That was the core group. But because the one-person/one-vote model on Usenet said, "Anyone who's on Usenet gets to vote on any group," sufficiently contentious groups could simply be voted away.

Imagine today if, in the United States, Internet users had to be polled before any discussion group opposed to the war in Iraq could be created, or French users had to be polled before any pro-war group could be created. The people who want to have those discussions are the people who matter, and absolute citizenship, with the idea that if you can log in, you are a citizen, can actually be a harmful pattern, because it allows the tyranny of the majority. The core group needs ways to defend itself so that it can keep the larger group concentrated on its sophisticated goals and away from its basic instincts.

The Wikipedia (the group-created online encyclopedia) has a similar system today, with a "volunteer fire department," a group of people who care to an unusual degree about the success of the Wikipedia. And since they have enough leverage (because of the way wikis work, they can always roll back graffiti and so forth), that thing has stayed up despite repeated attacks. So leveraging the core group is a really powerful system.

And because of the difficulty in maintaining a focus on sophisticated goals, all groups of any integrity have a constitution. There is always an informal piece of the Constitution, and there is sometimes a formal piece as well, an explicit and publicly examinable piece. At the very least, the formal part is what's instantiated in code—"the software works this way." The informal part is the sense of "how we do it around here." And no matter how it is substantiated in code or written in charter, whatever, there will always be an informal part as well. You can't separate the two.

Now, when I say these are three things you have to accept, I mean you *have* to accept them, because if you don't accept them up front, they'll happen to you anyway. And then you'll end up writing one of those documents that says, "Oh, we launched this and we tried it, and then the users came along and did all these weird things. And now we're documenting it so future ages won't make this mistake"—even though you didn't read the thing that was written in 1978.

Four Things to Design For

In addition to the things you have to accept, the forced moves, I also believe there are a handful of things designers of group software need to design for:

1.) The first thing you would design for is handles the user can invest in. Now, I say "handles" because I don't want to say "identity"; identity has recently become one of those ideas where, when you pull on the little thread you want, this big bag of stuff comes along with it. Identity is such a hot-button issue now, but for the lightweight stuff required for social software, it's really just a handle that matters.

It's pretty widely understood that anonymity doesn't work well in group settings, because "who said what when" is the minimum requirement for having a conversation. What's less well understood is that weak pseudonymity doesn't work well, either, because I need to associate who's saying something to me now with previous conversations.

The world's best reputation management system is right here, in the brain. And actually, it's right here, in the back, in the emotional part of the brain. Almost all the work being done on reputation systems today is either trivial or useless or both, because in most human situations, reputations aren't easy to make explicit. eBay has done us all an enormous disservice, because eBay works in noniterated atomic transactions, which are the opposite of social situations. eBay's reputation system works incredibly well, because it starts with a simple transaction ("How much money for how many Smurfs?") and turns that into a metric that's equally linear. That doesn't work well in social situations, where karma, a.k.a. nonreciprocal altruism, is a much subtler and more diffuse thing than eBay's reputation is.

Reputation is also not generalizable or portable. There are people who will cheat on their spouse but not at cards, and vice versa, and both, and neither. Reputation in one situation is not necessarily directly portable to another.

If you want a good reputation system, just let me remember who you are. And if you do me a favor, I'll remember it. And I won't store it in the front of my brain; I'll store it here, in the back. I'll just get a good feeling next time I get email from you; I won't even remember why. And if you do me a disservice and I get email from you, my temples will start to throb, and I won't even remember why. If you give users a way of remembering one another, reputation will happen, and that requires nothing more than simple and somewhat persistent handles.

Users have to be able to identify themselves and there has to be a penalty for switching handles. The penalty for switching doesn't have to be total. But if I change my handle on the system, I have to lose some kind of reputation or some kind of context. This keeps the system functioning.

Of course, this pulls against the sense that we've had since the early psychological writings about the Internet. "Oh, on the Internet we're all going to be changing identities and genders like we change our socks." But this sense of completely fluid identity is disrupted by things like the Kaycee Nicole story.

The story is baroque, but the basic outline is simple: a woman in Kansas was living online in an alternate persona, a high school student named Kaycee Nicole, and then, because the invented high school student's friends got so emotionally involved, the woman decided to kill her persona off, and so she began reporting, in the persona of Kaycee Nicole, that she had contracted a fatal disease.

So here's this attractive young woman everyone has befriended and now she's dying, and what happens? Everyone wants to fly to meet her before she goes. So then woman sort of panicked and Kaycee Nicole vanished. And a bunch of places on the Internet, particularly the MetaFilter community, started to smell a rat. And dozens of those people spent *hundreds* of hours trying to find out what was going on—it was sort of a distributed detective movement—and they eventually uncovered the hoax by putting all the various pieces together from Nicole's various posts.

Now a number of people point to this and say, "See, I told you about how fluid identity is online!" But that's not the lesson of the Kaycee Nicole story; the important lesson is this: changing your identity is really weird. And when the community understands that you've been doing it and you're faking, that is seen as a huge and violent transgression. And they will expend an astonishing amount of energy to find you and punish you. So identity is much less slippery than the early literature would lead us to believe, because although the technology makes fluid identity easy, social life demands some degree of fixity. And all you need is a system with some sort of persistent handle, and users will invest them with all the trappings of identity and even the layers above that like reputation.

2.) Second, you have to design a way for there to be members in good standing, some way in which good works get recognized. The minimal way is, posts appear with identity. You can do more sophisticated things like having formal karma or listing "member since" dates or noting who is a Pro user who helps fund the system.

I'm on the fence about whether or not this is a design worth accepting, because in a way I think members in good standing will rise. But more and more of the systems I'm seeing launching these days are having some kind of additional accretion so you can tell how much involvement members have with the system.

There's an interesting pattern I'm seeing among the music-sharing group that operates between Tokyo and Hong Kong. They operate on a mailing list, which they set up for themselves. But when they're trading music, what they're doing is, they're FedExing one another 180-gig hard-drives. So they're sending each other .wav files and not MP3s, and they're sending them in bulk.

Now, you can imagine that such a system might be a target for organizations that would frown on this activity. So when you join that group, your username is appended with the username of the person who is your sponsor. You can't get in without your name being linked to someone else. You can see immediately the reputational effects going on there, just from linking two handles.

So in that system, you become a member in good standing when your sponsor link goes away and you're there on your own report. If, on the other hand, you defect, not only are you booted, but your sponsor is booted. There are lots and lots of lightweight ways to accept and work with the idea of member in good standing.

3.) Three, you need some barriers to participation, however small. This is one of the things that killed Usenet, because there was almost no barrier to posting, leading to both generic system failures like spam, and also specific failures, like constant misogynist attacks in any group related to feminism, or racist attacks in any group related to African-Americans. You have to have some cost to either join or participate, if not at the lowest level, then at higher levels. There needs to be some kind of segmentation of capabilities.

Now, the segmentation can be total—you're in or you're out, as with the music group I just listed. Or it can be partial—anyone can read Slashdot, anonymous cowards can post, non-anonymous cowards can post with a higher rating. But to moderate, you really have to have been around for a while. It has to be hard to do at least some things on the system for some users, or the core group will not have the tools that they need to defend themselves.

Now, this pulls against the cardinal programming virtue of ease of use, but ease of use is the wrong goal for social software. Ease of use is the wrong way to look at the situation, because you've got the Necker cube flipped in the wrong direction, toward the individual, when in fact, the user of a piece of social software is the group.

The groups' goals sometimes differ from those of the individual members, and the user of social software is the group, so ease of use should be for the group. If the ease of use is only calculated from the user's point of view, it will be difficult to defend the group from the "group is its own worst enemy" style attacks from within.

I think we've all been to meetings where everyone had a really good time, everyone was telling jokes and laughing, and it was a great meeting, except we got nothing done. Everyone was amusing themselves so much that the group's goal was defeated by the individual interventions.

4.) Finally, you have to find a way to spare the group from scale. Scale alone kills conversations, because conversations require dense two-way conversations. In conversational contexts, Metcalfe's Law—the number of connections grows with the square of the number of nodes—is a drag. Since the number of potential two-way conversations in a group grows so much faster than the size of the group itself, the density of conversation falls off very fast as the system scales up even a little bit. You have to have some way to let users hang onto the "less is more" pattern, in order to keep associated with one another.

This is an "inverse value to scale" issue. Think about your Rolodex: a thousand contacts, maybe 150 people you can call friends, 30 people you can call close friends, two or three people you'd donate a kidney to. The value is inverse to the size of the group. And you have to find some way to protect the group within the context of those effects.

Sometimes you can do soft forking. LiveJournal does the best soft forking of any software I've ever seen, where the concepts of "you" and "your group" are pretty much intertwined. The average size of a LiveJournal group is about a dozen people. And the median size is around five.

But each user is a little bit connected to other such clusters, through their friends, and so while the clusters are real, they're not completely bounded—there's a soft overlap, which means that although most users participate in small groups, most of the half-million LiveJournal users are connected to one another through some short chain.

es of social software, like IRC channels and mailing lists,
erating with scale, because as the signal-to-noise ratio gets
e start to drop off, until it gets better, so people join, and so
it gets worse. You get these sorts of oscillating patterns, but the overall
system is self-correcting.

And then my favorite pattern is from MetaFilter, which is: when we
start seeing effects of scale, we shut off the new user page. "Someone
mentions us in the press and how great we are? 'Bye!" That's a way of
raising the bar; that's creating a threshold of participation. And anyone
who bookmarks that page and says, "You know, I really want to be in
there; maybe I'll go back later," that's the kind of user MeFi wants to
have.

You have to find some way to protect your own users from scale.
This doesn't mean the scale of the whole system can't grow. But you
can't try to make the system large by taking individual conversations
and blowing them up like a balloon; human interaction, many-to-many
interaction, doesn't blow up like a balloon. It either dissipates, or turns
into broadcast, or collapses. So plan for dealing with scale in advance,
because it's going to happen anyway.

~

Conclusion

Now, those four things are of course necessary but not sufficient condi-
tions. I propose them more as a platform for building the interesting
differences off. There are lots and lots and lots of other effects that make
different bits of software interesting enough that you would want to
keep more than one kind of pattern around. But those are commonali-
ties I'm seeing across a range of social software for large and long-lived
groups.

In addition, you can do all sorts of things with explicit clustering,
whether it's guilds in massively multiplayer games, or communities on
LiveJournal or what have you. You can do things with conversational
artifacts, where the group participation leaves behind some record.
Right now, the Wikipedia is the most interesting conversational artifact

I know of, where product is a result of process. Rather than "We're specifically going to get together and create this presentation," it's just "What's left is a record of what we said."

There are all these things, and of course they differ platform to platform. But there is, I believe, this common core of things that will happen whether you plan for them or not, and things you should plan for, that I think are invariant across large communal software.

Writing social software is hard. And, as I said, the act of writing social software is more like the work of an economist or a political scientist. And the act of hosting social software, the relationship of someone who hosts it is more like a relationship of landlords to tenants than owners to boxes in a warehouse.

The people using your software, even if you own it and pay for it, have rights and will behave as if they have rights. And if you abrogate those rights, you'll hear about it very quickly.

That's part of the problem that the John Hegel theory of community—"community leads to content, which leads to commerce"—never worked. Because lo and behold, no matter who came onto the Clairol chat boards, they sometimes wanted to talk about things that weren't Clairol products.

"But we paid for this! This is the Clairol site!" say the sponsors. Doesn't matter. The users are there for one another. They may be there on hardware and software paid for by you, but the users are there for one another.

The patterns here, I am suggesting, both the things to accept and the things to design for, are givens. Assume that addressing these issues is a forced move in the social platform, and then you can start going out and building on top of that the interesting stuff that I think is going to be the real result of this period of experimentation with social software.

Thank you very much.

Clay Shirky

GROUP AS USER: FLAMING AND THE DESIGN OF SOCIAL SOFTWARE[1]

Moments after announcing the need to study the sociology of human-to-human, computer-mediated software, Clay Shirky brilliantly gets busy, drilling down into the specific phenomenon of flaming, reminiscent of the great ethnographies of yore, more like Margaret Mead's studies of the sexual habits of Pacific Islanders than a typical software paper.[2] – Ed.

~

When we hear the word "software," most of us think of things like Word, PowerPoint, or Photoshop, tools for individual users. These tools treat the computer as a box, a self-contained environment in which the user does things. Much of the current literature and practice of software design—feature requirements, UI design, usability testing—targets the individual user, functioning in isolation.

And yet, when we poll users about what they actually do with their computers, some form of social interaction always tops the list—conversation, collaboration, playing games together, and so on. The practice of

---

1. Clay Shirky, "Group as User: Flaming and the Design of Social Software," Clay Shirky's Writings About the Internet (http://shirky.com), November 5, 2004. See http://shirky.com/writings/group_user.html.

2. "Flaming" refers to criticizing someone strongly online, for example through email or on discussion groups. – Ed.

software design is shot through with computer-as-box assumptions, while our actual behavior is closer to computer-as-door, treating the device as an entrance to a social space.

We have grown quite adept at designing interfaces and interactions between people and machines, but our social tools—the people-to-people software the users actually use most often—remain badly mis-fit to their task. Social interactions are far more complex and unpredictable than human/computer interaction, and that unpredictability defeats classic user-centric design. As a result, tools used daily by tens of millions are either ignored as design challenges, or treated as if the only possible site of improvement is the user-to-tool interface.

The design gap between computer-as-box and computer-as-door persists because of a diminished conception of the user. The user of a piece of social software is not just a collection of individuals but a group. Individual users take on roles that only make sense in groups: leader, follower, peacemaker, process enforcer, and so on. There are also behaviors that can only occur in groups, from consensus building to social climbing. And yet, despite these obvious differences between personal and social behaviors, we have very little design practice that treats the group as an entity to be designed for.

There is enormous value to be gotten in closing that gap, and it doesn't require complicated new tools. It just requires new ways of looking at old problems. Indeed, much of the most important recent work in social software has been technically simple but socially complex.

~

Learning from Flame Wars

Mailing lists were the first widely available piece of social software. (The PLATO system beat mailing lists by a decade, but had a limited user base.) Mailing lists were also the first widely analyzed virtual communities. And for roughly 30 years, almost any description of mailing lists of any length has mentioned flaming, the tendency of list members to forgo standards of public decorum when attempting to communicate with some ignorant moron whose to stupid to know how too spell and deserves to DIE, die a PAINFUL DEATH, you PINKO SCUMBAG!!!

Yet despite three decades of descriptions of flaming, it is often treated by designers as a mere side effect, as if each eruption of a caps-lock-on argument were surprising or inexplicable.

Flame wars are not surprising; they are one of the most reliable features of mailing list practice. If you assume a piece of software is for what it does, rather than what its designer's stated goals were, then mailing list software is, among other things, a tool for creating and sustaining heated argument. (This is true of other conversational software as well—the WELL, Usenet, web BBSs, and so on.)

This tension in outlook, between "flame war as unexpected side effect" and "flame war as historical inevitability," has two main causes. The first is that although the environment in which a mailing list runs is computers, the environment in which a flame war runs is people. You couldn't go through the code of the Mailman mailing list tool, say, and find the comment that reads "The next subroutine ensures that misunderstandings between users will be amplified, leading to name-calling and vitriol." Yet the software, when adopted, will frequently produce just that outcome.

The user's mental model of a word processor is of limited importance—if a word processor supports multiple columns, users can create multiple columns; if not, then not. The users' mental model of social software, on the other hand, matters enormously. For example, "personal home pages" and weblogs are very similar technically—both involve local editing and global hosting. The difference between them was mainly in the user's conception of the activity. The pattern of weblogging appeared before the name weblog was invented, and the name appeared before any of the current weblogging tools were designed. Here the shift was in the user's mental model of publishing, and the tools followed the change in social practice.

In addition, when software designers do regard the users of social software, it is usually in isolation. There are many sources of this habit: ubiquitous network access is relatively recent, it is conceptually simpler to treat users as isolated individuals than as social actors, historical design practice has focused on individuals, and so on. The cumulative effect is to make maximizing individual flexibility a priority, even when that may produce conflict with the group goals.

Flaming, an un-designed-for but reliable product of mailing list software, was our first clue to the conflict between the individual and the group in mediated spaces, and the initial responses to it were likewise an early clue about the weakness of the single-user design center.

~

Netiquette and Kill Files

The first general response to flaming was netiquette. Netiquette was a proposed set of behaviors that assumed that flaming was caused by (who else?) individual users. If you could explain to *each* user what was wrong with flaming, *all* users would stop.

This mostly didn't work. The problem was simple—the people who didn't know netiquette needed it most. They were also the people least likely to care about the opinion of others, and thus couldn't be easily convinced to adhere to its tenets.[3]

Interestingly, netiquette came tantalizingly close to addressing group phenomena. Most versions advised, among other techniques, contacting flamers directly rather than replying to them on the list. Anyone who has tried this technique knows it can be surprisingly effective. Even here, though, the collective drafters of netiquette misinterpreted this technique. Addressing the flamer directly works not because it makes him realize the error of his ways, but because it deprives him of an audience. Flaming is not just personal expression, it is a kind of performance, brought on in a social context.

This is where the "direct contact" strategy falls down. Netiquette docs typically regarded direct contact as a way to engage the flamer's rational self, and convince him to forgo further flaming. In practice, though, the recidivism rate for flamers is high. People behave differently in groups, and while momentarily engaging them one-on-one can have a calming effect, that is a change in social context rather than some kind of personal conversion. Once the conversation returns to a group setting, the temptation to return to performative outbursts also returns.

Another standard answer to flaming has been the kill file, sometimes called a bozo filter, which is a list of posters whose comments you want filtered by the software before you see them. (In the lore of Usenet, there

---

3. Besides, they were having fun. – *Ed.*

is even a sound effect—*plonk*—that the kill-file-ee is said to make when dropped in the kill file.)

Kill files are also generally ineffective, because merely removing one voice from a flame war doesn't do much to improve the signal-to-noise ratio[4]—if the flamer in question succeeds in exciting a response, removing his posts alone won't stem the tide of pointless replies. And although people have continually observed (for 30 years now) that "if everyone just ignores user X, he will go away," the logic of collective action makes that outcome almost impossible to orchestrate—it only takes a couple of people rising to the bait to trigger a flame war, and the larger the group, the more difficult it is to enforce the discipline required of all members.

∿

The Tragedy of the Conversational Commons

Flaming is one of a class of economic problems known as the Tragedy of the Commons.[5] Briefly stated, the Tragedy of the Commons occurs when a group holds a resource but each of the members has an incentive to overuse it. (The original essay used the illustration of shepherds with a common pasture. The group as a whole has an incentive to maintain the long-term viability of the commons, but with each individual having an incentive to overgraze, to maximize the value they can extract from the communal resource.)

In the case of mailing lists (and, again, other shared conversational spaces), the commonly held resource is communal attention. The group as a whole has an incentive to keep the signal-to-noise ratio high and the conversation informative, even when contentious. Individual users, though, have an incentive to maximize expression of their point of view, as well as maximizing the amount of communal attention they receive.

---

4. The term "signal-to-noise ratio" comes from high-end audio gear. A high signal-to-noise ratio implies that there's a lot of signal (the valuable stuff you want to hear) and very little noise. A low signal-to-noise ratio implies a lot of noise. In the context of discussion groups and online communities, a high signal-to-noise ratio implies a high proportion of interesting discussion topics. – Ed.

5. See http://dieoff.org/page95.htm.

It is a deep curiosity of the human condition that people often find negative attention more satisfying than inattention, and the larger the group, the likelier someone is to act out to get that sort of attention.

However, proposed responses to flaming have consistently steered away from group-oriented solutions and toward personal ones. The logic of collective action, alluded to earlier, rendered these personal solutions largely ineffective. Meanwhile, attempts at encoding social bargains weren't made because of the twin forces of door culture (a resistance to regarding social features as first-order effects) and a horror of censorship (maximizing individual freedom, even when it conflicts with group goals).

~

Weblog and Wiki Responses

When considering social engineering for flame-proofed-ness, it's useful to contemplate both weblogs and wikis, neither of which suffer from flaming in anything like the degree mailing lists and other conversational spaces do. Weblogs are relatively flame-free because they provide little communal space. In economic parlance, weblogs solve the tragedy of the commons through enclosure, the subdividing and privatizing of common space.

Every bit of the weblog world is operated by a particular blogger or group of bloggers, who can set their own policy for accepting comments, including having no comments at all, deleting comments from anonymous or unfriendly visitors, and so on. Furthermore, comments are almost universally displayed away from the main page, greatly limiting their readership. Weblog readers are also spared the need for a bozo filter. Because the mailing list pattern of "everyone sees everything" has never been in effect in the weblog world, there is little opportunity for anyone to hijack existing audiences to gain attention. Even comments appended to a particular weblog post are seen only by a minority of the readers of the post itself.

Like weblogs, wikis also avoid the Tragedy of the Commons, but they do so by going to the other extreme. Instead of everything being owned, nothing is. Whereas a mailing list has individual and inviolable posts but communal conversational space, in wikis even the writing is communal. If someone acts out on a wiki, the offending material can be subsequently edited or removed. Indeed, the history of the Wikipedia, host to communal entries on a variety of contentious topics ranging from Islam to Microsoft, has seen numerous and largely failed attempts to pervert or delete entire entries. And because older versions of wiki pages are always archived, it is actually easier to undo damage than cause it. (As an analogy, imagine what cities would look like if it were easier to clean graffiti than to create it.)

Weblogs and wikis are proof that you can have broadly open discourse without suffering from hijacking by flamers, by creating a social structure that encourages or deflects certain behaviors. Indeed, the basic operation of both weblogs and wiki—write something locally, then share it—is the pattern of mailing lists and BBSs as well. Seen in this light, the assumptions made by mailing list software looks less like The One True Way to design a social contract among users and more like one strategy among many.

~

Reviving Old Tools

This possibility of adding novel social components to old tools presents an enormous opportunity. To take the most famous example, the Slashdot moderation system puts the ability to rate comments into the hands of the users themselves. The designers took the traditional bulletin board format—threaded posts, sorted by time—and added a quality filter. And instead of assuming that all users are alike, the Slashdot designers created a karma system, to allow them to discriminate in favor of users likely to rate comments in ways that would benefit the community. And, to police *that* system, they created a meta-moderation system, to solve the "Who will guard the guardians?" problem. (All this is documented in the Slashdot FAQ,[6] our version of Federalist Papers #10.[7])

---

6. See http://slashdot.org/faq/com-mod.shtml#cm600.
7. See http://www.yale.edu/lawweb/avalon/federal/fed10.htm.

Rating, karma, meta-moderation—each of these systems is relatively simple in technological terms. The effect of the whole, though, has been to allow Slashdot to support an enormous user base, while rewarding posters who produce broadly valuable material and quarantining offensive or off-topic posts.

Likewise, Craigslist took the mailing list and added a handful of simple features with profound social effects. First, all of Craigslist is an enclosure, owned by Craig (whose title is not Founder, Chairman, and Customer Service Representative for nothing). Because he has a business incentive to make his list work, he and his staff remove posts if enough readers flag them as inappropriate. Like Slashdot, he violates the assumption that social software should come with no group limits on individual involvement, and Craigslist works better because of it.

And, on the positive side, the addition of a "Nominate for 'Best of Craigslist'" button in every email creates a social incentive for users to post amusing or engaging material. The "Best of" button is a perfect example of the weakness of a focus on the individual user. If Craigslist were software optimized for the individual, such a button would be incoherent—if you like a particular post, you can just save it to your hard drive. But users don't merely save those posts to their hard drives; they click that button. Like flaming, the "Best of" button also assumes the user is reacting in relation to an audience, but here the pattern is harnessed to good effect. The only reason you would nominate a post for "Best of" is if you wanted other users to see it—if you were acting in a group context, in other words.

~

Novel Operations on Social Facts

Jonah Brucker-Cohen's Bumplist[8] stands out as an experiment in the social aspect of mailing lists. Bumplist, whose motto is "an email community for the determined," is a mailing list for six people, which anyone can join. When the seventh user joins, the first is bumped and, if they want to be back on, they must re-join, bumping the second user, ad infinitum. (As of this writing, Bumplist is at 87,414 subscribers and

---

8. See http://www.runme.org/feature/read/+BumpList/+86/.

81,796 re-subscribers.) Bumplist's goal is more polemic than practical; Brucker-Cohen describes it as a reexamination of the culture and rules of mailing lists. However, it is a vivid illustration of the ways simple changes to well-understood software can produce radically different social effects.)

You could easily imagine many such experiments. What would it take, for example, to design a mailing list that was flame-retardant? Once you stop regarding all users as isolated actors, a number of possibilities appear. You could institute induced lag, where, once a user contributed five posts in the space of an hour, a cumulative 10-minute delay would be added to each subsequent post. Every post would be delivered eventually, but it would retard the rapid-reply nature of flame wars, introducing a cooling-off period for the most vociferous participants.

You could institute a kind of thread jail, where every post would include a "Worst of" button, in the manner of Craigslist. Interminable, pointless threads (e.g., Which Operating System Is Objectively Best?) could be sent to thread jail if enough users voted them down. (Though users could obviously change subject headers and evade this restriction, the surprise, first noted by Julian Dibbell, is how often users respect negative *communal* judgment, even when they don't respect the negative judgment of individuals.[9])

You could institute a "Get a room!" feature, where any conversation that involved two users ping-ponging six or more posts (substitute other numbers to taste) would be automatically redirected to a sublist, limited to that pair. The material could still be archived, and so accessible to interested lurkers, but the conversation would continue without the attraction of an audience.

You could imagine a similar exercise, working on signal/noise ratios generally, and keying off the fact that there is always a most active poster on mailing lists, who posts much more often than even the second most active, and much, *much* more often than the median poster. Oddly, the most active poster is often not even aware that they occupy this position (seeing ourselves as others see us is difficult in mediated spaces as well), but making them aware of it often causes them to self-moderate. You can imagine flagging all posts by the most active poster, whoever that

---

9. See Rape in Cyberspace (http://www.juliandibbell.com/texts/bungle.html). Search for "aggressively antisocial vibes."

happened to be, or throttling the maximum number of posts by any user to some multiple of average posting tempo.

And so on. The number of possible targets for experimentation is large and combinatorial, and those targets exist in any social context, not just in conversational spaces.

~

Rapid, Iterative Experimentation

Though most of these sorts of experiments won't be of much value, rapid, iterative experiment is the best way to find those changes that are positive. The Slashdot FAQ makes it clear that the now-stable ratings + karma + meta-moderation system could only have evolved with continued adjustment over time. This was possible because the engineering challenges were relatively straightforward, and the user feedback swift.

That sort of experimentation, however, has been the exception rather than the rule. In 30 years, the principal engineering work on mailing lists has been on the administrative experience—the Mailman tool now offers a mailing list administrator nearly a hundred configurable options, many with multiple choices. However, the *social* experience of a mailing list over those three decades has hardly changed at all.

This is not because experimenting with social experience is technologically hard, but because it is conceptually foreign. The assumption that the computer is a box, used by an individual in isolation, is so pervasive that it is adhered to even when it leads to investment of programmer time in improving every aspect of mailing lists except the interaction that makes them worthwhile in the first place.

Once you regard the group mind as part of the environment in which the software runs, though, a universe of untried experimentation opens up. A social inventory of even relatively ancient tools like mailing lists reveals a wealth of untested models. There is no guarantee that any given experiment will prove effective, of course. The feedback loops of social life always produce unpredictable effects. Anyone seduced by the idea of social perfectibility or total control will be sorely disappointed, because users regularly reject attempts to affect or alter their behavior, whether by gaming the system or abandoning it.

But given the breadth and simplicity of potential experiments, the ease of collecting user feedback, and most importantly the significance users place on social software, even a few successful improvements, simple and iterative though they may be, can create disproportionate value, as they have done with Craigslist and Slashdot, and as they doubtless will with other such experiments.

Eric Sink

CLOSING THE GAP, PART 1[1]

I started writing a long introduction to this article, but gave up because I'm so deeply in agreement with everything Eric Sink says that there's no point. It's simple. Everything Eric Sink says is right. Do what Eric says and you can't go wrong. – Ed.

~

At some point in the many activities of a small independent software vendor (ISV)[2], the customer trades money for software. No column on "The Business of Software" could be complete without some discussion of this magical event.

I'll start by defining some of my terminology. Before the customer makes the purchase, I like to say that there is a "gap." This gap is the distance between the prospective customer and your product, and it looks something like this:

Product ←————————————→ **Customer**

---

1. Eric Sink, "Closing the Gap, Part 1," Eric.Weblog() (http://software.ericsink.com). See http://software.ericsink.com/bos/Closing_the_Gap_Part_1.html.

2. ISV (Independent Software Vendor) is a weird TLA (Three-Letter Acronym) used almost exclusively by Microsoft to mean "software company that is not Microsoft." For some reason many people in the software industry have taken to calling themselves ISVs when they really mean "software companies." – *Ed.*

In order for the sale to occur, this gap must be closed. Until that happens, the gap represents all of the issues and obstacles that are preventing the customer from making the purchase:

- The customer has never heard of your product.
- The customer doesn't know enough about your product.
- Your product is too expensive.
- The customer needs two levels of management approval for the purchase.
- Your product lacks a feature the customer needs.
- Your product doesn't interoperate with the customer's other stuff.
- Your product isn't mature enough to meet the customer's expectations.

To continue to exist as a business, your small ISV must find a way to close this gap, over and over again. There are exactly two ways to close the gap:

- **Move your product to the right.** Tell the world about your product. Make your product better so that people will want to buy it.
- **Move your customer to the left.** Find people who might want your product. Convince them to buy it.

We will begin by talking about the challenge of moving your customer toward your product.

~

Proactive Sales

Let's define some more terminology. The word "sales" is somewhat overloaded, but in the context of a job function, I prefer to reserve this term for the process of proactively finding new prospective customers and working with them individually to try and convince them to make a purchase. A person who performs this job function is called a "sales guy."

#ifdef apology

I confess that the gender implication of this label is a bit inappropriate, but I've been calling these people "sales guys" for so long that I can't break the habit. Early in my career, it just so happened that all the sales professionals I knew were men. For years, I wondered if excellence in proactive selling required a level of obnoxiousness that simply isn't present in most females. More recently, I have come to know a number of women who are excellent "sales guys." (One in particular has a disturbingly successful track record of selling me advertising, which is something I truly hate to buy.)[3] Anyway, if you will forgive the apparent political incorrectness, I'm going to stick with my usual terminology for this article.

#endif

To sharpen the definition, I need to clarify two things that are not included in "sales":

Marketing is not sales. Marketing is an area all its own. It includes many different activities, ranging from strategy to communications. None of these activities is sales. The sales guy is a customer of the marketing group. Marketing activities are usually "one-to-many." Sales is almost always "one-to-one." Sales is strictly about closing the deal.

The person in your office who processes incoming orders from customers is not a sales guy. Yes, he deals with "sales" in the accounting sense, but I refer to this job function as "customer service."

A defining characteristic of a sales guy is the way he is paid. The compensation package of a sales guy includes commissions. He gets a percentage of every sale he closes. The percentages vary widely based on all kinds of factors, so I'm not even going to mention any ballpark figures. However, I will point out that these commissions can really add up to a lot of money. In many organizations, the highest paid individual is a sales guy, often making more than the CEO herself.

---

3. See http://software.ericsink.com/Magazine_Advertising.html.

~

Working with a Sales Guy

It is quite common for people in other job functions to have some resentment of the sales guy because of these commissions. For example, the lead architect who designed your product will be wondering why the sales guy gets a cut of every sale when she does not. Is the sales guy more valuable than the person who actually created the product?

Good sales guys understand this problem and work very hard to counteract it by "sucking up" to the developers at every opportunity. For example, in any situation where your sales guys and developers end up together in a bar, there should be absolutely no question about who is buying the drinks.

On the other hand, you can't allow your sales guy to spend *too* much time with your developers. Left without limits, a sales guy will start to routinely bring a developer with him on his customer visit. Suddenly, your overpaid coder has become an *extremely* overpaid sales assistant. The usual solution to this problem is to put your sales guys in a separate office, preferably in a different city. Sales guys need to be very close to a major airport anyway.

~

Characteristics of a Sales Guy

A sales guy needs a special set of skills. They tend to be extraverts. They are usually excellent communicators with incredible interpersonal skills. They are self-confident, sometimes to a fault. They're usually very good-looking and snappy dressers. Sales guys know enough about technology to be dangerous. They know how to handle themselves well in surprising situations. They know exactly when to move toward closure and ask for the deal.

A certain amount of variation from the sales guy stereotype is acceptable, but there is one trait that is absolutely a requirement: a good sales guy is someone who is motivated only by money. One of the most dangerous personnel mistakes is to hire a sales guy who cares about anything else.

A good sales guy will do only those things for which you have provided him a financial incentive (a commission). Everything else is a waste of time, and he is essentially immune to management influence through any other means.

Note that every coin has two sides. Although I consider this mercenary nature to be an important trait for a sales guy, there is a downside that accompanies this benefit. A good sales guy has incredible listening skills that only seem to work when he is working on a deal. When listening to a prospective customer, he will catch and understand every single detail, never missing something that might help close the sale.

On the other hand, when that sales guy's manager walks in and says:

"Fred, we need to talk. I heard a rumor from the developers that a couple of them had to buy their own beer at the pub last night even though you were right there. What's the problem here? Those beers are only going to cost you a few bucks. With the kind of money you make, I certainly think you can afford to pick up the check in situations like that."

A truly excellent sales guy will hear this:

"Blah, blah blah blah blah. Blah blah blah blah blah blah blah blah blah blah blah blah blah blah **BUY** blah blah blah blah blah blah blah blah blah blah blah blah blah. Blah's blah blah blah? Blah blah blah blah blah blah **COST** blah blah blah **BUCKS**. Blah blah blah blah **MONEY** blah blah, blah blah blah blah blah blah blah blah blah **CHECK** blah blah blah blah."

So while the greed gene can obviously create some challenges, the pros definitely outweigh the cons. Managing a money-driven sales guy ends up being simple and largely devoid of surprises. You don't have to spend all kinds of time figuring out what motivates your sales guy like you do with your developers. All you have to do is make sure his compensation is carefully correlated with the set of things you want him to accomplish.

The corollary to this principle is this: if your sales guy is doing something that you don't want him to do, there are only two possible explanations:

He is a bad sales guy, because he cares about something other than money.

It's your fault, because he is simply doing things that you have "incentivized" him to do.

For example, suppose your sales guy is rapidly closing deals with customers, but a lot of those customers end up unhappy shortly after buying the product. This usually happens when the sales guy is selling products to people who don't really need them. By the time the customer has realized this, the sales guy has already collected his commission and has moved on to his next victim. You forgot to make customer satisfaction part of his incentive, so he spends no time on it. Luckily, the solution to this particular example is rather simple. For example, you can just hold back the majority of his commission until you verify that the customer is still happy 90 days after the purchase.

Similarly, if the sales guy is spending too much time with your developers, you can just start charging him for it. Deduct $100 from his commission for every hour he spends with a coder. To be fair, give him a few hours for free, since he needs technical information to get his deals closed.[4]

~

One More Mandatory Trait for a Sales Guy

Any sales guy who is offended by all the vicious jokes in this article is probably not competent.

A sales guy simply must have a thick skin. If he can't handle my caricature, how will he cope when a customer tells him "no"? Even the best sales guy is going to hear "no" more often than "yes." If he can't accept all that rejection without getting discouraged, he's probably in the wrong job.

---

4. You may find yourself trapped in an endless cycle of incentive-tweaking to get it right. Any tweaks you come up with, your sales guy will find workarounds until you tweak *those*, and on and on in a Sisyphean cycle. Don't feel bad about this; it's a fundamental problem of the human condition. – *Ed.*

~

Reasons to Have a Sales Guy

A good sales guy is worth his weight in silicon. Yes, he gets paid an awful lot of money in commissions, but he brings in even more, by definition.

Still, not every organization needs a sales guy. The decision to hire one is a toughie, and needs to be considered very carefully. Hiring a sales guy will forever change your company. Don't do it unless you really need to. Here are a few common reasons why you do:

Reason #1: Nobody Really Wants Your Product

By their very nature, some products require a lot more effort to sell. Some products are just basically not any fun. For example, nobody really *wants* to buy life insurance. People buy life insurance, but not with the same enthusiasm they show when buying a hot new movie just released on DVD. This is why you can't swing a 5-iron anywhere in America without hitting an insurance salesman. Without these guys, far less insurance would ever get sold.

Similarly, some products are targeted at people who don't realize they have a problem.

If your product solves a problem that is not a strongly felt need, you've got to have a sales guy to help your prospective customers realize how miserable they really are. This tactic is called "creating dissatisfaction with the status quo."

If by chance you are just getting started with a new small ISV, now is the time to avoid these bugs. Start out with a small gap. Choose a product that people know how to get excited about.

Reason #2: Your Product Is Very Expensive

More expensive products are far more likely to require a sales guy to help the customer through the decision. Cars and houses are usually (but not always) sold by sales guys. Expensive software products face a similar cycle. Big purchase orders are big decisions, and most organizations will need a lot of handholding before they finally pull the trigger.

Reason #3: Your Product Is No Longer Being Improved

As a software product matures over the years, it tends to gain sales guys and lose developers. For a product that is nearing its twilight, it is not uncommon to see a company with lots of sale guys and no developers at all. The reason for this is reasonably intuitive: the product is no longer moving toward the customer. Closing the gap requires us to constantly be dragging customers over to the product.

(I am dying to name a few examples of this phenomenon, but my editors at Microsoft have been working very hard to teach me some manners. I'd like them to get the impression that their efforts are having some sort of an effect.)

~

The "No Sales Guy" Approach

Most small ISVs are better off not having any sales guys at all.

I realize that this opinion will be considered heresy in the church of conventional business wisdom, but I'm sticking to it. The bishops of that denomination already don't like me very much anyway. If I could ever find out where their cathedral is located, I plan to grab some Groucho Marx glasses and go dance on the altar.

As usual, I am happy to admit that there are exceptions to my rule. However, too many companies start looking to hire a sales guy before they should do so.

Moving customers is very difficult to do, especially for a small company with very little clout. Customers are heavy and unwieldy. They don't want to be moved, and they often get offended when somebody tries. It is easy to spend a lot of effort trying to push the customer toward the product without ever successfully closing the gap.

All that effort is better spent on the other side of the gap. Improve your product. Moving your product toward the customer is a lot easier. Listen to your customers and give them what they want. Keep your customers happy (they'll tell all their friends how great you are).

Focusing your efforts on the product side of the gap is an approach with two very nice features:

- **It is entirely within your core competencies.** You know how to make your product better. More specifically, if you don't know how to make your product better, your ISV is going to fail anyway, and the presence of a sales guy will not save you.
- **It is a leveraged activity.** When you make your product better for one customer, you are making it better for others as well.

~

The Bottom Line

Somewhere along the way, somebody is going to tell you that you're not a real company because you don't have any sales guys. Horse hockey.[5] Don't get forced into this until you're ready.

---

5. See http://www.imdb.com/title/tt0068098.

Eric Sink

CLOSING THE GAP, PART 2[1]

~

L ast month we introduced a concept that I call "the gap":

Product ◄——————————► Customer

This gap is the distance between the prospective customer and your product. As long as it continues to exist, your customer has less software and you have less money. In order for the sale to occur, this gap must be closed. Until that happens, the gap represents all of the issues and obstacles that are preventing the customer from making the purchase.

As Chief Sales Geek in your ISV, it is your responsibility to figure out how this gap is going to get closed. You have exactly two ways to do it:

- Move your product to the right.
- Move your customer to the left.

Last month, we talked about "proactive sales," or "moving your customer to the left." This month, we will talk about the other way of closing the gap: moving your product to the right.

1. Eric Sink, "Closing the Gap, Part 2," Eric.Weblog() (http://software.ericsink.com), May 10, 2004. See http://software.ericsink.com/bos/Closing_the_Gap_Part_2.html.

~

Responsive Sales

In Part 1 of this two-part column, I claim that most small ISVs do not need a sales guy and should not use the proactive sales approach. This month, I describe an alternative approach. Instead of proactive sales, we will talk about "responsive sales." Let us first highlight the differences between these two models:

- In **proactive sales,** the sales guy is in charge. He initiates contact with prospective customers. He tells them about the product. He answers all their questions. He stays in regular contact. He provides all the energy and all the momentum. Eventually, he convinces the customer to make a purchase. He receives money from the customer and delivers the product.

- In **responsive sales,** the customer is in charge. He initiates contact with your company only if and when he wants to do so. He hears about your product from a friend or an ad or a weblog. He reads everything he can find about your product and its features. He contacts your company to ask questions. He makes his decision at whatever pace makes sense for him and his organization. Eventually, he decides to make a purchase. He contacts your company to exchange money for product.

These contrasting descriptions may actually make responsive sales seem unappealing to you. After all, do we really want to trust the customer to handle all these important tasks?

Yes, we do.

I acknowledge that responsive sales can be scary. It feels like we are delegating a critical project to somebody we don't know and have probably never even met.

But a reward lies behind this risk. The truth is that customers *like* being trusted. They *like* making their decisions without pressure from a sales guy. They *like* to be in charge.

For all these reasons, responsive sales works very well, as long as we hold up our end of the deal. We have to be responsive. Yes, we are letting the customer be in charge, but we are not powerless.

In fact, we will be quite busy, indeed. It is our job to make the whole process as easy as possible for customers. They will choose to cross the gap. We will move our product to the right so the gap will be easier for them to cross.

To succeed in responsive sales, there are seven things we must do:

~

1. Make Sure Customers Know About Your Product

Customers cannot buy your product if they have never heard of it. Those of you who find this statement to be insightful will be similarly enlightened to learn that the sky is blue.

Seriously, I know I'm stating the obvious here, but awareness of your product is a pretty important precondition, especially for responsive sales. If the customer never contacts you, then you cannot be responsive. If you don't have a way of letting people know your product exists, then you may not need to read the remainder of this article. Responsive sales won't work for you until you start getting some awareness built up.

Still, we should remind ourselves that building awareness is the task of marketing, not sales. Specifically, this is part of a subcategory called marketing communications, or "marcomm" for short. A full treatment of marcomm is well beyond the scope of this article. For now, I want to mention three quick items:

Be Careful with Advertising

Q: What's the difference between buying magazine ads and setting dollar bills on fire?

A: Flaming cash actually produces a benefit, since it generates heat.

This joke is excerpted from the beginning of an article[2] I wrote last year about advertising for small ISVs. The rest of the article goes on to

---

2. See http://software.ericsink.com/Magazine_Advertising.html.

say that I am only half joking. Advertising is scary and dangerous. You can spend lots of cash and have no idea where it went.

I am not saying small ISVs should never advertise. Rather, I am saying that you should be very careful. If you have any reservations, just wait. Tell *their* sales guy to call you again in six months.

Try a Tradeshow

Among the traditional marcomm activities, tradeshows are my favorite. Remember the old joke about pizza and sex? A tradeshow falls into the same category: when it's bad, it's still pretty good. Even at the worst show I ever attended, I learned a few things and met some interesting people. If your market segment has any good tradeshows, consider being an exhibitor.

SourceGear will be an exhibitor next month at TechEd in San Diego.[3] Since we're currently finalizing preparations for the show, I plan to use the occasion as an excuse to devote next month's column to the topic of exhibiting at a tradeshow. Stay tuned!

Develop "in the Open"

Traditional marcomm has its place, but there are new approaches. With the ubiquity of the Internet today, one of the best ways to build awareness of your product is to develop it "in the open." In other words, using a combination of weblogs, public discussions, and preview downloads, let your prospective customers watch and talk with you as you make your software. Think of yourself as a chef in a Chinese restaurant, your customers watching as you stir-fry their shrimp and peapods.

Start out with a weblog—an open journal of your development progress. Every so often, post an update of how your application is progressing.

At some point, your application will be ready to demo for prospective customers. Release a public preview for download. Make sure you provide a mailing list or a web-based forum so you can receive their feedback.

Developing software takes time. Doing it "in the open" can be a great way of using that time to build awareness as you go.

---

3. See http://www.microsoft.com/seminar/teched2004/default.mspx.

~

2. Make Sure Your Product Is Something Customers Want

Pardon me for again stating the obvious, but this fact remains: if you're not selling something that people want, your gap is enormous.

A good proactive sales guy can overcome this problem. The tactics for selling things that nobody wants are very well understood. How many people would buy rustproofing for their new car if they had to specifically ask for it?

In the responsive sales approach, you have basically no hope of selling a product that is not fundamentally appealing. It is therefore extremely important that you do your homework and convince yourself that you are building a product that will be desirable. This is the other half of marketing.

Choose Your Position

If you have read anything at all about classical marketing, you have probably heard the word "positioning" at least once. Basically, positioning[4] is the process of figuring out how your target market will perceive your product. How do you want your product to be known? To what other products will yours be compared? Answering these questions is a critical step toward ensuring that your product is something people want.

Choose Your Competition

Avoiding competition is perhaps the most common way of ending up with a product nobody wants. You need competition.[5] By avoiding competition, you are simultaneously avoiding customers. Your product concept is validated by the presence of other ISVs who are profitably selling something similar. If there is nothing on the market that resembles your product, be afraid.

---

4. See http://software.ericsink.com/Positioning.html.
5. See http://software.ericsink.com/Choose_Your_Competition.html.

Develop "in the Open"

You've got that deja vu feeling right now, don't you?

Yes, I already made this point about developing "in the open," but now I'm making it again for a different reason. Developing in the open is not just a great way of building awareness. It is also a way of measuring how much people care.

For example, let us suppose that you choose to develop in the open, releasing lots of information and preview downloads very early in your development cycle. You make appropriate announcements in the right newsgroups and forums. However, very few people come to get the download. Hardly anyone posts to your mailing list. Nobody gives you any feedback.

The bad news is that you may be developing an application that nobody wants. The good news is that you find out a lot earlier by developing in the open. You have time to adjust the feature set. You may even decide to cut your losses and kill the project. Either way, you are better off getting the bad news earlier instead of waiting until the application ships.

~

3. Make Sure They Can Afford Your Product

The price of your product affects the size of the gap.

When writing about the subject of pricing, it is far more fashionable to claim that pricing should be higher, not lower. The basic idea is that you are making a statement with the price you choose. When you set the price of your product high, you are telling the world that you think your product is very valuable. This tends to make your product more highly desired.

Some purchasers actually prefer to buy higher-priced products. At the moment, I can use myself as an example. I am currently training to walk a half-marathon. It is important that I have really good shoes. I should probably go to one of those fancy stores where they analyze a videotape of your stride and help you select the perfect shoe. But I'm always in too much of a hurry, so I have simpler approach. I only buy shoes if they are of a strong brand and cost at least $85 per pair. This approach is low tech, but it is simple, and it works for me.

Some people buy software the same way I buy shoes. Buying the most expensive product is a convenient shortcut for the shopper who doesn't have time to research everything thoroughly.

A higher price point can be attractive to customers who are seeking either prestige or exceptional quality. However, lower pricing has its advantages, too. The fact is that many of your prospective customers have a budget. If your price is higher than their limit, the gap might as well be infinite.

A few months ago, my company lowered the price of our version control product (SourceGear Vault). At its original price, Vault was already one of the least expensive tools in its market segment. With the new pricing, all of the comparable competing products are several times our price. We knew this was a big risk. Some customers will automatically assume that a competing product that costs seven times more must certainly be seven times better than ours.

So far, the risk is paying off. We made this decision because we believed that the gap was simply too large for many customers to cross. Apparently we were right. Our total revenue has been significantly higher since the price change.

~

Further Reading

These first three items are basic elements of marketing. They are important preconditions for responsive sales, but there is much more to be said. This article only scratches the surface.

I am always a little hesitant to recommend marketing books. There are some truly excellent books, but they are not written for the geek audience. For the sake of staying safe, I'm going to confine my recommendations here to books written by folks who are legends in the field.

Philip Kotler is sometimes describes as "the father of modern marketing." I have several of his books, including *Marketing Insights from A to Z: 80 Concepts Every Manager Needs to Know*, which is very good.[6] It has 80 chapters, each of which is very short and focused. The chapters on advertising, customers, and price are particularly relevant to this article.

Speaking of Kotler, he wrote the preface for another book on my shelf entitled *Kellogg on Marketing* by Dawn Iacobucci.[7] It's a collection of articles by the faculty of the Kellogg Graduate School of Management at Northwestern. The stuff here is rather academic and not terribly easy to read, but there is a lot of substance. The chapter on pricing is 30 pages long and dense enough to keep anyone busy for a while.

Finally, I would be remiss if I did not mention Al Ries and Jack Trout. I try to read everything I can find by these guys. They invented the term "positioning," and their book of the same title (*Positioning: The Battle for Your Mind, 20th Anniversary Edition*[8]) is still the one to get. I also like *The 22 Immutable Laws of Marketing*.[9] Just keep in mind that these books are classics. For example, Law #2 of 22 mentions that "Today, the Commodore Amiga is a big success..." The stories age, but the principles are timeless.

OK, let's get back to this article. We've covered three of our seven keys to closing the gap.

~

4. Offer a Full-Featured Demo Download

Every small ISV today should give its customers an opportunity to try before they buy. It is officially now absurd to do otherwise. Customers will come to your website and *expect* to find a demo download.

---

6. See http://www.shopping.msn.com/search/detail.aspx?pcId=12005&prodId=303524&ptnrid=141&ptnrdata=0.

7. See http://www.shopping.msn.com/search/detail.aspx?pcId=12005&prodId=280769&ptnrid=141&ptnrdata=0.

8. See http://www.shopping.msn.com/search/detail.aspx?pcId=11891&prodId=815632&ptnrid=141&ptnrdata=0.

9. See http://software.ericsink.com/laws/Immutable_Laws_Marketing.html.

There are several opportunities here to make things easy for your customer. Don't miss out on any of the following:

Make the Download Easy to Find

You probably think your download is easy to find. After all, you know right where it is, right?

Don't assume. Grab a stranger (don't actually grab them) and ask them to visit your website and find the demo download. Watch them search and see how long it takes.

Make the Download Full-Featured

The best demo download is the product itself. Every SourceGear product has only one binary available for download. The demo version is exactly the same binary as the full product. Every feature is enabled, but only for 30 days. To make a purchase, the customer simply enters a serial number and does not have to reinstall.

Polish Your Installer

Your demo download is your opportunity to make a positive first impression. It is indescribably important that your demo "just works." If anything goes wrong, your customer will probably just lose interest and you will have lost the chance to be responsive.

Let the Customer Remain Anonymous

The hyperlink to your demo download should link directly to the actual binaries. Don't make users fill out a form and give their contact information. This is responsive sales, and the users are in charge. Let them decide when they want to make themselves known to you, if at all.

~

5. Answer the Customers' Questions

I am a big believer in the importance of giving excellent technical support. When your customers have problems, you need to stop and help them. Furthermore, I believe that happy customers are the responsibility of *every* employee in a small ISV.

At SourceGear, every developer is involved with helping customers. We do have "level 1" tech support people whose full-time responsibility is helping our customers. But when level 1 either overflows or escalates a problem, every developer is available to help with "level 2." Our customers like the fact that when they have a problem, they can talk to the person who actually wrote the code.

With very few exceptions, everyone on your staff should be prepared to stop what they are doing and help a customer when needed. An important key to the responsive sales model is that you have to treat your *prospective* customers exactly the same way.

~

6. Provide a Place for Community

Prospective customers want the ability to talk to current customers about you and your product. This concept may seem scary. After all, what if some of your customers are disappointed with your product in some way? Do you really want prospective customers talking with people who might say negative things?

Yes, you do. This is responsive sales, and the customer is in charge. Not only should you let your prospects talk to your customers, you should provide them with a place to do it.

I wish more vendors would do this. Last year, I bought a Chevy Avalanche from a dealer in my area. Think how nice it would be if my sales guy had made arrangements for me to speak with his past customers!

Before finalizing my decision, he escorts me to a special waiting room, and there I find everybody who has ever purchased an Avalanche from this particular sales guy. Immediately I start asking questions: How do you like the truck? Does water leak into the back? Should I upgrade to the bigger engine? What about this sales guy, is he a jerk? Has he ever lied to you?

Regardless of the answers I get, one thing is clear: this sales guy has impressed me. He is unafraid of his past choices. He believes in the quality of his product and in the level of customer service he provides. He has nothing to hide.

Obviously it's just not feasible for my Chevy dealer to offer this kind of benefit, but it's downright simple for a small ISV.

SourceGear provides a web-based forum where our customers and prospects can talk to us and to each other. Users of this site are free to express their opinions. When a customer gripes about us (SourceGear) or our products, we don't dismiss the comment.

Prospective customers often visit the site and ask questions from other users. If one of our current customers gripes about us, then we probably deserved it. Instead of trying to impede the truth, we instead try to fix the problem.

Sometimes this approach isn't much fun at all, but it provides a nice feedback mechanism that forces us to constantly improve our product and keep our customers happy. Prospective customers can see this.

~

7. Make It Easy to Buy Over the Web

The final step in closing the gap is the moment when someone gives you money and you give that person software. Just like every other step, the customer is in charge, but it is your job to make everything easy for them.

There are several different ways to get an online storefront. You can find lots of companies offering to host a store for you. There are also a number of software packages that you can buy. I lack the experience to recommend any of these options because we (SourceGear) have always written our own online store software.

One of the reasons we wrote our own store is because it gives us complete control over the experience of our user. We are always trying to make it easier for people to buy our product. We want our online store to immediately generate serial numbers and email them to customers.

Whatever approach you choose, the following suggestions may help you in your quest to keep things simple:

Don't Make Customers Log In

The last thing your customer needs is yet another username and password to remember.

Does your online store *really* need to create a user account for everybody who makes a purchase? Probably not.

Can't you just take their money and give them software? Probably.

You Don't Need a Shopping Cart

I think Amazon[10] too heavily influences the expectations for online shopping. In my opinion, Amazon has a really incredible shopping cart system. It is extremely powerful, and yet it feels extremely simple.

So we convince ourselves that our online store needs to be as cool as Amazon's, but that just isn't true. Amazon truly is an online store. The shopping cart metaphor makes sense. The Amazon store is immensely large and contains a staggering number of products. It's a pleasant place. It only makes sense that we would want to leisurely wander around the store, selecting various products as we go, stopping at the checkout line on our way out to pay the bill.

Your small ISV simply doesn't function on that kind of scale. You are more like a hot dog stand than a store. You sell only a few products; perhaps only one. Your customer has no interest in leisurely walking around and browsing the vastness of your product offerings. They came to buy a hot dog and they don't understand why you expect them to place it in a big shopping cart and walk halfway down the block to go pay for it.

I speak from experience and mistakes. Until recently, the SourceGear online sales system was an extremely poor clone of Amazon. In a major rewrite, we eliminated the shopping cart and simplified the entire ordering process to a single form. Everything is much simpler now.

Give Customers the Product Right Away

It's fine if you need to ship some sort of physical object to your customers. However, don't make them wait for the media or documentation before they can get started. Immediately after the user places an order, let the user download the bits and start using it right away.

Even better, give serial numbers to the users to simply activate the demo(s) they are already using.

---

10. See http://www.amazon.com.

~

But We *Can't* Do It This Way!

Why not?

I know that lots of people are going to disagree with me on the opinions in this article. Trusting the customer is scary. If you don't like what I've written here, then at least give serious consideration to the following:

Have I not described exactly how you want to be treated when you are the customer?

If so, then shouldn't you be treating your customers the same way? Why not?

~

We're Not Perfect

At every seminary and religious school, preachers are taught to "preach above themselves." After all, pastors are just people. They have problems just like the rest of us. It takes a lot of audacity to stand up before a congregation every Sunday and talk about how to live a better life. If perfection were a requirement for the job, then the pulpit would always be empty.

I face a similar problem in my writings, but especially in this article. Several times here I have used my own company as an example, but we are very far from perfect. Our demo doesn't always just work. Our online store has quirks. Sometimes we are too slow in responding to technical support. Just like every sermon I have ever heard in church, I preach to myself, and Monday morning I will try and do better.

For most small ISVs, responsive sales are the way to close the gap. Let the customer be in charge, but make the gap easy to cross by moving your product as close to them as possible.

Eric Sink

HAZARDS OF HIRING[1]

It's always much, much harder to fire someone than to not hire them in the first place. There are a lot of people who are doing a decent job, a 90% job, and you really wish you had the 100% person doing that job, but the 90% person just doesn't deserve to get fired, so you hobble along, suboptimally.

*For small software companies, having the right people is **super** important. On a team of five, one bad hire can literally wreck the team.*

*And that one 90% person causes other problems. Someone takes just a **little bit too long** to deliver their component, and it gets pushed off to the Next Major Release, which never comes, because you go out of business by then. Not because the person was terrible, just because it took them 10 months to deliver instead of 9.*

Or the person you hired to answer the phones doesn't really do a good job of talking to potential customers, so you decide that you need to hire a salesperson to take phone calls, and now you have two employees instead of one.

Or the junior programmer you hired turns out to be merely "OK," and they end up writing code that looks 90% right but that is so deeply buggy it needs to be debugged from the top down, with a senior programmer going over every line of code rewriting and refactoring just to get it to stop leaking memory all over the place.

*So now they're a **negative** asset, soaking up other people's time, because they're not quite bad enough to fire, and besides, you*

---

1. Eric Sink, "Hazards of Hiring," Eric.Weblog() (http://software.ericsink.com), July 08, 2004. See http://software.ericsink.com/bos/Hazards_of_Hiring.html.

uprooted them and their family and flew them 3000 miles across the country to get them to work for you, and their kids are just starting to get adjusted to school, and their spouse is in the hospital again, and they're having trouble making ends meet, and you couldn't live with yourself if you fired them for being merely a 90% programmer instead of a 100% programmer.

Much better not to hire the wrong people in the first place. – Ed.

~

Several months ago, I wrote an MSDN column entitled "Make More Mistakes."[2] This column was one of the most popular things I have ever written. People seemed to really enjoy reading about my screw-ups. As human beings, we are fascinated by the failures of others.

In the many emails I received about that column, one of the most common questions was why I didn't list any hiring mistakes. "Eric, is it possible that you have simply never made a mistake in a hiring decision?"

Au contraire, I've made plenty. But those are stories I would rather not tell. It is one thing for me to air my own idiocy in public, but quite another thing for me to recount tales that might hurt someone else.

Nonetheless, hiring decisions are tricky, and I think I've learned enough to say a few worthwhile things on this topic.

I'll start with four general guidelines for how to proceed with a hiring decision.

After that, I'll finish the article by saying a few things about the specific challenges of hiring software developers.

~

1. Hire After the Need, Not Before

The first step in hiring is to make sure that you actually need to be hiring. For small independent software vendors (ISVs), my rule is: don't fill a position until *after* the need for that position is painfully clear.

---

2. See http://software.ericsink.com/bos/Make_More_Mistakes.html.

In other contexts, it often makes sense to "staff up" in anticipation of growth. Many venture capital–funded companies work this way. Your investors didn't give you millions of dollars because they want their cash sitting in your bank instead of their own. They expect you to grow your company aggressively, and that often means hiring more staff.

But in a small company that is funded by its own revenues, it is almost always a mistake to hire for a position before it is absolutely clear that hiring is the right thing to do.

This is an easy mistake to make. Version 7.0 of your product is going to ship in eight weeks. You are expecting lots of new orders, so you decide to hire another customer service person to be ready for the deluge of phone calls.

Better idea: have one of your existing staff take those calls, or take them yourself. Don't increase your payroll until you are 100% certain that you have a permanent need for one more person than you have now.

Several years ago, I decided to get very aggressive about growing SourceGear "to the next level." We made several new hires, including a human resource (HR) person. We convinced ourselves that the company was going to be growing so fast that we needed an HR person to help coordinate policies and benefits. We hired a top-notch individual for that job. Let's call her Wilma.

Wilma was a dear friend of mine and still is. She did a fine job for us here at SourceGear.

But the fact remains that our company was not really big enough to have a real need for a full-time person in HR. We knew this, but we were "staffing up for growth." And then the dotcom bubble burst, and SourceGear never did get that big.

~

2. Realize That Hiring Is All About Probabilities

Hiring is all about probabilities. When we evaluate a candidate, we are basically just trying to predict whether that candidate will be a success in the position being filled. We're trying to know the future, but we have no prophets and no Oracle.[3]

So, we use various indicators that we believe will be correlated with future success. We look at past experience. We look at educational background. We call references.

But there are no certainties. Sometimes all our indicators are positive, but the employee just doesn't work out. Last year I helped a charitable organization hire a new staff member. We found a candidate with an incredibly solid résumé. Let's call him Wilbur.

We interviewed Wilbur at considerable length. We checked his references. There was no question he had the necessary experience to handle the job. The decision seemed clear, so we did the hire.

Shortly after Wilbur started on the job, things turned surreal. Was this the same guy we hired? The chemistry between him and the team was a nightmare. Wilbur is clearly a sharp guy with solid abilities, but this situation simply didn't work out at all.

On the other side of the coin, sometimes we miss out on a great employee because our indicators steered us away. Most of the time, we never know about these situations. We turn down a candidate, and we don't hear where that person ends up. Some of them go on to be a big success.

~

3. Know the Law

In the United States (and probably elsewhere as well), there are laws that you need to know before you even start the process of trying to hire someone. There are federal statutes and there may be state and local regulations as well. I am not an attorney, so I will not even attempt to explain these laws, but it is very important that you understand them.

The various materials from Nolo Press are usually a good starting point for beginning to understand legal matters. Nolo Press has a web page on employment law[4] that has lots of information. Even still, it is always advisable to consult a local attorney.

---

3. See http://www.neoandtrinity.net/oracle.html.

4. See http://www.nolo.com/lawcenter/ency/category.cfm/catID/4BEF1F62-722F-435E-98AB18960A6EAB0E.

One final remark: even if you discover that you are exempt from the laws due to the small size of your company, it is well worth your time to understand the law and begin making habits out of following them. In most situations, complying with the discrimination laws will actually improve your decision making anyway.

~

4. Get a Variety of Opinions

The general principle here is that good decisions happen when you have several different perspectives. If you want to consistently make the worst hiring decisions you can make, just make all the decisions by yourself without listening to anybody else.

But if you want wise decisions, get a variety of opinions and different perspectives. In my own hiring decisions, I make sure at least one of those perspectives comes from a woman in my company.

The simple fact is that the software industry has a lot more men than women. Julia Lerman[5] noticed that the Tech-Ed[6] speakers list had more people named Brian than women. Our field is perhaps 90% male, and that means I have to work a little harder to get balance on this aspect of our hiring decisions.

I've observed a pattern over the years, and of the bad hiring decisions we've made, many of them happened when the decision was made entirely without a woman's voice.

Fortunately, my approach has worked well in ways that I could not have anticipated. In 1998, SourceGear was looking to hire a full-time person in technical support. The decision was primarily being driven by myself and one of my coworkers named Mary. We interviewed several candidates. Mary and I disagreed on which candidate should be chosen. I deferred the decision to Mary, confident that I would eventually be proven right. But the person Mary chose turned out to be one of the best employees we've ever had.

---

5. See http://www.devsource.ziffdavis.com/article2/0,1759,1572759,00.asp.

6. Tech-Ed is a big conference Microsoft puts on regularly for its highly technical customers to learn about all the latest Microsoft goodies. – Ed.

~

Hiring Programmers: The Usual Advice

Most of the writings on the subject of hiring programmers tend to sound the same. The usual advice is to "only hire the very best."

I'll confess that I'm not terribly fond of this advice. It is simply too vague.

Please understand that I am not advising anyone to deliberately seek out mediocrity. We obviously want to hire the most talented and experienced people we can. In a hiring decision, the stakes are high. Your decision will affect your team, and it will affect the individual. As Joel says, "It is much better to reject a good candidate than to accept a bad candidate.... If you have any doubts whatsoever, **No Hire.**"[7]

But the usual advice still annoys me. The problem isn't so much with the advice itself, but with its tendency to be misunderstood. When applied with no additional precision, the primary effect of the usual advice is to create a sense of arrogance. This effect is especially common among programmers, since elitism comes naturally to us anyway. When we hear that we should "only hire the very best," we internally translate this to mean:

> The "very best"? Why, that's me! I am the "very best." Obviously, I should only hire people who are as gifted, as smart, and as good-looking as I am. After all, why should I pollute my perfect team with riffraff?

It is not surprising that this attitude provides a poor framework for hiring decisions. The usual advice works much better when it is understood quite differently:

> I want to build the most effective team that I can build. When I hire another person for my team, my goal is not merely to make the team larger. Each person I hire should be chosen to make my team better in some specific way. I am not looking for someone as talented as me. Rather, I am looking for someone who is more talented than me, in at least one significant way.

---

7. See http://www.joelonsoftware.com/articles/fog0000000073.html.

The very worst kind of manager is the one who feels threatened by his team. Consciously or not, he is afraid of those who are "the very best," so he consistently staffs his team with people who will not challenge him.

I suppose he might be able to get away with this in a big company. After all, I doubt that the Pointy-Haired Boss in the Dilbert comic strip was created with no source of inspiration at all.

But things are very different in the world of small software companies. If you are the founder or "chief geek" in your small ISV, take a careful, honest, and objective look at yourself. If you are the type of person who feels threatened by your own staff, stop and rethink. Until you move yourself past this problem, you have exactly zero chance of building an effective team.

The real point of the usual advice is not to inflate our egos—it is to remind us that we should not be afraid to search for the best people.

But we still need a more specific understanding of what the word "best" really means.

~

Look for Self-Awareness

The "very best" people never stop learning.

When I evaluate a candidate, one of the most important criteria is what I call "the first derivative." Is this person learning? Is this candidate moving forward, or have they stagnated? (For more of my thoughts on this topic, see the "Career Calculus" article on my weblog.[8])

People who are seriously focused on their own future success are very likely to be successful. This is often the strongest predictive indicator in the hiring process.

I'm not saying you should just hire people who want to succeed. Everybody wants to succeed. I'm talking about hiring people who are

---

8. See http://software.ericsink.com/Career_Calculus.html.

serious about constant learning. These people don't spend their time trying to convince you of how much they know. They don't focus on their past very much. They are always focused on their future. As you interview them, they are interviewing you, trying to figure out how much they can learn from you.

How do you find this kind of person? It turns out that this posture has a precondition that is rather easily observed: people who are committed to constant learning are people who know what they don't know. They know their own weaknesses, and they're not insecure in talking about them.

One of the popular interviewing questions is to ask the candidate to describe their biggest weaknesses. Even though this question is terribly "old school," I really like it.

Unfortunately, most candidates try to duck the question. They go to their local bookstore and they buy a book on interviewing. That book warns them that I am going to ask this question. The book tells them creative ways to avoid giving a genuine answer:

- Sometimes I work too hard.
- Sometimes other team members get frustrated with my attention to detail.

When I ask candidates to tell me about their weaknesses, I am hoping for a wise, honest, and self-confident answer. When I hear a candidate rationally admit a weakness, I am impressed. When I hear a candidate duck the question with language straight out of a book, I start thinking about the next candidate.

~

Hire Developers, Not Programmers

For a small ISV, the "very best" programmers are the ones who can do more than just write code. You should hire developers, not programmers.

Although the words "developer" and "programmer" are often used interchangeably, I make a distinction between them. That distinction is the difference between simply coding and being a part of product team.

I wrote an article on this topic on my weblog, from which I quote:

> For the purpose of this article, a "programmer" is someone who does nothing but code new features and [if you're lucky] fix bugs. They don't write specs. They don't write automated test cases. They don't help keep the automated build system up to date. They don't help customers work out tough problems. They don't help write documentation. They don't help with testing. They don't even read code. All they do is write new code. In a small ISV, you don't want any of these people in your company.
>
> Instead of "programmers" (people that specialize in writing code), what you need are "developers" (people who will contribute in multiple ways to make the product successful). [9]

What does the usual advice really mean? Exactly what attribute do I measure to determine if the candidate is "the very best"?

Most of the time, the usual advice is understood to apply only to coding skills. It really is true that the best coders are gifted with an aptitude. They understand things that generally cannot be taught. They are perhaps 10 times more productive than average coders. It obviously makes good sense to try to find one of these "10X" individuals, especially in larger environments where specialists like pure coders can fit in well.

But in a small ISV, we need versatility. We often need the people on our teams to wear multiple hats, not just write code. In these cases, it is often very important to look for the best developer, and that person is not necessarily the best programmer.

~

Education Is Good

People with a solid education in the fundamentals often turn out to be the "very best" developers.

The issue of education is quite controversial in the software field. Right now, somewhere on the Internet, there is a discussion board or a chat room where people are arguing about how much education is

---

9. See http://software.ericsink.com/No_Programmers.html.

needed to be a software developer. The arguments go on, all day, all night, 365 days a year, and they never find the answer to the question.

And they never will. Hiring is about probabilities. Educational experience is an indicator that can be used in predicting success, but it is not always accurate.

Two of SourceGear's best developers have no degree. One of them is an excellent programmer who is gradually becoming an excellent developer. The other is an excellent developer who is gradually becoming an excellent programmer.

Nonetheless, I still sort résumés by educational level. These two developers are exceptions from the norm. The bulk of my experience has taught me that a college degree is a useful predictor of future success. When I hire developers, I want to see a bachelor's degree from a highly regarded computer science department. Yes, yes, I have two obvious counterexamples right here among my coworkers. But hiring is about probabilities. When I see a BS from someplace like University of Illinois or Stanford, I believe the probability of ending up with a successful employee in the future is higher.

~

But Too Much Education Is a Yellow Light

On the other hand, when I see a PhD in computer science, I believe the probability goes down.

Universities don't teach people to be developers, anyway. They don't even teach people to be programmers. Universities teach their students to be computer scientists. Becoming a programmer or even a developer is usually left as an exercise for the student to complete on her own time.

A bachelor's degree gives you a solid grounding in fundamentals and it proves that you can finish. Those issues are important, but when it comes to the specific set of skills we need in a small ISV, you are approaching the point of diminishing returns on your first day of graduate school.

People tend to get terribly offended by these opinions. Please understand that I do have a lot of respect for people who have finished a PhD. It takes a tremendous amount of discipline, intelligence, and desire to finish a doctoral degree. I admire those "PhD Qualities." I seriously doubt whether I could finish a PhD myself.

But I still believe that those "PhD Qualities" are not the same skills that are needed in a small ISV. Shipping a shrink-wrapped product requires a *different* kind of discipline, intelligence, and desire. These "Shrink-wrap Qualities" are similar to "PhD Qualities," and yet are very different.

Furthermore, I believe that very rare is the person who has both PhD Qualities and Shrink-wrap Qualities. Some people have the talents to finish a PhD. Some have the talents to finish products. Some people have both, but not very many people. When I see someone who has finished a PhD, I know for certain that they have PhD Qualities. I will therefore consider it unlikely that they have Shrink-wrap Qualities as well.

Obviously, I may be wrong, but hiring is all about probabilities. We use guidelines to predict the future success of a candidate, but those guidelines are not always correct. There are exceptions to every rule, and playing the odds will cause me to miss out on those exceptions. That's unfortunate, because a PhD with Shrink-wrap Qualities would be an incredible person. Suppose, for example, that I received a résumé from somebody with a PhD in computer science and with several years of experience as a developer on the Adobe Photoshop team. Obviously, I would want to interview this person. I don't think there is a shrink-wrap product I admire more than Photoshop. PhD or not, this person clearly has Shrink-wrap Qualities. The PhD is not inherently negative. It is merely a predictive indicator, and sometimes it's wrong.

~

Look at the Code

Although I do place a high value on the noncoding aspects of software development, the code is important, too. The "very best" developers still ought to be darn good programmers.

Don't be afraid to look at the code. When you interview developers, ask for code samples. Ask them to write some code during the interview.

One of my favorite questions is to ask candidates how many lines of code they have written in their entire career. The answers vary widely. Some people don't even know. Some people tell me it's a stupid question and spout all the research showing that "line count" isn't a terribly good measure of programmer productivity. Fine, I'll stipulate to all that, but I still like the question. I believe that people tend to become better programmers as they write more and more code. I want to know how much code you've got behind you.

During college I wrote a C compiler, just for fun. It was written in C, entirely from scratch, with a handwritten recursive descent parser. I even did some peephole optimizations on the back-end. It wasn't very fast, but it could compile itself with no errors. I released it under the GPL, but I was only the person who ever used it.

When I applied for a developer job at Spyglass, I showed my compiler to the hiring manager. I got the job, and my compiler project was one of the factors in his decision. He said he looked at my code and realized that I had already gotten a lot of the bad code out of my system, so my next hundred thousand lines of code ought to be pretty good. ☺

Twelve years later, I think there is some wisdom in hiring people who have made significant contributions to an open source community project. After all, I don't have to ask for code samples; I can just grab a tarball[10] and read it myself.

But the availability of code for review is one just minor reason why I like to see open source experience on a résumé. Working on this kind of project also says something about the person.

Granted, a lot of these coders are driven purely out of hatred for Microsoft. Regardless of your opinions about Microsoft, that kind of motivation is not likely to be a good foundation for success in any developer job.

But a lot of people work on an open source project simply because they have a passion for coding. It's their hobby, and as hobbies go, it's

---

10. A "tarball" is a bunch of source code bundled up in one file, named after the Unix utility *tar*, which bundles multiple files into one. – *Ed.*

not a bad one. Some folks look at projects like AbiWord[11] or ReactOS[12] and all they see are people who are wasting their time by cloning mature Microsoft products. I'll concede that these projects don't make much sense if you're trying to find a business case for them. But the typical contributor to these projects is coding for fun. Watching TV is a waste of time. Coding is not.

People who genuinely love to write code often turn out to be the "very best" developers.

∿

The Very Best

It turns out that the usual advice works just fine, but we have to move from the vague to the specific. To summarize the various points I made in the previous sections, here are 10 questions to ask yourself when considering a candidate for a developer position:

1. Can this candidate bring something to the team that nobody else has?
2. Is this candidate constantly learning?
3. Is this candidate aware of his/her weaknesses and comfortable discussing them?
4. Is this candidate versatile and willing to do "whatever it takes" to help make the product successful?
5. Is this candidate one of those "10X coders"?
6. Does this candidate have a bachelor's degree from a good computer science department?
7. If this candidate has a PhD, is there other evidence to suggest that s/he is one of those rare people who also has "Shrink-wrap Qualities"?

---

11. See http://www.abisource.com.
12. See http://www.reactos.com.

8. Does this candidate have experience on a team building shrink-wrap software?

9. Does this candidate write good code?

10. Does this candidate love programming so much that s/he writes code in their spare time?

It's not necessary to answer "yes" to all 10 of these questions. I'm not even going to specify a minimum number of "yes" answers needed for a positive hiring decision. Hiring is all about probabilities, and each of these questions can serve as an indicator to help you predict whether the candidate will be a success for you.

In the end, every hiring decision will be made with your own judgment, and there are no guarantees. However, giving consideration to these issues can help raise the probability of making a hiring decision that you will not later regret.

Aaron Swartz

POWERPOINT REMIX[1]

In my own speeches I try to avoid the boring PowerPoints with the bullets. I either put up pictures of really hot actors (by which I mean, hot-looking: Jennifer Aniston, Brad Pitt, etc.), or puppies, or jokes, and I think I have the whole bullet thing isolated to one slide with three bullet points. Of course, when I'm so busy telling jokes and showing pictures of hot actors it's hard to find time to get to the bullets.

In 2003 Edward R. Tufte, famous for his brilliant and beautiful books on the visual display of information, decided he had had just about enough PowerPoint for a lifetime, and launched a campaign to rid the world of this scourge. "Alas," Tufte wrote, "slideware often reduces the analytical quality of presentations. In particular, the popular PowerPoint templates (ready-made designs) usually weaken verbal and spatial reasoning, and almost always corrupt statistical analysis." His excellent essay, "The Cognitive Style of PowerPoint," makes the case in just 28 concise pages.

Aaron has a summary. – Ed.

---

1. Aaron Swartz, "PowerPoint Remix," http://www.aaronsw.com, May 23, 2003. See http://www.aaronsw.com/weblog/000931.

~

EDWARD R. TUFTE'S "THE COGNITIVE STYLE OF POWERPOINT"[2] PRESENTED IN THE FORM OF A POWERPOINT PRESENTATION

Overview

- PowerPoint is standard...
- ...but bad.
- Why?

Cognitive Style

- Is presenter-oriented
- Audience and content suffer
  - Low resolution
  - Deeply hierarchical
  - Preoccupied with form

Low Resolution

- Nearly content-free
- Only slightly better than 1982 Pravda propaganda

Dilutes Thought

- Bullets make us stupid
  - Too generic
  - Omit relationships
  - Omit assumptions
  - Omit subjects, verbs

\terlude: analysis of Columbia disaster PowerPoint][3]

The Cognitive Style of PowerPoint. Cheshire, CT: Graphics Press, 2003.
\dwardtufte.com/bboard/q-and-a-fetch-msg?msg_id=0000Rs&topic_id=
'2eT%2e.

Deeply Hierarchical

- Often six levels deep
- Feynman only needed 2

Why?

- Based on software corporation itself
  - Big bureaucracy
  - Programming computers
    - Deeply hierarchical
  - Marketing
    - Misdirecting
    - Sloganeering
    - Exaggerating

Why? (cont'd)

- What could be worse?
  - Stalin?
- Pushy
  - Bullets are to be followed
- Based on great leader on pedestal

What else?

- Better: good teaching
  - Explanation, reasoning, etc.
  - Credible authority

PowerPoint in schools

- Disturbing!
- Must find replacement
  - Good: teaching kids to smoke
  - Better: close school, go to Exploratorium
  - Best: write illustrated essay

[Interlude: performance of the Gettysburg PowerPoint][4]

[Interlude: what if we presented cancer survival rates in PowerPoint?]

Stylesheets

- Corporate logowear
  - Gives name of corporate dept.
  - Not actual people (too embarrassed? – *A.S.*)
- Emulates reading primers for 6-year-olds
- Poor typography is key
- Break things up to prevent comparisons
- Useless tables

World Domination

- Printed PowerPoints: 50 slides = 1 page of Physician's Desk Reference
- Online PowerPoints: 20% of density of popular websites
- Worse signal-to-noise ratio known

Sequentially

- Bullet-point striptease
- Dissolves like random jump-cuts
- Handouts would let audience control order and pace

What to do?

- Immediate worldwide product recall
- It's like an out-of-control prescription drug

---

4. See http://www.norvig.com/Gettysburg.

Improving Presentations

- Get better content
- Provide handouts
- Don't have pointless ones

Final Thoughts – *A.S.*

- Good essay
- Buy lots of copies
- Hand out to annoying PowerPoint presenters

why the lucky stiff

A QUICK (AND HOPEFULLY PAINLESS) RIDE THROUGH RUBY (WITH CARTOON FOXES)[1]

Way back in the glory days of computers, i.e., when I was a teenager, there was a tradition of funny, light, pleasant books about programming that actually taught you something.

The Apple][came with a user's guide full of Monty Python–style humor that told you how to treat your floppy disks, including the stern admonition that one must never staple them to a notebook. I giggled for three weeks over that and read it out loud to everyone who would listen. Can't remember why. I think it was funny to my young mind.

Daniel Friedman's The Little LISPer *(Science Research Associates, 1974) was a slim, crystal-clear gem of a book, possibly the best-written programming tutorial ever written even though it was teaching a language that many people, honestly, couldn't wrap their heads around.*

*And C would never have become a standard if it weren't for the eponymous book by Brian Kernighan and Dennis Ritchie (*The C Programming Language, *Prentice-Hall, 1978), which was a paradigm of clear writing and brilliant pedagogy, albeit completely lacking in cartoon foxes or indeed any kind of cartoon animals.*

Unfortunately, the business of programming language books changed for the worse when publishers noticed that the bestseller

---

1. why the lucky stiff, "A Quick (and Hopefully Painless) Ride Through Ruby (with Cartoon Foxes)," why's poignant guide to ruby (http://poignantguide.net/ruby/index.html). See http://poignantguide.net/ruby/chapter-3.html.

was usually the book with the thickest spine. Befuddled shoppers, faced with learning Java or getting out of the IT industry, went to the neighborhood Buns 'n' Noodles to be confronted with an entire Wall of Java, and the only reasonable way to pick a book was to pick the fattest one. Which is how we got the scary red books with 24 mugshots taken from FBI wanted posters on the front cover that didn't teach you anything.

Thankfully, why the lucky stiff, along with a couple of cartoon foxes, is resurrecting the tradition of great, entertaining programming tutorials with a tutorial on the Ruby programming language. Sometimes it gets a little bit off topic, but I'm hardly one to complain about that. – Ed.

~

Yeah, these are the two. My asthma's kickin' in so I've got to go take a puff of medicated air just now. Be with you in a moment.

I'm told that this chapter is best accompanied by a rag. Something you can mop your face with as the sweat pours off your face.

Indeed, we'll be racing through the whole language. Like striking every match in a box as quickly as can be done.

~

Language and I *Mean* Language

My conscience won't let me call Ruby a *computer* language. That would imply that the language works primarily on the computer's terms. That the language is designed to accommodate the computer, first and foremost. That therefore, we, the coders, are foreigners, seeking citizenship in the computer's locale. It's the computer's language and we are translators for the world.

But what do you call the language when your brain begins to think in that language? When you start to use the language's own words and colloquialisms to express yourself? Say, the computer can't do that. How can it be the computer's language? It is ours, we speak it natively!

We can no longer truthfully call it a *computer* language. It is *coder-speak*. It is the language of our thoughts.

Read the following aloud to yourself.

```
5.times { print "Odelay!" }
```

In English sentences, punctuation (such as periods, exclamations, parentheses) are silent. Punctuation adds meaning to words, helps give cues as to what the author intended by a sentence. So let's read the above as: *Five times print "Odelay!"*.

Which is exactly what this small Ruby program does. Beck's mutated Spanish[2] exclamation will print five times on the computer screen.

Read the following aloud to yourself.

```
exit unless "restaurant".include? "aura"
```

Here we're doing a basic reality check. Our program will **exit** (the program will end) **unless** the word **restaurant** contains (or **includes**) the word **aura**. Again, in English: *Exit unless the word restaurant includes the word aura.*

Ever seen a programming language use question marks so effectively? Ruby uses some punctuation, such as exclamations and question marks, to enhance readability of the code. We're asking a question in the above code, so why not make that apparent?

Read the following aloud to yourself.

```
[toast, cheese, wine].each { |food| eat food }
```

While this bit of code is less readable and sentence-like than the previous examples, I'd still encourage you to read it aloud. Although Ruby may sometimes read like English, it sometimes reads as a shorter English. You might read the above, fully translated into English, as: *With toast, cheese, and wine, take each type of food and eat that food.*

This program won't actually work if you run it. Ruby doesn't know how to **eat**. But the beautiful thing is that you can add your own words to Ruby. Your own actions. Your own objects.

At this point, you're probably wondering how these words actually fit together. Smotchkkiss is wondering what the dots and brackets mean. I'm going to discuss the various *parts of speech* next.

All you need to know thus far is that Ruby is basically built from sentences. They aren't exactly English sentences. They are short collections of words and punctuation that encompass a single thought. These sentences can form books. They can form pages. They can form entire novels, when strung together. Novels that can be read by humans, but also by computers.

---

2. See http://www.whiskeyclone.net/ghost/L/lordonlyknows.html.

Concerning Commercial Uses of the (Poignant) Guide

The (Poignant) Guide is released under a Creative Commons license that allows unlimited commercial use of this text. Basically, this means you can sell all these bootleg copies of it and keep the revenues for yourself. I trust my readers (and the world around them) to rip me off. To put out some crappy Xerox edition with that time-tested clipart of praying hands on the cover.

Guys, the lawsuits just ain't worth the headache. So I'm just going to straight-up endorse authorized piracy, folks. Anybody who wants to read the book should be able to read it. Anybody who wants to market the book or come up with special editions, I'm flattered.

Why would I want the $$$? IGNORE ALL OTHER SIDEBARS: I've lost the will to be a rich slob. Sounds inhuman, but I like my little black-and-white television. Also my hanging plastic flower lamp. I don't want to be a career writer. Cash isn't going inspire me. Pointless.

So, if money means nothing to the lucky stiff, why rip me off when you could co-opt shady business practices to literally crush my psyche and leave me wheezing in some sooty iron lung? Oh, and the irony of using my own works against me! Die, Poignant Boy!

To give you an idea of what I mean, here are a few underhanded concepts that could seriously kill my willpower and force me to reconsider things like existence.

IDEA ONE: BIG TOBACCO

Buy a cigarette company. Use my cartoon foxes to fuel an aggressive ad campaign. Here's a billboard for starters:

Make it obvious that you're targeting children and the asthmatic. Then, once you've got everyone going, have the **truth** people do an expose on me and my farm of inky foxes.

Sensible Hipster Standing on Curb in Urban Wilderness: He calls himself the lucky stiff.

(Pulls aside curtain to reveal gray corpse on a gurney.)

Hipster: Some stiffs ain't so lucky.

(Erratic zoom-in. Superimposed cartoon foxes for subliminal Willy Wonka mind trip.)

Yo. Why you gotta dis Big Smokies like dat, Holmes?

IDEA TWO: HEY, FIRING SQUAD

Like I said, start selling copies of the (Poignant) Guide, but corrupt the text. These altered copies would contain numerous blatant (and libelous) references to government agencies, such as the U.S. Marshals and the Pentagon. You could make me look like a complete traitor. Like I have all these plans to, you know, kill certain less desirable members of the U.S. Marshals or the Pentagon.

Not that there are any less desirable members of the U.S. Marshals or the Pentagon. Yeah, I didn't mean it like that.

Oh, crap.

Oh, crap. Oh, crap. Oh, crap.

Turn off the lights. Get down.

IDEA THREE: BILLBOARDS, PART II

How about making fun of asthmatics directly?

IDEA FOUR: ALEC BALDWIN

Adapt the guide into a movie. And since, you know, I'm a character in this guide, you could get someone like Alec Baldwin to play me. Someone who's at a real low point in his career.

You could make it seem like I did tons of drugs. Like I was insane to work with. Like I kept firing people and locking them in the scooter room and making them wear outfits made of bread. Yeah, like I could actually be *baking* people into the outfits.

You could have this huge mold that I strap people into. Then, I pour all the dough on them and actually bake them until the bread has risen and they've almost died. And when the television crews come and I'm on *Good Morning America*, they'll ask, "So, how many people have you employed in the production of your guide?" And I'd respond, "A baker's dozen!" and erupt into that loud maniacal laughing that would force audience members to cup their hands over their ears.

Of course, in the throes of my insanity, I would declare war on the world. The bread people would put up quite a fight. Until the U.S. Marshals (or the Pentagon) engineer a giant robotic monkey brain (played by Burt Lancaster) to come after me.

Here's where you'll make me look completely lame. Not only will I sacrifice all of the bread people (the Starchtroopers) to save myself, not only will I surrender to the great monkey brain like a coward, but when I narrowly escape, I'll yell at the audience. Screaming insistently that it's MY movie and no one should see it any more, I'll rip the screen in half and the film projector will spin with its reel flapping in defeat. And that will be the end of the movie. People will be *so* pissed.

Now, I've got to thinking. See, and actually, Alec Baldwin did a decent voiceover in *The Royal Tenenbaums*. His career might be okay. You might not want to use him. He might not do it.

Tell ya what. I'll play the part. I've made a career out of low points.

~

The Parts of Speech

Just like the white stripe down a skunk's back and the winding, white train of a bride, many of Ruby's parts of speech have visual cues to help you identify them. Punctuation and capitalization will help your brain to see bits of code and feel intense recognition. Your mind will frequently yell *Hey, I know that guy!* You'll also be able to name-drop in conversations with other Rubyists.

Try to focus on the look of each of these parts of speech. The rest of the book will detail the specifics. I give short descriptions for each part of speech, but you don't have to understand the explanation. By the end of this chapter, you should be able to recognize every part of a Ruby program.

Variables

Any plain, lowercase word is a variable in Ruby. Variables may consist of letters, digits, and underscores.

x, y, banana2, or phone_a_quail are examples.

Variables are like nicknames. Remember when everyone used to call you Stinky Pete? People would say, "Get over here, Stinky Pete!" And everyone miraculously knew that Stinky Pete was you.

With variables, you give a nickname to something you use frequently. For instance, let's say you run an orphanage. It's a mean orphanage. And whenever Daddy Warbucks comes to buy more kids, we insist that he pay us **one-hundred twenty-one dollars and eight cents** for the kid's teddy bear, which the kid has become attached to over in the darker moments of living in such nightmarish custody.

```
teddy_bear_fee = 121.08
```

Later, when you ring him up at the cash register (a really souped-up cash register that runs Ruby!), you'll need to add together all his charges into a **total**.

```
total = orphan_fee + teddy_bear_fee + gratuity
```

Those variable nicknames sure help. And in the seedy underground of child sales, any help is appreciated I'm sure.

Numbers

The most basic type of number is an *integer*, a **series of digits** that can start with a **plus** or **minus sign**.

1, 23, and -10000 are examples.

Commas are not allowed in numbers, but underscores are. So if you feel the need to mark your thousands so the numbers are more readable, use an underscore.

```
population = 12_000_000_000
```

Decimal numbers are called *floats* in Ruby. Floats consist of numbers with a **decimal place** or **scientific notation**.

3.14, -808.08, and 12.043e-04 are examples.

Strings

Strings are any sort of characters (letters, digits, punctuation) surrounded by quotes. Both single and double **quotes** are used to create strings.

"sealab", '2021', or "These cartoons are hilarious!" are examples.

When you enclose characters in quotes, they are stored together as a single string.

Think of a reporter who is jotting down the mouthnoises of a rambling celebrity. "I'm a lot wiser," says Avril Lavigne. "Now I know what the business is like—what you have to do and how to work it."

```
avril_quote = "I'm a lot wiser.  Now I know
what the business is like -- what you have
to do and how to work it."
```

So, just as we stored a number in the teddy_bear_fee variable, now we're storing a collection of characters (a string) in the avril_quote variable. The reporter sends this quote to the printers, who just happen to use Ruby to operate their printing press.

```
Tabloid.print oprah_quote
Tabloid.print avril_quote
Tabloid.print justin_timberlake_pix
```

Symbols

Symbols are words that look just like variables. Again, they may contain letters, digits, or underscores. But they **start with a colon**.

:a, :b, or :ponce_de_leon are examples.

Symbols are lightweight strings. Usually, symbols are used in situations where you need a string but you won't be printing it to the screen.

You could say a symbol is a bit easier on the computer. It's like an antacid. The colon indicates the bubbles trickling up from your computer's stomach as it digests the symbol. Ah. Sweet, sweet relief.

Constants

Constants are words like variables, but constants are **capitalized**. If variables are the nouns of Ruby, then think of constants as the proper nouns.

Time, Array, or Shake_It_Like_A_Polaroid_Picture are examples.

In English, proper nouns are capitalized. The Empire State Building. You can't just move the Empire State Building. You can't just decide that the Empire State Building is something else. Proper nouns are like that. They refer to something very specific and usually don't change over time.

In the same way, constants can't be changed after they are set.

```
EmpireStateBuilding = "350 5th Avenue, NYC, NY"
```

If we try to change the constant, Ruby will complain to us. Such things are frowned upon.

Methods

If variables and constants are the nouns, then methods are the verbs. Methods are usually attached to the end of variables and constants by a **dot.** You've already seen methods at work.

```
front_door.open
```

In the above, open is the method. It is the action, the verb. In some cases, you'll see actions chained together.

```
front_door.open.close
```

We've instructed the computer to open the front door and then immediately close it.

```
front_door.is_open?
```

The above is an action as well. We're instructing the computer to test the door to see if it's open. The method could be called Door.test_to_see_if_its_open, but the is_open? name is succinct and just as correct. Both exclamation marks and question marks may be used in method names.

Method Arguments

A method may require more information in order to perform its action. If we want the computer to paint the door, we should provide a color as well.

Method arguments are attached to the end of a method. The arguments are usually surrounded by **parentheses** and separated by **commas**.

```
front_door.paint( 3, :red )
```

The above paints the front door three coats of red.

Think of it as an inner tube the method is pulling along, containing its extra instructions. The parentheses form the wet, round edges of the inner tube. The commas are the feet of each argument, sticking over the edge. The last argument has its feet tucked under so they don't show.

Like a boat pulling many inner tubes, methods with arguments can be chained.

```
front_door.paint( 3, :red ).dry( 30 ).close()
```

The above paints the front door three coats of red, dries for 30 minutes, and closes the door. Even though the last method has no arguments, you can still use parentheses if you like. There is no use dragging an empty inner tube, so the parentheses are normally dropped.

Some methods (such as print) are kernel methods. These methods are used throughout Ruby. Since they are so common, you won't use the dot.

```
print "See, no dot."
```

Class Methods

Like the methods described above (also called *instance* methods), class methods are usually attached after variables and constants. Rather than a dot, a **double colon** is used.

```
Door::new( :oak )
```

As seen here, the new class method is most often used to create things. In the above example, we're asking Ruby to make a new oak door for us. Of course, Ruby has to have an understanding of how to make a door—as well as a wealth of timber, lumberjacks, and those long, wiggily, two-man saws.

Global Variables

Variables that begin with a **dollar sign**, are global.

$x, $1, $chunky, and $CHunKY_bACOn are examples.

Most variables are rather temporary in nature. Some parts of your program are like little houses. You walk in and they have their own variables. In one house, you may have a dad that represents Archie, a traveling salesman and skeleton collector. In another house, dad could represent Peter, a lion tamer with a great love for flannel. Each house has its own meaning for dad.

With global variables, you can be guaranteed that the variable is the same in every little house. The dollar sign is very appropriate. Every American home respects the value of the dollar. We're crazy for the stuff. Try knocking on any door in America and hand them cash. I can guarantee you won't get the same reaction if you knock on a door and offer Peter, a lion tamer with a great love for flannel.

Global variables can be used anywhere in your program. They never go out of sight.

Instance Variables

Variables that begin with an **at** symbol are instance variables.

@x, @y, and @only_the_chunkiest_cut_of_bacon_I_have_ever_seen are examples.

These variables are often used to define the attributes of something. For example, you might provide Ruby with the width of the front_door by setting the @width variable inside that front_door. Instance variables are used to define characteristics of a single object in Ruby.

Think of the **at** symbol as meaning **attribute**.

Class Variables

Variables that begin with **double at** symbols are class variables.

@@x, @@y, and @@i_will_take_your_chunky_bacon_and_raise_you_two are examples.

Class variables, too, are used to define attributes. But rather than defining an attribute for a single object in Ruby, class variables give an attribute to many related objects in Ruby. If instance variables set attributes for a single front_door, then class variables set attributes for everything that is a Door.

Think of the **double at** prefix as meaning **attribute all**. Additionally, you can think of a swarm of **AT-ATs** from *Star Wars*, which are all commanded by Ruby. You change a class variable and not just one changes, they all change.

Blocks

Any code surrounded by **curly braces** is a block.

{ print "Yes, I've used chunky bacon in my examples, but never again!" } is an example.

With blocks, you can group a set of instructions together so that they can be passed around your program. The curly braces give the appearance of crab pincers that have snatched the code and are holding it together. When you see these two pincers, remember that the code inside has been pressed into a single unit.

It's like one of those little Hello Kitty boxes they sell at the mall that's stuffed with tiny pencils and microscopic paper, all crammed into a glittery transparent case that can be concealed in your palm for covert stationery operations. Except that blocks don't require so much squinting.

The curly braces can also be traded for the words **do** and **end**, which is nice if your block is longer than one line.

```
do
  print "Much better."
  print "Ah.  More space!"
  print "My back was killin' me in those crab pincers."
end
```

Block Arguments

Block arguments are a set of variables surrounded by **pipe** characters and separated by **commas**.

|x|, |x,y|, and |up, down, all_around| are examples.

Block arguments are used at the beginning of a block.

```
{ |x,y| x + y }
```

In the above example, |x,y| are the arguments. After the arguments, we have a bit of code. The expression x + y adds the two arguments together.

I like to think of the pipe characters as representing a tunnel. They give the appearance of a chute that the variables are sliding down. (An x goes down spread eagle, while the y neatly crosses her legs.) This chute acts as a passageway between blocks and the world around them.

Variables are passed through this chute (or tunnel) into the block.

Ranges

A range is two values surrounded by **parentheses** and separated by an **ellipsis** (in the form of two or three dots).

(1..3) is a range, representing the numbers 1 through 3.

('a'..'z') is a range, representing a lowercase alphabet.

Think of it as an accordion that has been squeezed down for carrying. (Sure, you can build a great sense of self-worth by carrying around an unfolded accordion, but sometimes a person needs to wallow in self-doubt, carefully concealing the squeeze-box.) The parentheses are the handles on the sides of a smaller, handheld accordion. The dots are the chain, keeping the folds tightly closed.

Normally, only two dots are used. If a third dot is used, the last value in the range is excluded.

(0...5) represents the numbers 0 through 4.

When you see that third dot, imagine opening the accordion slightly. Just enough to let one note from its chamber. The note is that end value. We'll let the sky eat it.

Arrays

An array is a list surrounded by **square brackets** and separated by **commas**.

[1, 2, 3] is an array of numbers.

['coat', 'mittens', 'snowboard'] is an array of strings.

Think of it as a caterpillar that has been stapled into your code. The two square brackets are staples that keep the caterpillar from moving, so you can keep track of which end is the head and which is the tail. The commas are the caterpillar's legs, wiggling between each section of its body.

Once there was a caterpillar who had commas for legs. Which meant he had to allow a literary pause after each step. The other caterpillars really respected him for it and he came to have quite a commanding presence. Oh, and talk about a philanthropist! He was notorious for giving fresh leaves to those less fortunate.

Yes, an array is a collection of things, but it also keeps those things in a specific order.

Hashes

A hash is a dictionary surrounded by **curly braces**. Dictionaries match words with their definitions. Ruby does so with **arrows** made from an equals sign, followed by a greater-than sign.

{'a' => 'aardvark', 'b' => 'badger'} is an example.

This time, the curly braces represent little book symbols. See how they look like little, open books with creases down the middle? They represent opening and closing our dictionary.

Imagine our dictionary has a definition on each of its pages. The commas represent the corner of each page, which we turn to see the next definition. And on each page: a word followed by an arrow pointing to the definition.

```
{
  'name' => 'Peter',
  'profession' => 'lion tamer',
  'great love' => 'flannel'
}
```

I'm not comparing hashes to dictionaries because you can only store definitions in a hash. In the example above, I stored personal information for Peter, the lion tamer with a great love for flannel. Hashes are like dictionaries because they can be very easy to search through.

Unlike arrays, the items in a hash are not kept in a specific order.

Regular Expressions

A regular expression (or *regexp*) is a set of characters surrounded by **slashes**.

/ruby/, /[0-9]+/ and /^\d{3}-\d{3}-\d{4}/ are examples.

Regular expressions are used to find words or patterns in text. The slashes on each side of the expression are pins.

Imagine if you had a little word with pins on both side and you held it over a book. You pass the word over the book and when it gets near a matching word, it starts blinking. You pin the regular expression onto the book, right over the match, and it glows with the letters of the matching word.

Oh, and when you poke the pins into the book, the paper sneezes, *reg-exp!*

Regular expressions are much faster than passing your hand over pages of a book. Ruby can use a regular expression to search volumes of books very quickly.

Operators

You'll use the following list of operators to do math in Ruby or to compare things. Scan over the list, recognize a few. You know, addition + and subtraction - and so on.

```
**  !   ~   *   /   %   +   -   &
<<  >>  |   ^   >   >=  <   <=  <=>
||  !=  =~  !~  &&  +=  -=   =
..  ...  not and or
```

Keywords

Ruby has a number of built-in words, imbued with meaning. These words cannot be used as variables or changed to suit your purposes. Some of these we've already discussed. They are in the safe house, my friend. You touch these and you'll be served an official syntax error.

alias	and	BEGIN	begin	break	case	class	def	defined
do	else	elsif	END	end	ensure	false	for	if
in	module	next	nil	not	or	redo	rescue	retry
return	self	super	then	true	undef	unless	until	when
while	yield							

Good enough. These are the illustrious members of the Ruby language. We'll be having quite the junket for the next three chapters, gluing these parts together into sly bits of (poignant) code.

I'd recommend skimming all of the parts of speech once again. Give yourself a broad view of them. I'll be testing your mettle in the next section.

Seven Moments of Zen from My Life

1. 8 years old. Just laying in bed, thinking. And I realize. *There's nothing stopping me from becoming a child dentist.*

2. 21. Found a pencil on the beach. Embossed on it: *I cherish serenity.* Tucked it away into the inside breast pocket of my suit jacket. Watched the waves come and recede.

3. 22. Found a beetle in my bathroom that was just about to fall into a heating vent. Swiped him up. Tailored him a little backpack out of a leaf and a thread. In the backpack: a Skittle and AAA battery. That should last him. Set him loose out by the front gate.

4. Three years of age. Brushed aside the curtain. Sunlight.

5. 14. Riding my bike out on the pier with my coach who is jogging behind me as the sun goes down in the original Nintendo version of Mike Tyson's Punch-Out.

6. 11. Sick. Watching Heathcliff on television. For hours, it was Heathcliff. And he was able to come right up close to my face. His head spun toward me. His face pulsed back and forth, up close, then off millions of miles away. Sound was gone. In fractions of a second, Heathcliff filled the universe, then blipped off to the end of infinity. I heard my mother's voice trying to cut through the cartoon. Heathclose, Heathaway, Heathclose, Heathaway. It was a religious rave with a cat strobe and muffled bass of mother's voice. (I ran a fever of 105 that day.)

7. 18. Bought myself a gigapet. A duck. Fed it for a while. Gave it a bath. Forgot about it for almost a couple months. One day, while cleaning, I found a chain and he was there on the end. Hey, little duck. Mad freaky, hoppin' around with his hair out, squawking diagonal lines. In a tuxedo.

~

If I Haven't Treated You Like a Child Enough Already

I'm proud of you. Anyone will tell you how much I brag about you. How I go on and on about this great anonymous person out there who scrolls and reads and scrolls and reads. "These kids," I tell them. "Man, these kids got heart. I never..." And I can't even finish a sentence because I'm absolutely blubbering.

And my heart glows bright red under my filmy, translucent skin and they have to administer 10cc of JavaScript to get me to come back. (I respond well to toxins in the blood.) Man, that stuff will kick the peaches right out your gills!

So, yes. You've kept up nicely. But now I must begin to be a brutal schoolmaster. I need to start seeing good marks from you. So far, you've done nothing but move your eyes around a lot. Okay, sure, you did some exceptional reading aloud earlier. Now we need some comprehension skills here, Smotchkkiss.

Say aloud each of the parts of speech used below.

```
5.times { print "Odelay!" }
```

You might want to even cover this paragraph up while you read, because your eyes might want to sneak to the answer. We have a *number* 5, followed by a *method* .times. Then, the first crab pincers of a *block*. The kernel *method* print has no dot and is followed by a *string* "Odelay!". The final crab pincers close our *block*.

Say aloud each of the parts of speech used below.

```
exit unless "restaurant".include? "aura"
```

Like the print method, exit is a kernel *method*. If you were paying attention during the big list of keywords, you'll know that unless is just such a *keyword*. The *string* "restaurant" is clung to by the *method* include?. And finally, the string "aura".

Say aloud each of the parts of speech used below.

```
[toast, cheese, wine].each { |food| eat food }
```

This caterpillar partakes of finer delicacies. An *array* starts this example. In the array, three *variables* toast, cheese, and wine. The whole array is trailed by a *method* each.

Inside of a *block*, the *block argument* food, traveling down its little waterslide into the block. The *method* eat then is able to use the block argument, which has become the *variable* food.

Look over these examples once again. Be sure you recognize the parts of speech used. They each have a distinct look, don't they? Take a deep breath, press firmly on your temples. Now, let's dissect a cow's eye worth of code.

An Example to Help You Grow Up

Say aloud each of the parts of speech used below.

```
require 'net/http'
Net::HTTP.start( 'www.ruby-lang.org', 80 ) do |http|
    print( http.get( '/en/LICENSE.txt' ).body )
end
```

The first line is a method call. The *method* called require is used. A *string* is passed to the method containing 'net/http'. Think of this first line of code as a sentence. We have told Ruby to load some helper code, the Net::HTTP library.

The next three lines all go together. The *constant* Net::HTTP refers to the library we loaded above. We are using the *method* start from the library. Into the method, we're sending a *string* 'www.ruby-lang.org' and the *number* 80.

The word do opens a *block*. The block has one *block variable* http. Inside the block, the *method* print is called. What is being printed?

From the *variable* http, the *method* get is called. Into get, we pass a *string* containing the path '/en/LICENSE.txt'. Now, notice that another method is chained onto get. The *method* body. Then, the block closes with end.

Doing okay? Just out of curiousity, can you guess what this example does? Hopefully, you're seeing some patterns in Ruby. If not, just shake your head vigorously while you've got these examples in your mind. The code should break apart into manageable pieces.

For example, this pattern is used a number of times:

variable . method (method arguments)

You see it inside the block:

```
http.get( '/en/LICENSE.txt' )
```

We're using Ruby to get a web page. You've probably used HTTP with your web browser. HTTP is the Hypertext Transfer Protocol. HTTP is used to transfer web pages across the Internet. Conceptualize a bus driver who can drive across the Internet and bring back web pages for us. On his hat are stitched the letters HTTP.

The variable http is that bus driver. The *method* is a message to the bus driver. Go get the web page called /en/LICENSE.txt.

So where you see the chain of methods:

```
http.get( '/en/LICENSE.txt' ).body
```

Since we'll be getting back a web page from the http bus driver, you can read this in your brain as:

web page .body

And this bit of code:

```
print( http.get( '/en/LICENSE.txt' ).body )
```

This code gets the web page. We send a body message to the web page, which gives us all the HTML in a *string*. We then print that string. See how the basic dot-method pattern happens in a chain. The next chapter will explore all these sorts of patterns in Ruby. It'll be good fun.

So, what does this code do? It prints the HTML for the Ruby home page to the screen. Using an web-enabled bus driver.

~

And So, the Quick Trip Came to an Eased, Cushioned Halt

So now we have a problem. I get the feeling that you are enjoying this way too much. And you haven't even hit the chapter where I use jump-roping songs to help you learn how to parse XML!

If you're already enjoying this, then things are really going bad. Two chapters from now you'll be writing your own Ruby programs. In fact, it's right about there that I'll have you start writing your own blogging software, your own file-sharing network (a la BitTorrent), as well as a program that will instant-message you when you get email. And then, the mother of all scripts: a program that will spider the entire Internet for MIDI files!

And you know (you've got to know!) that this is going to turn into an obsession. First, you'll completely forget to take the dog out. It'll be standing by the screen door, darting its head about, as your eyes devour the code, as your fingers slip messages to the computer.

Thanks to your neglect, things will start to break. Your mounds of printed sheets of code will cover up your air vents. Your furnace will choke. The trash will pile up: take-out boxes you hurriedly ordered in, junk mail you couldn't care to dispose of. Your own uncleanliness will pollute

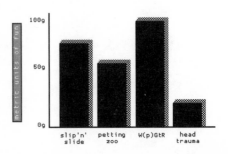

the air. Moss will infest the rafters, the water will clog, animals will let themselves in, trees will come up through the foundations.

But your computer will be well cared for. And you, Smotchkkiss, will have nourished it with your knowledge. In the eons you will have spent with your machine, you will have become part-CPU. And it will have become part-flesh. Your arms will flow directly into its ports. Your eyes will accept the video directly from DVI-24 pin. Your lungs will sit just above the processor, cooling it.

And just as the room is ready to force itself shut upon you, just as all the overgrowth swallows you and your machine, you will finish your script. You and the machine together will run this latest Ruby script, the product of your obsession. And the script will fire up chainsaws to trim the trees, hearths to warm and regulate the house. Builder nanites will rush from your script, reconstructing your quarters, retiling, renovating, chroming, polishing, disinfecting. Mighty androids will force your crumbling house into firm, rigid architecture. Great pillars will rise, statues chiseled. You will have dominion over this palatial estate and over the encompassing mountains and islands of your stronghold.

So I guess you're going to be okay. Whatdya say? Let's get moving on this script of yours?

INDEX

COLOPHON

We adopted the cover of this book from the title page of the first complete English edition of *Euclid's Elements*, published in 1571. Interestingly enough, that book was translated from the Greek by Sir Henry Billingsley, who became the Lord Mayor of London. (We aren't sure whether any politicians since then would have the knowledge of both mathematics and Greek needed to do such a wonderful job.) Also noteworthy is that Billingsley relied on John Dee for help in the translation; this is the same John Dee who became famous in fantasy literature—for example, in H. P. Lovecraft's short story "The Dunwich Horror." (Actually, most scientists of his time, including Newton himself, straddled the worlds of science and magic.) Anyway, John Dee contributed a wonderful preface to this book that argued the central importance of mathematics in the arts and sciences—which of course endeared him to all subsequent mathematicians such as our publisher, Gary Cornell. After all, it said, among other things

> O comfortable allurement, O ravishing persuasion to deal with a science whose subject is so ancient, so pure, so excellent, so surrounding all creatures, so used of the almighty and incomprehensible wisdom of the Creator.

Still, as important as this translation is, it isn't without its problems; most noteworthy is that the original title page (shown here) has an error: Billingsley ascribed the *Elements* to the wrong Euclid, Euclid of Megara, who alas, was not the Euclid of Alexandria who worked and taught at the great library and actually wrote the *Elements*!

Our copy of the title page comes from a copy held at the Bancroft Library of the University of California at Berkeley. It was scanned for us at 2400 dpi by the nice folks at Bancroft Library. The usual foxing found in a book so old was removed and the other needed modifications made to the title page through the wizardry of Kurt Krames, Apress's chief designer, using Adobe Photoshop 7 on a Mac G4.

Ptolomeus

Marinus

Aratus

Strabo

Hipparchus

Polibius

VIRESCIT VVLNERE VERITAS

THE ELEMENTS
OF GEOMETRIE
of the most aunci-
ent Philosopher
EVCLIDE
of Megara.

Faithfully (now first) translated into the Englishe toung, by
H. Billingsley, Citizen of London.
Whereunto are annexed certaine
Scholies, Annotations, and Inuenti-
ons, of the best Mathematici-
ens, both of time past, and
in this our age.

With a very fruitfull Preface made by M. I. Dee,
specifying the chiefe Mathematicall Sciêces, what
they are, and whereunto commodious: where, also, are
disclosed certaine new Secrets Mathematicall
and Mechanicall, vntill these our daies, greatly missed.

Geometria

Astronomia

Arithmetica

Musica

TB F

MERCVRIVS

Imprinted at London by *Iohn Daye.*

forums.apress.com

JOIN THE APRESS FORUMS AND BE PART OF OUR COMMUNITY. You'll find discussions that cover topics of interest to IT professionals, programmers, and enthusiasts just like you. If you post a query to one of our forums, you can expect that some of the best minds in the business—especially Apress authors, who all write with *The Expert's Voice*™—will chime in to help you. Why not aim to become one of our most valuable participants (MVPs) and win cool stuff? Here's a sampling of what you'll find:

DATABASES
Data drives everything.

Share information, exchange ideas, and discuss any database programming or administration issues.

PROGRAMMING/BUSINESS
Unfortunately, it is.

Talk about the Apress line of books that cover software methodology, best practices, and how programmers interact with the "suits."

INTERNET TECHNOLOGIES AND NETWORKING
Try living without plumbing (and eventually IPv6).

Talk about networking topics including protocols, design, administration, wireless, wired, storage, backup, certifications, trends, and new technologies.

WEB DEVELOPMENT/DESIGN
Ugly doesn't cut it anymore, and CGI is absurd.

Help is in sight for your site. Find design solutions for your projects and get ideas for building an interactive Web site.

JAVA
We've come a long way from the old Oak tree.

Hang out and discuss Java in whatever flavor you choose: J2SE, J2EE, J2ME, Jakarta, and so on.

SECURITY
Lots of bad guys out there—the good guys need help.

Discuss computer and network security issues here. Just don't let anyone else know the answers!

MAC OS X
All about the Zen of OS X.

OS X is both the present and the future for Mac apps. Make suggestions, offer up ideas, or boast about your new hardware.

TECHNOLOGY IN ACTION
Cool things. Fun things.

It's after hours. It's time to play. Whether you're into LEGO® MINDSTORMS™ or turning an old PC into a DVR, this is where technology turns into fun.

OPEN SOURCE
Source code is good; understanding (open) source is better.

Discuss open source technologies and related topics such as PHP, MySQL, Linux, Perl, Apache, Python, and more.

WINDOWS
No defenestration here.

Ask questions about all aspects of Windows programming, get help on Microsoft technologies covered in Apress books, or provide feedback on any Apress Windows book.

HOW TO PARTICIPATE:
Go to the Apress Forums site at **http://forums.apress.com/**.
Click the New User link.